THE OLD LEFT IN HISTORY
AND LITERATURE

Twayne's

LITERATURE

&

SOCIETY

SERIES

THE OLD LEFT
IN HISTORY AND
LITERATURE

Julia Dietrich

Twayne Publishers
AN IMPRINT OF SIMON & SCHUSTER MACMILLAN
NEW YORK

Prentice Hall International
LONDON • MEXICO CITY • NEW DELHI • SINGAPORE • SYDNEY • TORONTO

Twayne's Literature & Society Series No. 8

The Old Left in History and Literature

Julia Dietrich

Copyright © 1996 by Twayne Publishers

Twayne Publishers
An Imprint of Simon & Schuster Macmillan
866 Third Avenue
New York, New York 10022

Library of Congress Cataloging-in-Publication Data

Dietrich, Julia.
  The old left in history and literature / Julia Dietrich.
      p.   cm.—(Twayne's literature & society series ; no. 8)
  Includes bibliographical references and index.
  ISBN 0-8057-8861-1 (alk. paper)—ISBN 0-8057-7819-5 (pbk. : alk. paper)
  1. Radicalism—United States—History—20th century. 2. Communism—
United States—History. 3. Socialism—United States—History—20th
century. 4. Politics and literature—United States. 5. United States—
Politics and government—1901–1953. I. Title. II. Series.
E743.D495   1995
973.9—dc20   95-6126
                                                                                            CIP

10 9 8 7 6 5 4 3 2 1

Printed in the United States of America

CONTENTS

Preface   vii
Acknowledgments   xi

  1 The American Left, 1912–1919   1
  2 War and Revolution, 1917–1920   28
  3 From the Jazz Age to the Crash, 1920–1930   53
  4 From the Great Depression to the Popular Front, 1931–1935   85
  5 The Popular Front, 1935–1939   114
  6 From World War II to the Demise of the Movement   143
  7 The Struggle for the Past   177

Chronology   185
Notes and References   188
Selected Bibliography   201
Index   205

PREFACE

Since the Bolshevik revolution of 1917, the American popular imagination has tended to conflate all Leftists into "Reds" and to characterize Communism as the opposite number to American freedom, not only internationally but also within the United States. Characterizing Communism in this oppositional role has made it difficult for us to see the Communist experience as *part of* the American political experience and has also had the effect of highlighting its foreign connections but isolating the history of the Communist Party from that of other American Leftist groups. The end of Cold War hostilities invites us to look at American Communism less monolithically, seeing it not only as a revolutionary challenge to capitalism but also as a complex expression of people's hopes, supported by behavior from the heroic to the execrable; as the encounter between revolutionary theory and obdurate reality; and as one of a spectrum of Left political agendas.

Pioneering historians of American Communism, like Theodore Draper, Harvey Klehr, and Joseph Starobin, have given us organizational histories that have not been superseded. Theirs are primarily political histories, focused on the Party as an institution and on its relation to the Communism in Moscow.[1] A younger generation of historians, however, writing in the 1980s and 1990s, does not dispute the influence of the Comintern but takes a greater interest in the social history of the Party.[2] Historians like Michael Brown, Maurice Isserman, Ellen Schrecker, and Mark Naison find greater interest in individuals' lived experience of the Communist Party.

A parallel development is taking place in scholarship on the literature associated with Leftist movements in the United States. In the 1950s and 1960s, critics like Alan Rideout and James Burkhart Gilbert wrote valuable studies that did much to establish a radical canon and to place the works in the context of political history. The preface to Rideout's 1956 *The Radical Novel in the United States, 1900–1954*, demonstrates how radical literature was held in the same sort of isolation as radical groups themselves as long as Communism was perceived as a genuine threat. He writes, "The general reader may be put off by the subject matter, for nowadays in the United States the mention of anything having to do with radical politics is likely to be met by suspicion or anger."[3] The preeminence of the New Criticism during the period between World War II and the 1980s, focusing exclusively on aesthetic values in literature, served further to isolate the novels, poems, plays, and songs that supported radical analyses and radical agendas.

Recently, however, the literature of the Old Left has begun to come out of quarantine and be read as part of a radical tradition in American literature, stretching backward and forward from the 1930s and deserving recognition as a significant strand of the American literary tradition. The interest in integrating radical works into the mainstream of American literature is supported by a general turn in literary criticism, beginning in the 1980s, toward the social. Many contemporary critics look not only for the aesthetic values in a work but also into its role in the movement of power through the society. A novel, play, poem, or song is not simply an "art product" of its society but an active agent in the play of social forces.

The writers of explicitly political literature, generated from the Leftist radical groups of the first half of this century, did not speak about their work in the complex theoretical terms of contemporary critics, but they recognized an important social role for literature. In radical movements, literature and other cultural forms are particularly important because such movements are seeking to reach people, educate them, and change the way they think about basic social relations. What better than a novel or play to suggest to people that something they may have accepted as a given, such as corporate ownership of factories, is not an inevitable or immutable fact of life? How better to help people see what a different future might look like than to figure it forth in a novel or a play? How better to educate organizers or would-be strikers than with "strike novels" that tell them what to expect? How better than a poem or song to reach the public with a view of an event different from that given by the Hearst newspaper chain? On the other hand, what better means than a novel has the disillusioned radical to repudiate the movement and warn off others? or the yet-loyal radical to criticize the direction of the movement?

Throughout the twentieth century, Leftist groups of many varieties have attracted talented writers. Some, like John Reed, have had great influence on the movements themselves. Later, during the Popular Front the Party had great hope for what its writers could do to foster change; at other times, however, cultural work was at best an accessory to radical groups, which relied on economic forces and political organizing to move the masses leftward. Writers complained that in the Communist Party cultural work was at times downright suspect.[4] Cultural workers generally did not take direction well. Writers skilled enough to create complex and believable characters are likely to produce works with some ambiguities, unresolved tensions, and unanswered questions as they represent political ideas *lived out*. They may be aware of these ambiguities or they may not; writers cannot control every meaning that a reader may find in a text. Those ambiguities and tensions and contradictions take us inside the complex life of the Old Left.

It will be the project of this book to survey the history of the Old Left in all its sectarian variety and to examine a representative selection of literature that came out of and was written about the movement. We begin in 1912 with the reorientation of the *Masses* magazine toward revolutionary Socialism, and we follow the Old Left into the 1950s, when it ceases to be a major cultural force, and then look briefly at several works about the Old Left from 1956 to the present. The literature is so extensive that we can consider only a small portion of it, chosen to give us insight into thinking about radical issues from a variety of cultural perspectives and to help us understand the relationship between radical theory and radical aesthetics as it was formulated at the time.

We will consider not only literature written for an explicitly political purpose by adherents of Leftist parties but also works by writers who are interested in Left ideas but critical of Leftist organizations. Because the theory of the Old Left was based in certain assumptions about the individual and the community—the capacity of humankind for cooperation, the relationship between means and ends, and other encompassing questions about human experience—Leftist ideas and issues recur throughout twentieth-century American literature, not only in explicitly Leftist "political" literature. For that reason, a sense of the history of the Old Left is indispensable to a complete reading of many works in various American traditions.

Examining the history and the literature in relation to each other seems particularly useful as we try to understand the Old Left as a cultural as well as a political phenomenon. Likewise, it is within the rhetorical context created by the history that we can best understand the literature. Writers of the Old Left wrote during just the period when modern urban life was calling forth new developments in the American literary traditions. As they struggled to define an aesthetic, they might be guided by Left literary theory to a greater or lesser degree, but they had always to be responsible to the social conditions and political responses that called their works into being. As they consciously wrote from within history, they are best read that way.

ACKNOWLEDGMENTS

I gratefully acknowledge permission to reprint from the following material.

Frederick R. Benson, from *Writers in Arms: The Literary Impact of the Spanish Civil War*. Copyright © 1967 by New York University. Reprinted by permission.

James P. Cannon, from *The History of American Trotskyism*. Copyright © 1972 by Pathfinder Press. Reprinted by permission.

Malcolm Cowley, from "Echoes of a Crime." Reprinted by permission of The New Republic.

Selected excerpt from *The God That Failed* by *Richard Crossman*. Copyright 1949 by Richard Crossman, renewed © 1977 by Anne Crossman. Richard Wright material, copyright 1944 by Richard Wright. Reprinted by permission of HarperCollins Publishers, Inc.

Selected excerpts from *The Long Loneliness* by Dorothy Day. Copyright © 1952 by Harper & Row, Publishers, Inc. Copyright renewed © 1980 by

Tamar Teresa Hennessy. Reprinted by permission of HarperCollins Publishers, Inc.

Floyd Dell, from *Homecoming*. Copyright © 1933. Used by permission of Henry Holt and Company, Inc.

John Dos Passos, from *The Adventures of a Young Man*. Copyright © 1939. Used by permission of Elizabeth H. Dos Passos.

W. E. B. DuBois, from *Darkwater: Voices from within the Veil*. Copyright © 1920. Used by permission of David G. DuBois.

Excerpt from William Z. Foster in the *Daily Worker*, 30 December 1930, used by permission of International Publishers Co.

Mike Gold, selections from "A Letter to the Author of a First Book" and "A Keynote to Dos Passos' Works." Used by permission of the Evelyn Singer Agency.

Selected excerpt from *The Romance of American Communism* by *Vivian Gornick*. Copyright © 1977 by Vivian Gornick. Reprinted by permission of BasicBooks, a division of HarperCollins Publishers, Inc.

From *Scoundrel Time* by *Lillian Hellman*. Copyright © 1976 by Lillian Hellman. By permission of Little, Brown and Company.

Ernest Hemingway, from *For Whom the Bell Tolls*. Reprinted with permission of Scribner, an imprint of Simon & Schuster, Inc., from *For Whom the Bell Tolls* by Ernest Hemingway. Copyright 1940 by Ernest Hemingway. Copyright renewed © 1968 by Mary Hemingway.

Josephine Herbst, from *The Starched Blue Sky of Spain*. Copyright © 1991 by the Estate of Josephine Herbst. Reprinted with permission.

Granville Hicks, from "Dos Passos's Gifts." Reprinted by permission of The New Republic.

Langston Hughes, from *Phylon*: "My Adventures as a Social Poet," copyright © 1947, by Clark Atlanta University, Atlanta, Georgia. Reprinted with permission.

Selected excerpt from *The Heyday of American Communism: The Depression Decade* by *Harvey Klehr*. Copyright © 1984 by Harvey Klehr. Reprinted by permission of BasicBooks, a division of HarperCollins Publishers, Inc.

Meridel Le Sueur, from *Salute to Spring*. Copyright © 1940, renewed 1966. Used by permission of International Publishers Co., Inc.

David Madden, from the introduction to *Proletarian Writers of the Thirties*. Copyright © 1968. Reprinted with permission of Southern Illinois University Press.

Robert Nemiroff, from the introduction to *The Sign in Sidney Brustein's Window*. Copyright © 1965 by Random House, Inc. Reprinted with permission.

Material taken from *Bread upon the Waters* by Rose Pesotta. Used with permission of the publisher: ILR Press, School of Industrial and Labor Relations, Cornell University, Ithaca, New York 14853-3901. Copyright 1987 by Cornell University.

May Sarton, from *Faithful Are the Wounds*. Copyright © 1955 by May Sarton, © renewed 1983 by May Sarton. Reprinted by the permission of Russell & Volkening as agents for the author and by permission of W. W. Norton & Co., Inc.

From *The Anarchists' Convention* by John Sayles. Copyright © 1975, 1976, 1977, 1978, 1979 by John Sayles. By permission of Little, Brown and company.

Agnes Smedley, from *Daughter of Earth*. Copyright © 1973. Used with permission of The Feminist Press at The City University of New York.

Selected excerpt from *A People's History of the United States* by *Howard Zinn*. Copyright © 1980 by Howard Zinn. Reprinted by permission of HarperCollins Publishers, Inc.

I wish to express my gratitude to the Tamiment Library at New York University, the New York Public Library, the Library of Congress, and the Rare Books Department of the University of Louisville for allowing me access to collections that were essential for completing this project.

Man with an IWW hat card at an April 1914 rally. From the Baines Collection of the Library of Congress.

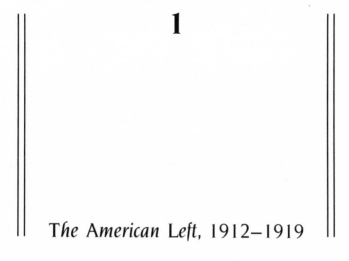

1

The American Left, 1912–1919

LEFT POLITICS IN AMERICA HAVE BEEN INSEPARABLE FROM AMERICAN culture in all its diversity. The American Left has never been simply or primarily class-based; as a result, it has never had the cultural homogeneity or the focused agenda of the European Left. There has never been a single Left, united on ends and means. Defining what is and what is not "Left," then, is no simple task, and it is complicated by the use of the term variously as a mantle of virtue and as a stigma; by various factions declaring each other to be "Left deviationists" or "Right deviationists"; by sectarian "more Left than thou" attitudes; and by how close the center was to the Right at any given time. To take the narrowest definition and limit our discussion in this book to the Communist Party would be to replicate a pointless sectarianism and to forego discussion of one of the most interesting problems of the Old Left: the struggle to find a form of Leftism that could be successful in America.

The preeminence of the Communist Party has complicated the task of understanding the movement and has skewed in one direction those questions asked about it. That the Old Left was much more than Communism is indicated not only by the variety of Left groups and philosophies that competed with Communism but also by the rate at which people joined and then exited the Party. The high turnover suggests not only that the Communist Party did not meet the needs of many seekers but also that there were indeed many seekers, many people looking for a way to realize a Leftist vision. Because their energy did not locate any organizational form to rival the Party, they have tended to disappear from the story of the Old Left or to appear as "ex-Communists." Likewise, those who never joined the Party but perhaps joined its front groups or were for a while "fellow travelers" have tended to be defined as being or not being Communists. The Party attracted powerfully enough to enlist the most dedicated cadre, and it repelled powerfully enough to make exmembers the friendliest witnesses before the House Un-American Activities Committee. The story of the Old Left is not just the story of the movement's interaction with mainstream American culture and politics. It is also the story of the movement's interaction with its own constituency. What did Leftists find in the Communist Party, and what did they fail to find? What alternatives did they create?

Because the Old Left is a movement (a series of efforts initiated by different groups and individuals), we should look beyond organized parties of any stamp to see it accurately. Richard Flacks, in *Making History: The American Left and the American Mind*,[1] identifies as Left any group or individual who works to democratize decision making and any group or individual who works to foster in others a willingness or readiness to participate in decision making for the common good. The common vision of the Left, then, is one in which people come together to make decisions about those things that affect their lives rather than having those decisions made by employers or government officials or other authorities. They have maximum control over their lives, and they make decisions not to benefit themselves at the expense of others but to further the common good. They are not just making individual lives; they are engaging in the highest human activity of making history, that is, determining the conditions in which life is lived. This vision required not just reform of American institutions (for example, restraining monopolies) but a displacement of power from the few to the many. The distinction between reformism and radicalism has been a difficult one to make throughout most of this century. Modern American liberalism is generally characterized as reformist because it does not challenge the existence of the capitalist system, but some reforms, like the extension of suffrage, meet the Leftist criterion of distributing power more widely. The idea of the "dictatorship of the proletariat," on the other hand, was acceptable to many Leftists because its authoritarianism was regarded as a necessary transitional stage.

Thus the difficulties in deciding what is "Left" are not merely definitional problems but, in fact, the very political problems agonized over and argued over by those who thought of themselves as Leftists. They agreed that there should be a redistribution of power, but how should this redistribution take place? Is violence an acceptable tool? Can the new society be brought about by evolution, education, and the ballot box? Is reform a good thing—a step toward empowerment—or is it a trap in which people get improvements in their living conditions but continue to be without power over their lives? Must the impulse for change come from the urban working class—the proletariat? Can an authoritarian movement ever deliver greater democracy? Is religion a help or a hindrance in preparing people to make responsible decisions?

These are some of the major questions that divided the Old Left. They are, of course, theoretical, but they are not merely intellectual; typically, one's stance on these and other issues was strongly influenced by the particular culture through which one came to Left politics. Church-based communities of believers in the Social Gospel, for example, were not only *unlikely* to accept a Marxist view of religion but were unable to do so without destroying the community itself, depriving it of the belief that made it a community. Likewise, immigrant Socialists whose politics and daily lives were organized around working-class solidarity would not be likely to accept a view of revolution in which class did not play a leading role; to do so would be to undermine the basis on which their own political community was built. It will be worth our while, then, to look briefly at some of the ways of being a Leftist in America in the years just before the Bolshevik revolution. We will focus particularly on the years 1912 to 1917, when the magazine *Masses* espoused revolutionary Socialism and opened its pages to just the sort of definitional and strategic questions that we have been considering.

Political categories like "anarchist" or "Socialist" are of limited use in describing the American Left; each category included a wide spectrum of opinion on goals and on appropriate political strategies, and the categories themselves overlapped. What label can we usefully give, for example, to Elizabeth Gurley Flynn, who worked as a strike coordinator for the Industrial Workers of the World (IWW) but was also a member of the Socialist Party and a Socialist orator and later a member of the Communist Party—an anarcho-syndicalist-Socialist-turned-Communist? A descriptor that inclusive is virtually useless. Most Americans who became Leftists in the twentieth century did so out of their specific cultural experience. It will be more helpful for our purposes, therefore, to look at cultural groupings within the Left, even though these too overlap and subsume a range of political thought.

=== The Greenwich Village Left ===

One strand of the Left tradition in America has been a self-consciously intellectual one, claiming its heritage in Emerson, Whitman, and Thoreau and in the American Revolution. One has only to think of "Song of Myself" and

Walden to recognize the mixture of radically democratic politics, individualism, and antibourgeois lifestyle that characterized one segment of the American Left over long years. In the 1910s Greenwich Village was not the only place where the mixture of intellectual bohemian culture and Left politics flourished, but it was the most well-known and became a mecca for young people fleeing towns like Sherwood Anderson's *Winesburg, Ohio*. They fled lives of conformity, strictly regulated sexuality, anti-intellectualism, and local cultures centered on small business and moneymaking.

The Village was the antithesis of Winesburg. In her autobiography, *My Thirty Years' War*, Margaret Anderson describes the rooms on Sixteenth Street, in the margins of the Village, that she and her partner Jane Heap had taken: "We bought gold Chinese [wall] paper at a Japanese paper shop, in long oblong strips. The woodwork was pale cream, the floor dark plum, the furniture old mahogany. The feature of the room was a large divan hung from the ceiling by heavy black chains. It was covered by a dull-toned blue and on it were four silk cushions—emerald green, magenta, royal purple, and tilleul."[2] And a few pages later she adds, "It was one of those periods when money absolutely abstained from coming in" (Anderson, 157). One suspects that the motive for Anderson's rather uncharacteristic inclusion of these details of decor is the same as the motive for the decor itself: to indicate that this is really, *really* not "Winesburg."

By the standards of the time, the Village Left was fairly diverse in its background. Most of its "members" were native-born Americans with a European background, though some, like Emma Goldman, were immigrants, and in the 1920s African Americans had a discernible voice. Most supported themselves with intellectual or artistic work, but some, like Mabel Dodge, had independent incomes, and others, like William Haywood of the IWW, worked as organizers. Yet others combined intellectual and cultural work: the editors of the *Masses* were eager to make their reputations as writers and artists; Emma Goldman lectured on birth control, on anarchism, and on the European dramatic tradition. Generally, they were well educated. The group included some seasoned veterans, but in the 1910s there was a preponderance of young people, who differed from their elders most notably in their enthusiasm for Freud.[3] His theories supported the freeing of sexuality from domesticity and procreation. Crystal Eastman, Max Eastman, John Reed, Louise Bryant, Henrietta Rodman, Floyd Dell, Dorothy Day, Ida Rauh, Hutchins Hapgood, Jessie Ashley, George Cram Cook, Susan Glaspell, Margaret and William Sanger, Margaret Anderson, and Jane Heap are names that recur in the accounts of life in the Village. In Provincetown on Cape Cod, some of the group produced theatricals that led to the founding of the Provincetown Players (M. J. Buhle, 258). Many of the women prominent in the Greenwich Village Left also belonged to Heterodoxy, the Village club that attracted and nurtured "New Women," requiring of its members only that they hold ideas that challenged conventional thinking.

From the writings of the Villagers, we are left with an impression of endless discussions carried on in restaurants and cafes, discussions in which they had the luxury of friendly, vociferous disagreement; unlike the members of a political party, they had no need to agree on points of unity. And unlike those belonging to an economically oppressed group, they were not struggling for their immediate survival. What they did share foremost, however, was a commitment to personal freedom: artistic freedom, uncensored speech, free love, unregimented education, control over one's own work. They supported labor, particularly the IWW, and they reviled the National Association of Manufacturers and its attempts to prevent labor from organizing. They strongly opposed government intervention on the side of capital in labor struggles. They strongly supported women's self-determination, though they disagreed about the usefulness of suffrage. They supported civil rights and improved living conditions for African Americans, but the issue did not loom large in their writing or in their activism. Some were committed anarchists; many were members of the Socialist Party.

The *Masses,* published from various locations in the Village, represented this intellectual, literary, anarcho-Socialist variety of Leftism. In December 1912 Max Eastman, once a student of John Dewey at Columbia, took over the editorship and changed the magazine's format and its politics.[4] On its founding by Piet Vlag in 1911, the *Masses* had advocated cooperatives and opposed direct action such as the law-defying strikes of the Wobblies (Industrial Workers of the World, supposedly nicknamed by the immigrant pronunciation of *IWW* as "I Woubble U Woubble U"). Eastman steered the magazine into support of the Wobblies, though he insisted that it not be tied to any single Leftist orthodoxy.

In his first issue, Eastman wrote, "[by revolution] we mean a radical democratization of industry and society, made possible by the growth of capitalism, but to be accomplished only when and if the spirit of liberty and rebellion is sufficiently awakened in the classes which are now oppressed. A revolution is a sweeping change accomplished through the conquest of power by a subjected class. The opposite of revolution is not evolution, but reform. . . . The Evolutionist is a man who talks about Evolution; the Revolutionist is a man who produces it."[5] And in his "Editorial Notice" he wrote that the magazine would not be a vehicle for factional debates in the Socialist Party. It would oppose dogmatism. "Our appeal will be to the masses, both Socialist and non-Socialist, with entertainment, education, and the livelier kinds of propaganda."[6]

John Sloan, Maurice Becker, Alice Beach Winter, Cornelia Barnes, and George Bellows were among those who contributed artwork to the *Masses.* They took their subject matter from urban life, insisting that a prostitute in night court, shop girls coming home from work, and tenement dwellers filling the summer streets were a part of the American reality. The literary taste of the *Masses* was not for bold experiment; avant-garde developments like imagism and stream-of-consciousness narration seemed a bit precious and beside the point to Eastman, who preferred literature with revolutionary content when he could get it. He complained that there was not enough *good* revolutionary literature, and he would not print bad literature just because it was revolutionary.

Eastman favored a literature of ideas that would appeal to open-minded and thoughtful people, a literature that concerned itself with the same human situations, relations, and problems to which Socialism addressed itself. Because the Socialism of the *Masses* was undoctrinaire, the literature could reflect the writer's observation from life; it need not demonstrate the truths of any one particular political analysis. Rather, it would be political simply because the writer's consciousness was informed by Socialist concerns and values. Literature would be political in an organic rather than a formulaic way.

Eastman elaborated his ideas on the relation between literature and politics in "Confessions of a Suffrage Orator" in the November 1915 issue.[7] After noting that all of the arguments for and against woman suffrage had long been familiar and that there was not much to be gained by argument and refutation, he wrote, "What our times respond to, is a propagandist who knows how to respect the wishes of other people and yet show them in a sympathetic way that there is more fun for them as well as for humanity in general in the new direction. *Give them an hour's exercise in liking something else*—that is worth all the proofs and refutations in the world."

The editorial board of the *Masses* was fairly fluid, but over the years it included, along with Eastman, Floyd Dell, John Reed, Eugene Wood, Mary Heaton Vorse, William English Walling, and Louis Untermeyer, along with a number of lesser-known writers. The issues that recurred most often were labor and free-speech issues and woman suffrage. In the December 1912 issue, for example, Eastman's "Knowledge and Revolution" column expressed outrage that Joseph Ettor and Arturo Giovannitti, IWW organizers of the textile strike in Lawrence, Massachusetts, were receiving an unfair trial on the trumped-up charge of having murdered a fellow worker. Eastman ended by noting that a minister and the mayor of Schenectady had both been jailed in connection with the Lawrence strike for publicly reading, respectively, the Bible and the U.S. Constitution.

In that same issue, Eugene Wood's "Foolish Female Fashions" argued that American business uses women to sell clothes that advertise their husbands' or fathers' wealth.[8] Mary Heaton Vorse's "The Two-Faced Goddess" is a story told by a male narrator about men so desperate to escape domesticity that they buy a leaky, anchor-dragging boat as a reason to be away from home.[9] The story, like Floyd Dell's "Feminism for Men" in the July 1914 issue, focuses on *men's* unhappiness with traditional gender roles.[10]

Margaret C. Jones in *Heretics and Hellraisers: Women Contributors to the "Masses," 1911–1917*, notes that women editors, writers, and artists played a determining role in the character of the *Masses* and that, overall, they presumed a vital link between feminism and Socialism: suffrage alone would not give real freedom to poor and working-class women.[11] The combination of political power (through the ballot) and self-determination (through economic democracy) would be required to liberate women (Jones, 27). These women also seem to have believed that their sex must have social freedom (from rigid gender roles and repressive sexual mores), but even in the *Masses* they presented a view of gender relations that was less than radical even for the time. Their autobiographies speak of liaisons with men, and in some cases with women, outside of marriage, sometimes of lives in which work is more important than relationship. But their essays and fiction in the *Masses* generally assume that a relationship with a man is important to women. Mary Bradley's "A Stranger in the City" (March 1917) and Jeannette Eaton's "Rebellion" (August 1917), for example, take as their theme the moments of loneliness experienced by independent women (Jones, 18–19). Likewise, the writers seem to have thought it radical enough to defend heterosexual desire in the still-Puritan culture of early twentieth-century America; that "sex is not wicked" was a bold idea, even if it was between a man and a woman (Jones, 19). The poetry of Lydia Gibson, who sometimes signed herself Lydia Lesbia Gibson, is rare in its celebration of lesbian desire. It seems, then, that the women who contributed to the *Masses* were conscious of writing for an audience not quite as "advanced" as they were themselves.

The Socialism of the *Masses*' editors, springing as it did from commitment to personal freedom, sexual freedom, and self-expression, was heavily tinged with anarchism. Thus their compatibility with those, like Emma Goldman, who named themselves anarchists is not surprising. Anarchism, fittingly, is a label applied to a variety of political theories having in common only the opposition to external authority. Like Marxism, it developed in the nineteenth century, when industrialization and urban living deprived so many people of control over their work and their lives. Images of factory workers as cogs in a wheel were reinforced by images of families interchangeably "boxed" into identical rows of tenements, unable to feed and house themselves if their jobs were taken away. Anarchists insist that people should have sovereign control over their lives, bound only by those structures that they create voluntarily and over which they retain practical control.

The theory of anarchism in modern times can be traced to William Godwin's *An Inquiry Concerning Political Justice* (1793) and to Max Stirner's (Johann Kaspar Schmidt's) *The Ego and His Own* (1844), two books that share only an assertion of the rights of individuals to complete autonomy. Such an assertion is as likely to lead rightward as leftward, politically. Libertarian and conservative political philosophies hold as their highest principle the individual's right to be free from restraint; therefore they oppose regulation of business or trade or personal contracts, even if the absence of restraint leads to much more power of self-determination for some and much less for others. Left anarchism, in contrast, is devoted to gaining greater power of self-determination for the many, even though that imposes some limits on individual self-assertion.

Within Left anarchism a fairly broad spectrum of thought developed in the nineteenth century.[12] Pierre Joseph Proudhon (1809–65), in spite of his famous slogan, "Property is Theft," allowed for some ownership of private property as an incentive to hard work, but only after everyone had had the same opportunities for education and employment. He envisaged factories as workers' cooperatives, bringing into the industrial setting the combination of independence and mutual cooperation that characterized preindustrial communities of artisans and peasant farmers.[13]

With government removed, people would create voluntary organizations to do what needed to be done or simply what they wanted done. These organizations would be purely local, thus enabling everyone to participate in decision making and creative development of the project. Such voluntary groups would send representatives to federations that would work out solutions to problems affecting more than one locale (for example, rights to use natural resources), but the federations would be problem-solving, not legislating, bodies, and the job of representing one's commune at the federation would be short-term and rotating. Proudhon believed that development of economic independence for workers, through such tools as producer and consumer cooperatives and an interest-free credit bank, was the means through which society would be transformed; political action was useless. Workers controlling their own workplaces would prepare themselves to be entirely self-determining and to institute voluntary associations of many sorts when the time was right to do away with government.

Less theorist than activist, Michael Bakunin (1814–76) was a friend and admirer of Proudhon. Despite Marxist claims to the contrary, it was Proudhon and not Marx who was key to the founding of the International Workingmen's Association, commonly called the First International. It was established in 1864 by the European labor movement to promote class solidarity after the uprisings of 1848 and to prevent cross-border strike breaking. When Proudhon died a year after the founding of the International, Bakunin became the standard-bearer for anarchism against Marxism, and, in fact, the First International was effectively torn apart by disagreement between these two nonproletarians.

Whereas Marx opposed capitalist states, Bakunin, as an anarchist, opposed all states.[14] Marx believed that revolution would result from the uprising of the masses, after which the masses would control the government. Bakunin envisaged a revolution in which a small group of conspirators would seize control and abolish the government, leaving the masses to govern themselves without any state authority to interfere and exploit them. Marx thought that only the proletariat, the urban working class, was sufficiently developed to make a revolution; Bakunin championed the equal ability of the poorest peasants to throw off their masters and control their own lives.

In a lengthy section of the *German Ideology* (1845–46), Marx attacks Max Stirner, accusing him of being hopelessly theoretical, of believing that revolution will come when people *decide* to liberate themselves.[15] He continued to distinguish his theory from anarchism, publishing in 1847 *The Poverty of Philosophy* in answer to Proudhon's book *The Philosophy of Poverty*, published the previous year. Marx's critique ended his friendship with Proudhon, whom he accused of misunderstanding economics and especially exchange value.[16] Indeed, the most consequential of the differences between anarchists and Marxists lies in the role each gives to economic self-determination.

Marxists generally regard economic power as preeminent, the only kind of power that matters. As a result, they see class as *the* category around which to build theory and as *the* determiner of historical agency. After the revolution, the dictatorship of the proletariat will be authoritarian, but justified by the need to redistribute economic power. Typically, in a Marxist analysis, it is assumed that the liberation of oppressed racial or ethnic groups and of women will follow from the establishment of a classless society. Anarchists insist that economic self-determination, while essential to liberation, is not the only necessary form of self-determination, even in the short-run. Patriarchy, racist and ethnic hierarchies, and bureaucracy are evils in their own right and not simply side effects of capitalism. Anarchists will not grant legitimacy to any form of government, even one that professes to exist to redistribute economic power, because they do not see all forms of oppression as stemming from class.

Bakunin's involvement in a number of underground movements in various European countries, his penchant for conspiracy, and his belief that a dedicated few can overturn a government have given anarchism a legacy of *direct action*, an interest in "the propaganda of the deed." To some anarchists, this was license to engage in terrorism, assassination, and, at worst, random violence. Although it was always a small minority of anarchists that engaged in terrorism, the characterization of the anarchist as a bomb thrower was pervasive in Europe and America at the end of the nineteenth century and in the early decades of the twentieth. The association of symbols like the black flag, the black cat, and the wooden shoe ("sabot," therefore sabotage) with anarchism helped to reinforce the image of anarchists as a secret terrorist society.

The Russian aristocrat Peter Kropotkin (1842–1921), using his training as a scientist, made significant contributions to anarchist theory by buttressing with evolutionary arguments the anarchist belief in the human ability to cooperate.[17] Darwin, in emphasizing competition, had appeared to undercut the anarchist vision of a peaceful society in which everyone works for the common good without coercion. Basing his argument of animal studies,

Kropotkin said in *Mutual Aid* (1902) that cooperation is more important than competition in ensuring the survival of a species. Taking as his model the medieval village or commune, Kropotkin believed that everyone should do both mental and physical work and that property should be held in common, from which belief his theory is sometimes called "Communist anarchist."

Though radically at odds with the peaceful societies envisaged by Proudhon and Kropotkin, violence remained a problematic issue within anarchism. A political philosophy that eschewed electoral politics and mass-movement building and pictured the revolution as a spontaneous uprising left open the door to violent acts by individuals hoping that their action would be the one to spark the general uprising. Among late twentieth-century Leftist anarchists, violence is discredited as a strategy; they insist that means and ends must be consistent.[18] George Woodcock, a contemporary anarchist writer, describes terror as a perversion of anarchist intentions.[19]

At the turn of the twentieth century, the strongest political expression of anarchism in western Europe and in America was the anarcho-syndicalist movement, that concentrated on building trade unions which could then be the vehicles for self-government in the Socialist, stateless society to come. In the 1880s and 1890s, anarcho-syndicalism attracted many adherents, offering an alternative both to Marxian Socialism and to the reform-through-legislation approach. In the United States, the most influential anarcho-syndicalist group was the Wobblies (IWW), founded in 1905. Theirs was not a philosophically "pure" anarcho-syndicalism, however: the emphasis on "One Big Union"—the IWW slogan—conflicted with anarchist insistence on decentralization and local control; and the IWW was intermittently involved with Socialist political parties.

Emma Goldman emigrated to the United States from Russia in 1886, the same year that the Haymarket Riot in Chicago created eight anarchist martyrs and a backlash against both anarchism and organized labor. Inspired by the example of the martyrs and educated by Johann Most's newspaper *Die Freiheit*, Goldman embraced anarchism. She soon became one of the best-known anarchists in America—newpapers favored the adjective "notorious."

In her early years in this country, she seems to have underestimated the difference between the American and the European working class. When she conspired with Alexander Berkman in the disastrous and failed 1892 attempt to assassinate Henry Clay Frick, she seems to have believed that this move against management in the midst of the Homestead steel strike would call forth a general uprising of American labor. What it did do was reinforce the native-born equation of immigrant radicalism with terrorism.[20] Anarchists in America were beginning to disavow the use of the *attentat,* or the violent act, but Goldman defended Berkman, and in 1901 she was virtually a lone voice defending Leon Czolgosz, the self-proclaimed anarchist who assassinated President William McKinley. One of her biographers, Marian Morton, suggests that she felt obligated to defend the *attentat* because to repudiate it would be to repudiate Berkman's act, which she had joined in planning (Morton, 34). Later, after Berkman was released from prison, she urged against terrorism.

At odds with the immigrant anarchist circles over Czolgosz, Goldman forged closer ties with native-born anarchists and other Leftists in the first decade of the twentieth century, particularly through work in the Free Speech League (Morton, 41). She made friends among other Leftists in Greenwich Village, especially John Reed, Hutchins Hapgood, and Margaret Anderson. In 1906 she began publication of an English-language magazine, *Mother Earth,* to educate the American public about anarchism. More than any other individual, she bridged the gap between the immigrant radical circles of the Lower East Side and the native-born Left in New York and throughout the country.[21] Whereas on her early tours she had given her speeches in German, after the turn of the century she spoke in English, drawing large crowds all across the country.

Working with Goldman in the collective that published *Mother Earth* were Hippolyte Havel, Harry Kelley, Leonard Abbott, Max Baginski, and Alexander Berkman, released from prison in 1906. Among the contributors were Theodore Dreiser, Arturo Giovannitti, and Voltairine de Cleyre, who sent essays from Philadelphia tracing anarchist ideas not only to European roots but also to Jefferson, Paine, Emerson, and Thoreau. The circulation of *Mother Earth* has been estimated at various points between 3,500 and 10,000 (Morton, 47).

Who were these readers? Who shared Goldman's form of Leftism or was at least interested enough in it to read *Mother Earth* regularly? Some, no doubt, were IWW leaders and supporters. It is unlikely that great numbers of IWW activists were subscribers, as they characteristically moved across the country on the rails and lacked such amenities as permanent mailing addresses. Others likely were members of the Socialist Party or were independent Leftists or liberals, perhaps also subscribing to the *Masses*. Committed anarchist readers would have included both those English-speaking members of the immigrant Left and native-born proponents of individualist anarchism, a rightward leaning form of anarchism that had earlier found expression in Benjamin Tucker's magazine *Liberty*.

Margaret S. Marsh, in *Anarchist Women, 1870–1920,* profiles in some detail three groups of women who were attracted to anarchism: women who had emigrated or whose parents emigrated from southern or eastern Europe, regions where anarchism was more dominant than Marxian Socialism, and who were relatively unskilled workers; women, usually native born, with professional jobs who found that the suffrage-feminist domestic vision of women had nothing to contribute to *their* liberation; and women from all classes who were drawn to anarchism as a means of psychological liberation, that is, as a theory that legitimated the overthrow of conventions about sexuality and propriety.[22] Of these, the first group was most likely to choose a Left form of anarchism and to maintain a commitment to it; the third group was most likely to gravitate toward individualist anarchism and to spend the least time in the movement. Anarchism seems to have recommended itself to a number of radical women because its vision of liberation was neither tied to the (largely male) industrial proletariat—as was that of Marxian Socialism—nor focused narrowly on the ballot—as was that of the suffrage feminists.

Men seem to have been attracted to anarchism for reasons that sometimes parallel those of the women: unskilled workers were drawn to the IWW because it was the only union interested in organizing them; activist immigrant radicals from southern and eastern Europe and especially Russia—largely unindustrialized countries—had a vision of revolution based on peasant uprisings, not proletarian ascendancy; and native-born anarchists, from individualist to Leftist, sought psychological liberation, personal freedom, or social justice. In short, anarchists in America at that time were divided into distinct cultural groups; their preference for anarchism over Marxism derived from a broad range of cultural experiences and led to different agendas. The person of Emma Goldman, moving across the country and "at home" in both the Village and the Lower East Side, gave American anarchism the appearance of more unity than it actually had.

In the years leading up to the Bolshevik revolution, a reader of *Mother Earth* would have found birth control, labor advocacy, protest against corrupt courts and abridgement of free speech, and opposition to World War I and to militarism to be central anarchist issues. The issue of woman suffrage was at best moot for the anarchists. In the 1910s, the women's movement was focused strongly on the single issue of suffrage; getting the vote for women was seen as a crucial step to further liberation. To win suffrage, the movement chose to present women as mothers, guardians of domesticity and decency and in need of the ballot to secure such virtues for society. Given the profamily feeling running high in the country at the time, it was probably a good strategic move (Marsh, 63). Anarchists, however, wanted no part of arguments that reinforced the association of women with domesticity and motherhood; they wanted careers opened to women, and they wanted sexual freedom (Marsh, 63). Anarchists traditionally scorned the ballot as useless, and, for many immigrants, suffrage was completely irrelevant because they were not citizens.

Emma Goldman derided the suffrage feminists, viewing women's liberation as largely a matter of *deciding* to be free and to live without constraints. Although Goldman always thought of herself as a Left anarchist, this reliance on the will as an agent of change underscores the individualist strain in her philosophy (Morton, 64–65). Emancipation may indeed begin in a woman's soul, as she wrote in *Anarchism and Other Essays*,[23] but the path from the liberated soul to a living wage was too important an issue to gloss over as Goldman did. Her anarchist commitment to personal freedom, however, made her a committed and effective advocate of birth control at a time when the Comstock Act made it illegal to distribute any information on the subject.

In the October 1916 issue of *Mother Earth*, Ben Reitman wrote that Emma Goldman was the first person actually to explain from a public podium what some of the methods of birth control were and not merely to urge that information be made available. He went on to note that birth control is now becoming respectable, and so the anarchists will now focus on labor struggles, antiwar preparedness work, and advocacy for jailed comrades. The previous month's issue had carried a request for funds to be sent to the IWW, which was feeding striking miners at the Mesabi Iron Range, and an article by Berkman on the frame-up of Tom Mooney in the open-shops fights on the West Coast. Berkman's article ends almost wistfully, asking why labor does not use the one tool anarchists think most likely to cripple authority: "Is the General Strike only a dream? And yet, it could open every door of every prison in the land."[24] Use of the General Strike as a means of overthrowing the government was a central element in the anarchist vision; that we should find Berkman wondering aloud whether it is a chimera suggests that fall 1916 was a depressing time as well as an ominous one, as the United States prepared to enter World War I.

For a contemporary portrait of the Greenwich Village Left from 1913 to 1924, we can turn to Floyd Dell, an editor of the *Masses* and one of the central figures in Village life. Dell had spent his childhood in small Illinois towns, where his father lost his butcher shop and struggled to find work. At an early age, Dell pronounced himself an atheist, explaining in his autobiography, *Homecoming* (1933), that it was a way of rebelling against respectability.[25] At 16 he joined the Socialist Party:

> Frank Norris's novel "The Octopus" stirred my mind. And that spring, down in a small park near my home, I heard a man make a Socialist speech to a small and indifferent crowd. Afterward I talked to him; he was a street-sweeper. . . . And my long-slumbering Socialism woke up. Of course I was a Socialist! . . . And now it seemed to me that I had always been a Socialist. I remember old Jimmy Houseweart, the Socialist farmer with the white beard, and the book he had lent my father; I remembered the Socialist book I had read on Danton and the French Revolution; I remembered Kennan, and Kropotkin, and the Nihilists. My life seemed now to have some meaning, to be a whole. (Dell 1933, 73)

Thus was Dell radicalized by street oratory and the Quincy public library. His route leftward was not an unusual one. Indeed, writing—both fiction and nonfiction—and oratory have been central to many forms of Leftism. The task of the Left is to make people see the world differently, to make them see capitalism not as a system in which the hardworking prosper while the shiftless and less skilled descend into poverty but rather a system in which factory owners prosper while working people, hardworking or not, have only minimal control over their future. In Marxian terms, the task is to substitute "true consciousness" for "false consciousness"; that is, to put the blame on the oppressors rather than on the victims. For those forms of Leftism that believe in building a broad base of support for political change, oratory, journalism, and informational writing are important vehicles for changing consciousness. And fiction can make the invisible visible, whether it be the slums of the day or the fairer, more beautiful world to come. It is not surprising, then, that so many of the heroes of the Greenwich Village Left were writers, from Walt Whitman to Jack London. Nor is it surprising that Floyd Dell became a journalist, reviewer, dramatist, and novelist. In *Love in Greenwich Village* (1926),[26] he shows us how the Left politics of the Villagers were lived, and we will consider that aspect of the book in this chapter. He also helps us understand the ambivalence generated by the Bolshevik revolution, and in the next chapter we will return to look again at Dell's book in that light.

Using references to Schliemann's excavations at Troy and playful echoes of Biblical style, Dell begins his book with an account of the "founding" of the Greenwich Village he knew. In 1913, the old Liberal Club was split in two by the controversy over the marriage of "Egeria" (Henrietta Rodman). She then led the departing faction to a new home in the Village, where the new Liberal Club became the center of Village life for the artists, writers, professors, students, social workers, and social activists who formed a loose and ever-changing community. Polly, a restaurant owner willing to give a meal to those temporarily without funds, and her dishwasher, Hippolyte, an anarchist, were indispensable pillars of Village life.

Throughout the stories and poems that lead from this beginning to the last chapter, "The Fall of Greenwich Village," Dell's tone is nostalgic, even elegiac, as he describes the ideals and the revels of his bohemians, who live for art and ideas and disdain middle-class comforts and respectability. As the title suggests, *Love in Greenwich Village* focuses on human relationships, often the stories of young lovers who choose to be "modern," dispensing with marriage and with traditional gender roles and refusing to sacrifice their work—either his or hers—to domesticity. One such is "The Kitten and the Masterpiece," the story of Paul Sherwood, who has labored and starved in order to have one year in which to live in Village frugality and write his novel. He gets sidetracked by his grudging attachment to a stray kitten and his initially reluctant attachment to a young Village poet named Glory June. As his year goes by, the two become lovers, share their meager money, and have a wonderful time at Village masquerades, parties, and no-budget theatricals. After much soul-searching about what he wants most, on New Year's Eve he asks her to marry him. She refuses, telling him that as his wife she would be happy and that is what she is afraid of. She thought he understood that work is not so easily abandoned, and love doesn't mean marriage. Dell doesn't tell us Paul's reaction, but he leads us to see in it something of relief, and he notes that Paul and Glory have since achieved recognition in their fields.

"The Kitten and the Masterpiece" is followed by "Phantom Adventure," in which a man discovers that his vague discontent with his settled married life is shared by his wife, who had come to symbolize that very settledness to him. Yet another, less cheerful, view of men's and women's gender roles emerges from the next story, "The Button." Barbara Locke comes to the Village on the train from the Midwest, typewriter in hand, determined to be a writer. But on the train she has met Henry Riggs, a young man who wants to be a salesman. He progresses in that career as she leads her happy Village life. Then she marries him and is happy until one day he complains that she hasn't sewn back a missing button on his shirt. She is furious to be reduced to such trivial responsibilities, and she moves back to her old apartment in Greenwich Village. There she meets, shares her lunch with, and encourages a young writer who reminds her of Henry, confirming her landlady's view that such nurturing is women's natural role. Ultimately, she returns to Henry and the suburbs. Although not unhappy, she keeps the young writer's gift of a dictionary and says that its words will "help me to remember all the silly, lovely thoughts I had before I became just a woman. For hours at a time I shall be my old, free self" (Dell 1926, 119).

Feminism is one of the major concerns of Dell's book, central to nearly all of the stories and poems. In 1913 he had published *Women as World Builders*,[27] in which he argues that men were the real instigators of the feminist movement because they were tired of seemingly subservient women and wanted true companions instead. In his July 1914 *Masses* article, "Feminism for Men," he argues that the only reason some men oppose woman suffrage is that full citizenship for women will undermine the cult of masculine superiority, which men are nonetheless better off without because it prevents them from having honest relationships with women. In these writings, he takes it for granted that women's primary interest will always be in relationships with men, and in *Love in Greenwich Village* male-female relationships are the focus whenever the stories have female characters. Dell's interest is in the problems that his emancipated men and women have in being free together. Sometimes the problems seem to arise simply out of conflicting desires, sometimes from larger social forces.

Dell's focus is always on people and on the choices they make. The word *freedom* resounds throughout the stories and poems, and freedom is the hallmark of Village life. But his Villagers are not Utopians; they live in history. When his characters make choices, such as the choices about gender roles, they do so out of a mixture of personal desire and conviction but also within economic constraints. Their contempt for bourgeois show and comfort cannot isolate them entirely from economic forces. In the next-to-last story, "Green

Houses," a young woman from the South, raised only for leisure and unable to support herself with a job, lives in the Village with a young man named Carlo. Her family continues to send her money, but she knows it is only because she has misled them about her life. When her family announces a plan to visit her, she decides that she must go home and lead a conventional life. Carlo insists that she must stay. Finally, she agrees, but warns, "Without money to spend, I'll be unhappy, I know that. We'll be sick of each other many a time" (Dell 1926, 290). Framing this story is a narrative told by another character about a Japanese merchant's son and an elegant prostitute who fall in love but accept that their time together in the "Green House" must be just a lovely interlude before their social roles inevitably separate them. The story confronts the possibility that the Village life Dell so loves is also just an interlude, possible only briefly until economic realities pull it apart. Other stories in *Love in Greenwich Village* deal explicitly with the end of the Village as Dell knows it, an end brought on not only by economic forces but also by the politics of revolution and reaction.

= The Industrial Workers of the World =
and the Disenfranchised

"The working class and the employing class have nothing in common. There can be no peace so long as hunger and want are found among millions of working people and the few, who make up the employing class, have all the good things of life": thus begins the preamble to the constitution of the IWW, founded in Chicago in June 1905. The men and women who created and went on to lead the One Big Union had impressive credentials in frontline labor organizing. Some of the early leaders included William ("Big Bill") Haywood, leader of the Cripple Creek, Colorado, miners' strike in 1903–1904; Vincent St. John, leader of the Telluride, Colorado, strike of 1901; Elizabeth Gurley Flynn, the Socialist orator; Mother (Mary Harris) Jones, a labor militant since the 1870s; Thomas J. Haggerty, a radical Catholic priest; Joe Ettor, whose father had been wounded by the Chicago Haymarket bombing of 1886; and Arturo Giovannitti, who with Ettor would go on to lead the Lawrence, Massachusetts, textile strike of 1912.

In 1905 unskilled labor was being squeezed between steady or falling wages and the rising cost of living. Employers could play one immigrant group against another to keep wages down and raise the constant specter of unemployment. The American Federation of Labor (AFL), founded in 1886, had won some protections for skilled workers, leaving the unskilled at a particular disadvantage. The AFL unions were organized by crafts, much as the medieval guilds had been. Admission to the union conferred status, as it certified skill in a craft. In practical terms, however, it was often a disadvantage to labor to have the workers in a large factory divided into five or six different unions. The IWW, whose members referred to the AFL as the American *Separation* of Labor, wanted one union for all workers, skilled and unskilled, male and female, across ethnic lines. The One Big Union, as the IWW referred to itself, was composed of smaller unions organized not by craft but by industry. Thus, for example, all the workers in a large printing plant would belong to the same union, whether they were typesetters, pressmen, cutters, or maintenance workers. Industries relying not on craft skills but on assembly-line production, like the auto industry, would be organized according to the product being produced. The advantage of industrial organization, as the IWW saw it, was that it confronted the employer with a larger and more powerful labor force.

The IWWs had another, equally important, reason for promoting industrial unions: as syndicalists they saw unionization as a step toward worker ownership and management. They envisioned the One Big Union calling the General Strike, which would paralyze the country and necessitate the transfer of ownership to the workers themselves. (Throughout the life of the IWW there has been a tension between those who emphasize the One Big Union and those who emphasize the individual industrial unions.) The industrial union, drawing all the workers of a plant into one bargaining unit, was thereby preparing them to manage the plant cooperatively. This vision, of course, owes much to anarchism and particularly to the syndicalism of European thinkers like Georges Sorel and Edouard Hervé, but the energy in the IWW came less from European theory than from a particularly American combination of outrage and confidence.

Among the founders of the IWW had been prominent Socialists, including Eugene Debs and Daniel DeLeon, but they soon broke with the IWW over strategy. The Socialists had wanted the organization to be involved in electoral campaigns and legislative lobbying as well as labor organizing. The core that remained with the IWW put no faith in electoral work and determined to put all the effort into direct action "at the point of production." They reasoned that many workers—women, many African Americans, noncitizen immigrants, migrant workers without permanent addresses—had no vote. What they did have was their role in the economic system. If they stopped the machines, left the ore in the ground and the fruit on the trees, then they would be listened to.

Direct action usually took the form of the strike, and the Wobblies are credited with introducing the sit-down strike, a strategy entirely consistent with their vision of a worker takeover. But they were not above dropping hints about sabotage, even though it would be pointless to destroy the machinery they hoped one day to take over. Actual incidents of sabotage ascribed to the Wobblies are few.[28] Even hints of sabotage, however, contributed to the portrayal of the Wobblies as lawless and threatening. In spite of the break with Socialist Party leadership over strategy, many Wobblies continued as Party members.

Culturally, the IWW was very different from the reformist AFL. Seeing unions as the vehicle for self-government after the revolution, the Wobblies believed it necessary to organize *all* workers. The legions of women working in northeastern textile mills, the African Americans in the southern timber industry, production-line workers in mid-America, western miners, farm-workers, and itinerant laborers who couldn't afford a permanent home—all these could get a Wobbly red card, and for a fraction of what the AFL charged its members. And their dues bought something entirely different. Whereas the AFL unions bargained for contracts on wages and hours and working conditions, the IWW disparaged formal contracts between labor and management, believing that labor should never give up its right to press for more. A worker who signed a red card got not a bargaining agent but a sense of collective empowerment and a vision of labor always ready to take action on its own behalf.

Melvyn Dubofsky, in *We Shall Be All: A History of the Industrial Workers of the World*, theorizes that the appeal of the IWW lay in its gifts of hope and self-respect to the dispossessed. It offered them a vision of themselves as historical agents rather than victims.[29] If their lives must be blighted by poverty and brutality, then they would suffer in the interest of *change,* and their suffering would be meaningful. This change in self-concept, fired with a particularly American can-do attitude, was of tremendous importance in individual lives and essential in forming the character of IWW men and women as tough, endlessly resourceful, and independent. "Organizing" for the IWW went beyond chartering locals; change of consciousness was the heart of it.

When the IWWs attempted to organize miners and itinerant workers in the West, they often found themselves threatened, beaten, and jailed just for giving a soapbox speech. Their commitment to direct action—just *take* your rights—led them into the free speech fights for which they became famous. When a Wobbly was jailed for speaking in a certain town, others would hit the rails and travel to that town, taking the soapbox one after another until the jails were full and the Wobblies constituted a critical mass. At that point the attention and publicity they gained was used to spread the Wobbly message. Sometimes they were freed; at other times they served years of jail time, often on trumped-up charges of violence, or were themselves the victims of extralegal violence. Herb Edwards, an immigrant from Norway, describes the commitment of the Wobblies in the free speech fights as a "religious fervor": "they would ride box cars and ride the guts of a rattler to stay underneath the freight train to cross the country and take part in the fight, to take part in the dead of winter."[30]

As strike leaders, the IWWs had their most spectacular success with the Lawrence, Massachusetts, textile strike of 1912, when 25,000 workers struck to protest a pay cut. They represented more than a dozen nationalities, and the IWW's Joe Ettor and Arturo Giovannitti made cross-ethnic solidarity a major part of their agenda. The militia surrounded Lawrence, strikers sent their children to other cities for safety, and one official of the AFL protested that it was a revolution, not a strike, that was in progress.[31] Strikers enlarged their agenda to include not just a rollback of wage cuts but also some pay increases, premium pay for overtime, and a promise of no retaliation against strikers. They won it all. A hand-lettered sign, reading "We Want Bread and Roses, Too," indicated that self-respect was at issue here along with wages, and it gave the strike its nickname.

The following year, silk workers in Paterson, New Jersey, struck to resist demands for increased production. The IWW sent Elizabeth Gurley Flynn, Carlo Tresca, and Bill Haywood. But the mill owners managed to outlast the workers this time. The IWW, as a low-overhead, low-dues revolutionary union, had no considerable strike fund with which to support workers, and the strike was lost. In spite of losses like Paterson, the IWW was strong and growing into the late 1910s, with good support in many AFL unions and in the Socialist Party; industrial organizing was succeeding, and daily newspapers were published by more than a dozen foreign-language Wobbly groups (Georgakas, 10).

The experience of the IWW has generated a good deal of writing, including the well-known memoirs by Haywood and Flynn, and Wobbly characters appear in a number of American novels, but the most important intersection between literature and Wobbly history is a collection of songs. Having gone through 19 editions and numerous title changes by 1923, the collection came to be known as the "Little Red Song Book."[32] Ralph Chaplin, T-Bone Slim, and Joe Hill consistently provided the IWW with ballads and anthems, but each successive edition of the book included new songs contributed by workers across the country and generally published first in a local IWW newspaper. Thus the literature of the movement was a product of personal initiative, group experience, and decentralized process—the Wobbly ideal.

Singing was no mere pastime for the Wobblies. Many of their songs, like "They'll Soon Ring Out," describe the postrevolutionary world; others, like "One Big Industrial Union," offer political analysis. Both constitute an effective form of political education. One of the most enduring genres of Wobbly song is the parody, which substitutes one interpretation of reality for another, creating the new within the shell of the old. "Dump the Bosses Off Your Back," sung to the tune of "Take It to the Lord in Prayer," is one of a number of songs that appropriate religious melodies but undercut religious faith, replacing it with political commitment. Joe Hill's "The White Slave," sung to "Meet Me Tonight in Dreamland," takes a romantic ballad and empties it of romance, instead connecting economic and gender exploitation.

As loosely organized a group as the IWW needed a shared culture to develop cohesiveness across different racial, ethnic, and regional divisions. The songs were the primary means of fostering a solidarity that was genuinely class-based and that transcended the divisions—doing culturally what the

IWW was trying to do politically.[33] A song created by women textile workers might be adapted by western miners, and that process would involve just the combination of solidarity and decentralization that the IWW was promoting. Simply humming the tune of "Take It to the Lord in Prayer" could remind other Wobblies present that they shared an alternative political philosophy and an alternative vision of the future; they heard more than most Americans heard.

= The Diverse Constituencies = of the Socialist Party

The Socialist Party, founded in 1901, brought together several very different constituencies whose agendas nonetheless converged or were compatible enough to make the Party a viable political force in the 1910s. Electorally, its agenda generally matched that of the Greenwich Village Left. It included many native-born and well-educated Americans, many of whom were of the upper-middle class. They saw the Socialist Party as continuing an American radical tradition that included Jefferson, Thoreau, and the abolitionists. During that decade the Party also included a significant number of native-born farmers and storekeepers, concentrated in the West and Midwest. In the small towns of plains states like Oklahoma and Kansas, people felt increasingly exploited by railroads, on whom they relied to get the crop to market, and by banks, on whose credit they relied to get the crop in the ground.[34] Their Socialism owed much to American Utopianism and the agrarian ideal. Their values were seriousness and hard work, and their politics were founded on a respect for those values. Politically, their goal was to restore self-determination and economic power to small, independent producers (P. Buhle, 88–89). On the subject of private property, their stand was based on experience rather than theory: everyone should be able to own land or a business that would sustain a family and allow it to prosper from hard work; no one should be able to acquire a monopoly or otherwise use the market to destroy others.

In the Southwest, families of tenant farmers and of independent farmers created out of their religious background and faith a uniquely American Socialist cultural expression, the tent meeting. People came from all over the district and camped out for days of lectures, singing, and communal meals, learning and celebrating the Socialist gospel.

The Socialist Party also had labor support. Eugene Debs, from Terre Haute, Indiana, the Party's leader throughout the 1910s, had come to Leftist thinking after a slow and agonizing loss of faith in the American dream of hard work and upward mobility. He had then founded the American Railway Union and led the Pullman strike of 1894 that was put down by government troops. That experience radicalized him further. Some native-born skilled labor followed Debs into the Socialist Party, believing as he did that labor would never get its due under the current political and economic system. Among such workers, however, the Party never garnered a mass following. Among the skilled, native-born workers, it had its greatest success in cities and towns where the workers were descendants of the radical German Socialists who had fled to America after the failed revolution of 1848.

Speaking to the native-born Socialist constituency, the *Appeal to Reason* was published from 1895 to 1922, from Girard, Kansas, for most of that time, with a remarkable circulation of 760,000 in 1913.[35] Though never officially sponsored by the Party, it was overtly Socialist, printing European and American Socialist thinkers and carrying news of strikes and of Socialists elected to office.

Another significant constituency was immigrant, at first largely Jewish but later including large numbers of Finns, Russians, Hungarians, Lithuanians, Letts, and Slovenians, and smaller numbers of other national groups. Theirs was a "scientific Socialism," so-named because of Marx's claim to have discovered the scientific law that revolutions occur to bring social relations in line with the forces of production (for instance, mass production has made work social rather than individual; therefore the proletariat will usher in Socialism to replace capitalist democracy). From the Lower East Side of Manhattan to the Mesabi Iron Range of Minnesota, Marxian Socialist ideas united intellectuals and manual laborers in ethnic communities. These communities produced a host of foreign-language Socialist newspapers, the best known being the *Jewish Daily Forward,* characteristic in its blend of community news, cultural fare, and political discussion.

Within even some large American cities, there flourished what has come to be called "sewer Socialism." Men like Morris Hillquit of New York City and Victor Berger, mayor of Milwaukee, believed that municipal administration could be a route to Socialism. They concentrated on winning support by giving people the things they wanted and needed: sewers, clean water, paved roads, and the like. Typically, these municipal Socialists developed political machines that structurally paralleled those of the major parties: they provided strong support for unions, deflected the claims of women and African Americans for civil rights and equal justice, and reviled the IWW (P. Buhle, 95).

Within the Socialist Party, women constituted a self-conscious presence. Some women, including many from middle America, came to the Party from the nineteenth-century women's movement, which emphasized solidarity among women and the moral influence women could bring to public institutions. Others were radicalized by Marxian theory, emphasized class over gender, and focused more on economic empowerment than moral influence. The Women's National Committee, founded in 1908 to bring independent women Socialists into the Party, created a program, replicated across the country, to teach Marxian principles to women Socialists, using women's study circles (M. J. Buhle, 157–59). Noting women's increasing dependence on paid work, the Party insisted on regarding women simply as members of the proletariat. In spite of this, there remained within the Socialist Party a strong contingent of women who viewed liberation primarily in terms of solutions to women's particular needs, especially enfranchisement, access to education and work, relief from the double burden of paid work and domestic work, freedom from sexual harassment, and birth control. Thus the tension between class struggle and gender struggle was submerged but unresolved.

When the Nineteenth Amendment to the Constitution gave women the right to vote in 1920, the Socialist Party could claim to have given important support, though the work had in fact been done by a dedicated minority and had not been a priority for the Party overall (M. J. Buhle, 240). It was those forces opposed to woman suffrage that exploited the Party's role in the suffrage campaigns for political gain (M. J. Buhle, 237). Evidence suggests that when, after enfranchisement, the Party nominated women candidates, it was rewarded with a large vote, but generally the women's vote seems to have neither helped nor hurt the Party (M. J. Buhle, 239).

By the mid- to late 1910s, the Party was well on its way to fragmentation. The decade from 1907 to 1917 has been called the Progressive Era because it delivered substantial reforms, such as the eight-hour day and child labor laws. Such reforms eased the pressure for radical change and deprived the Socialist Party of some of its previous support. With the U.S. entry into World War I, however, even the drive for reform was ended. The adjective *progressive* came to denote not social values but civic improvements, like paved roads and good lighting, intended to improve a town's commercial competitiveness.

The mixture of constituencies in the Party had always been unstable. By the late 1910s the changes in American society were changing the mixture and making it more volatile. Many of the young recruits were educated city dwellers, typified by the Greenwich Village Left, whose attraction to Socialism was based on a desire for personal, cultural, and sexual freedom. The fast pace of urban life and the pleasures of the city energized them, and they *liked* the popular culture that came with mass production (P. Buhle, 97). Modern art, jazz, and the neon advertising that lit the urban night were not merely unobjectionable, they were desirable. The nostalgic agrarian Socialism of the plains, religious and traditional, based its politics on a refusal of mass culture, and this new urban group based its Socialism on a desire to extend the freedom and material potential within mass culture. In place of seriousness and hard work, they elevated self-expression and self-development. The coexistence of these two factions limited what the Party as a whole could actually do without alienating one or the other.

The Socialist Party always espoused Marxist theory. Ernest Untermann's *Marxian Economics: A Popular Introduction to the Three Volumes of Marx's Capital* was widely circulated by the Party.[36] In a readable way, it explained

Women Socialists participating in the May Day Parade in New York City in 1914. From the Baines Collection of the Library of Congress.

Marx's theory that the value of a product depended on the amount of labor needed to produce it, thus the "labor theory of value." The product could then be sold for more than the cost of its production, creating a profit, or "surplus value," which the owners kept for themselves rather than passing it along to the workers—the ones who created the value. This "capitalist expropriation" enabled the owners to grow rich without working, while competition for sales required that production costs—chiefly wages—be kept as low as possible. Low wages would limit what working people could buy; the products they could not afford would pile up as inventory; the factory would close until the inventory had been reduced. Thus there would be cycles of boom and bust, and working people could expect periodic layoffs. Owners would constantly search for new markets, where people had money to buy their surplus inventory, and the search would lead them to imperialist adventures around the globe. Wars would break out over control of these distant markets. Under Socialism there would be no capitalist expropriation; the workers would divide the profits and thus have enough spending power to keep inventories from building up. There would be no motive for imperialism or war.

Guided by Marxian theory, the Socialist Party expected the proletariat to be the revolutionary element within society. It consequently devoted much of its energy to union building, even though much of the Party's support came from other groups with other agendas. Along with militant labor work, it pursued an electoral program, running candidates in presidential elections and in many local races and working for the passage of reform legislation. This electoral work won the Party the support of people who wanted and needed such reforms, but it alienated the militant Marxists. They denounced electoral work as useless at best, a buttress for capitalism at worst.

= The Religious Left =

Another group of American Leftists derived their convictions from the Christian Gospel. A reading of the Gospels as a call to end poverty and injustice in this temporal world is as old as Christianity itself, but it came to the fore in American Protestantism as the Social Gospel movement, which began to attract a sizable number of adherents in the 1880s and gained force steadily until the 1920s. Walter Rauschenbusch, Harry F. Ward, and Reinhold Niebuhr provided the theological underpinnings of the movement. In 1912, Rauschenbusch wrote in *Christianizing the Social Order* that the movement was now the dominant interpretation of Christianity among mainstream American Protestants.[37] Indeed, his judgment seems to have been well-founded. The Federal Council of Churches at its 1908 meeting had unanimously endorsed the Social Creed of Churches, calling its member denominations to social responsibility. In small towns as well as urban centers, churches took on social service work, feeding and clothing the poor and providing help for the unemployed, the working poor, and children. The pulpit and the Sunday school textbooks taught Christians that they had a responsibility not only to look after the poor but to work actively to change the social conditions that produced such poverty, and that these responsibilities were best discharged socially, that is, through government and institutions rather than private charity.

Politically, this responsibility was met more often by support for a reform program rather than by commitment to radical change. Christians from the middle and upper strata of society generally focused on improving conditions through better education, health services, and housing and through reform legislation, such as that prohibiting child labor. They were less inclined to support the initiatives for change that came from the poor themselves.[38] Christian reformers in the Progressive Era did little to support labor unions, even the reformist AFL. In culture and class, the reformers and the union organizers were separated by a gulf seldom bridged. Strikes and boycotts were not strategies with which the reformers were comfortable.[39]

For a smaller but important number of Christians, however, the tradition of the Social Gospel did lead to political Socialism. Frances Willard, the leader of the Women's Christian Temperance Union (WCTU), had come to Socialism by reading Edward Bellamy's *Looking Backward* (1888). Despite her many years as president of the WCTU, her main interest and her greatest legacy was the promotion of Christian Socialism and woman suffrage as mutually supporting ideals. Through her, many suffragists came to the Socialist Party, working from a theoretical base in Christian Socialism.

On the farms and in the small towns of the Midwest and West, Christian Socialism provided a framework of support for the Socialist Party. Ruth Norrick, interviewed in 1983 for the Tamiment Library's Oral History of the American Left, said, "You ask me where I became a radical. I would say it was in the First Congregational Church of Terre Haute, Indiana. . . . This was in 1920, '21, and '22." The thirst for justice, the willingness to sacrifice for the larger group and the greater future, the sense of life as a mission, the conviction that God sides with the downtrodden—these were commonly held principles among the Kansas farmers who read the *Christian Socialist* and the African-American Socialists in northern cities and southern towns, whose ministers might have belonged to the multiracial Christian Socialist Fellowship.

Whereas Karl Marx presented Socialist revolution as the working out of historical necessity, American Leftists at many points on the political spectrum were at least as likely to speak of it in moral and salvific terms. Whether they identified themselves as Christian Socialists or had simply come to Socialism through a moral commitment, the religious framework influenced their political action. They tended, for example, to be optimistic about the eventual triumph of righteousness and thus willing to struggle against long odds. They were also likely to be less immediately accepting of political strategies involving violence or deception.

The Roman Catholic Church, which enjoyed particular authority among many immigrant groups, including the large Irish-American population, did not participate in the Social Gospel movement and, in fact, was on terms of mutual suspicion with the Progressive reformers. Joseph McShane in *Sufficiently Radical* relates the conservatism of the Church to its social positioning.[40] To the Vatican, the United States was still a country in need of missionary work; therefore the Catholic Church in the United States was under the supervision of the conservative Congregation for the Propagation of the Faith in Rome. Among its Protestant and Jewish neighbors, the American Church was already suspect as a foreign influence because of its loyalty to Rome; it was therefore unwilling to support social change and call upon itself further charges of un-Americanism. Its response to social ills was a hit-or-miss program of charity (McShane, 16). In addition, many individual Catholics, as well as the institutional Church, resented the patronizing assumption of the reformers that their religion and culture played a role in keeping them poor (McShane, 17). Into the 1910s the Church opposed unionization and taught the most conservative possible interpretation of *Rerum Novarum,* issued by Pope Leo XIII in 1892 and taken by Socialists and unionists worldwide as legitimizing their politics. Spurred by the Bolshevik revolution and the unrest after World War I, however, the Catholic Church in America would unlock the door that opened leftward.

=== Conclusion ===

At the end of the 1910s, the American Left was a small but recognized segment of the political spectrum. It drew support and legitimacy from native traditions of Left thinking, ranging from the philosophies of Emerson and Thoreau to the Utopian vision of Charlotte Perkins Gilman in *Herland* to the "Nationalist" Clubs inspired by Edward Bellamy's *Looking Backward* and dedicated to public ownership of industry, to the various experiments in communal living undertaken by Utopian communities in the nineteenth century.[41] Immigrant Leftists brought to America Marxian, or scientific, Socialism and the revolutionary energy that was contributing to the volatility of Europe in the decade leading to World War I. In spite of the condemnations repeated by conservative newspaper chains, the Left nonetheless managed to garner support in every region of the country, among the poor and the wealthy, the educated and the illiterate, native-born and foreign, religious and atheist, male and female. The Left attracted adherents from those who wished to flee from modern culture and those who wished to embrace it.[42] Though its diversity indicated that it included many constituencies, diversity also made it difficult to get agreement from groups with widely divergent agendas, visions, and strategies. A Left to some degree paralyzed by its diversity created frustration among those who wanted immediate change. When World War I rearranged the boundaries and allegiances of the American Left, and when the Bolshevik revolution was led by a small vanguard party, some Leftists would embrace Communism as the swift and effective means to radical change; other Leftists would reject it as one more unacceptable, and highly disruptive, political competitor.

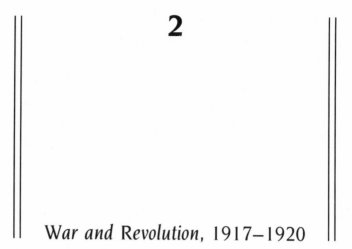

2

War and Revolution, 1917–1920

THE BEGINNING OF WORLD WAR I IN EUROPE PROFOUNDLY DISrupted and discouraged the Left, both in Europe and America. The war brought the collapse of the Second International, the European-based federation of Socialist parties and Socialist labor unions. The International had condemned the war as a war for markets, the sacrifice of millions of lives in the service of imperialist capitalism. The *Masses* carried in its September 1914 issue an editorial by Max Eastman, saying, "[W]e may as well call it a gamblers' war. Only so can we indicate its underlying commercial causes, its futility and yet also the tall spirit in which it is carried off. . . . It is not a national trait but a class trait that has given to Germany the position of grandiose aggressor in this inevitable outbreak of commercial war."[1]

The International had passed resolutions urging workers to call a general strike to make it impossible for their countries to wage war and also urging them to use the situation to hasten revolution. When the moment actually came, however, most Socialists supported their governments. "Internationalism"—class solidarity across national borders—collapsed. The crisis this created for Socialism was not only practical but theoretical: If internationalism was so fragile, was Socialism merely a Utopian dream, as its critics contended? Would Socialist leaders always support their national governments to keep what power they had in the country? And was the war *simply* a contest among imperialist nations, or was there reason to support democratic Britain against feudal Germany? Would the military defeat of the kaiser be the means to advance German Socialism?

In August 1917, John Reed wrote an article titled "This Unpopular War" for *Seven Arts*, saying,

> I have seen and reported many strikes, most of them desperate struggles for the bare necessities of life; and all I have witnessed only confirms my first idea of the class struggle and its inevitability. I wish with all my heart that the proletariat would rise and take their rights— I don't see how else they will get them. Political relief is so slow to come, and year by year the opportunities of peaceful protest and lawful action are curtailed. But I am not sure that the working class is capable of revolution, peaceful or otherwise; the workers are so divided and so bitterly hostile to each other, so badly led, so blind to their class interest. The war has been a terrible shatterer of faith in economic and political idealism.[2]

Against this background of practical discouragement and reexamination, the Russian Revolution shone all the brighter for being unexpected. Marx, of course, had predicted Socialist revolution as the natural outgrowth of bourgeois capitalism and industrialism; Russia was agrarian and barely beyond feudalism. But the Russian Revolution had a galvanic effect on world Socialism simply by creating, for the first time, a major power that claimed to be Socialist. Just when a Socialist future had seemed Utopian, or at best had seemed to recede into the distance, the Councils of Workingmen's and Soldiers' Delegates in Russia proclaimed that it was here, now.

The Left in America watched intently as the Russian Revolution proceeded, claiming to be the embodiment of their dreams. The response from the Left was far from unanimous, however. To some, the revolution was a signal of the new day dawning, a model for American revolution, a sign of hope long coming. For others, it was more ambiguous, convincing in its success but also disturbing in its acceptance of violence and authoritarianism and difficult to reconcile with American cultural traditions.

The *Masses*, of course, opposed World War I as an imperialist war. In the October 1914 issue, Eastman argued that there was no moral reason for preferring one set of capitalists over another, but from the standpoint of results, the war should be continued until the kaiser was defeated and deposed.[3] The August 1915 issue carried "The State of the War" by Arthur Bullard, who had been living in Paris and argued that the Germans must be defeated because they were motivated not only by economic interest but also by the belief that theirs was the superior culture, destined to be imposed on others.

For the staff and the readers of the *Masses*, the apparent collapse of internationalism was particularly disturbing. In the October 1914 issue, Eastman wrote that no one had really thought that the European Socialists were yet strong enough to prevent the war. In the same issue, William English Walling noted that about 40 percent of the German Social Democratic Party (SDP) in the Reichstag supported Karl Liebkneckt's antimilitarist stand, even though the Party required that all of its members vote as a bloc to support the government.[4] Arthur Bullard argued in November 1914 that it was useless to dwell on the breakdown of internationalism.[5]

In April 1917, noting that votes for the Socialist Party in America were down by a third and membership down by half, Eastman wrote that the Party would do well to engage in some honest analysis and stop relying on the formulas of Marxian, or scientific, Socialism. As he saw it, "Scientific thinking requires the power to suspend judgment, and that power has been habitually renounced as an automatic part of the act of becoming a party member. A ready-made first-aid solution of any question that might arise was assumed to be at hand in the *Communist Manifesto* and the party platform, and anyone who had anything else to say would be a heretic and a traitor to 'the working-class.' "[6] He went on to criticize the Socialist Party for its failure to be a working-class party, its failure to "focus on advancing the immediate economic interests of the working class."

The first mention of the Russian Revolution in the *Masses* came in John Reed's lead article of May 1917.[7] He called it then a middle-class revolution. But, writing again in June, he reported that it was looking more like a popular revolution.[8] The next month he reported that it was indeed a Socialist revolution, the purpose of it being "the establishment of a new human society upon the earth."[9] In August, Eastman wrote, "What makes us rub our eyes at Russia is the way all our own theories are proving true. . . . One by one the facts fall out exactly as they were predicted by Marx and Engels and the philosophers of Syndicalism."[10] He wrote that Lincoln Steffens, just back from Petrograd, reported that the workers were in control of the machines.

The August *Masses*, however, didn't reach its subscribers. The Postmaster General, invoking the Espionage Act of 1917, revoked the magazine's mailing license, citing specific editorials and cartoons and a poem as constituting an anticonscription campaign. Granville Hicks, in his 1936 biography of John Reed, asserts that one particular headline, "Knit a Strait-Jacket for Your Soldier Boy," above an article about mental illness in the armed forces, particularly incensed the district attorney against Reed.[11] Material for the August issue had been chosen by Dorothy Day, who did the editorial work while Eastman and Dell were away. According to her later account, no one on the magazine blamed her for the choices; they knew that a run-in with the government was inevitable.[12] In the issues from August to December

1917, when the magazine was forced out of business, it focused on the flagrant violations of the civil liberties of those who opposed the war: the silencing of the *Masses* itself; the unfair trial of Alexander Berkman and Emma Goldman; the raids on Socialist Party offices around the country; the burning of East St. Louis, an African-American town, by white vigilantes; the indictment of much of the IWW leadership for conspiracy against the government.

The September 1917 issue also carried, with an admiring preface, the "Program of the Russian Social Democratic Labor Party," and an editorial in which Eastman expressed extreme regret that Alexander Kerensky was forcing Russia to continue to wage war against Germany.[13] He blamed the U.S. government for driving Russia to this position by refusing to adopt Russia's peace proposals. In fact, the continuation of the war was a highly divisive issue for American Socialists at this point; in spite of the fact that they condemned the war as an imperialist adventure of capitalism, they also wanted the Allies to be in a strong enough position to depose the kaiser. They recognized too that Germany posed the most serious threat to Socialist Russia. A number of members had resigned from the Socialist Party when it refused to rescind its antiwar stand.

Eastman, Dell, H. J. Glintenkamp, Merrill Rogers, Art Young, Josephine Bell, John Reed (in absentia), and the *Masses* Publishing Company came to trial in April 1918 (Hicks, 304). For the defendants, the trial was more about free speech and the right to dissent than it was about the war. A hung jury freed them until a second trial in the autumn of 1918. Again, only a hung jury saved them. John Reed almost missed the questionable pleasure of trial by his peers; he was in Russia during the first, trial but returned in time to join the other defendants in the second. Oregon born and Harvard educated, Reed was a member of the left wing of the Socialist Party. For the *Masses* he had covered the Mexican Revolution and written reports on World War I from France and the Balkans. In September 1917, he went to St. Petersburg, just in time to get a sense of the Russian mood on the eve of the Bolshevik takeover. Because of his opposition to the war, he could find no magazine or newspaper to sponsor him. The *Masses* couldn't afford to send him, but one of its supporters underwrote his trip (Hicks, 249).

In March of 1917 food riots had broken out in St. Petersburg, the garrison had joined the rioters, and Tsar Nicholas II had abdicated. Propertied liberals generally supported this development, prompting radicals to call it a bourgeois revolution. A Council (Soviet) of Workingmen's and Soldiers' Delegates established itself in St. Petersburg, and several interim governments came and went. In July, the government was in the hands of Alexander Kerensky, a moderate Socialist who delayed social change, waiting for the Constituent Assembly, and continued the war against Germany, a war that lacked popular support. Kerensky invited General Kornilov to restore order and suppress the soviets (councils), but he soon realized that Kornilov intended to take over the government for tsarist forces. Kerensky appealed to the populace and the soviets and his old rivals the Bolsheviks—many of whom he had jailed—to save his government.

Lenin was in Finland, having returned from Switzerland by traveling across Germany in a sealed train arranged by the German army. Trotsky, hastily returned from exile in New York, was leading the St. Petersburg Soviet. The Bolsheviks controlled many of the soviets in important Russian cities, and they controlled the Red Guards, the newly formed revolutionary army that turned back Kornilov's forces.

═══ Ten Days That Shook the World ═══

At this point, in September 1917, Reed takes up the story in *Ten Days That Shook the World,* beginning, "This book is a slice of intensified history—history as I saw it."[14] As a journalist, Reed writes a fast-paced narrative full of the concrete detail that conveys immediacy and excitement. As a dedicated revolutionary Leftist, he sees "history" as more than a succession of political maneuvers, chance happenings, and vivid personalities. For him, history is the story of the defeat of capitalism and the beginning of the Socialist era. Telling the story in the first person, he invites the reader to experience the excitement, the confusion, the terror, and the exaltation of those days when it was not clear whether this was the historic Socialist breakthrough or merely a premature, abortive attempt.

The first two chapters of *Ten Days That Shook the World* are given to establishing background. Reed explains that in September 1917 the bourgeois class and the moderate Socialist government of Kerensky believed that the revolution was complete and that any remaining problems would be addressed by the Constituent Assembly that was scheduled to convene in December. But the poorer peasants, the factory workers, and the common soldiers wanted more radical change immediately: "Peace, Land, and Workers' Control of Industry" (Reed 1919, 30)—the program of the Bolshevik Party. Reed makes it clear that the Bolshevik triumph came not from political strength—they were a small party with little power—but from their position as a vanguard party, one that represents the most radical will of the masses. He describes a country that is radicalizing with amazing speed (Social Democratic support falls from 70 percent to 18 percent from June to September [Reed 1919, 33]), where the workers and peasants are simply taking control of machinery and land, and where the soldiers are "voting" for peace by deserting their units, while only the small Bolshevik Party is speaking for such a radical program.

Chapter 3, "On the Eve," describes the feverish atmosphere of expectation that filled St. Petersburg in early November. Saying that no one could tell which side would prevail, Reed writes, "In the barracks and the working-class quarters of the town the Bolsheviki were preaching, 'All Power to the Soviets!' and agents of the Dark Forces [reactionaries] were urging the people to rise and slaughter the Jews, shopkeepers, socialist leaders" (Reed 1919, 65). Reed has easy access to Smolny Institute, the suburban headquarters of the St. Petersburg Soviet, formerly a convent school for daughters of the nobility. It is there that on the night of 6 November one of the Bolshevik leaders tells him, "We're moving!" (Reed 1919, 87).

In his fourth chapter, "The Fall of the Provisional Government," Reed describes the eerie calm, the confusion, and the misinformation that attend the transfer of power. He describes Lenin predicting that the Russian Revolution will spark proletarian revolts all across industrialized Europe. The middle third of the book then is given to the defense of the Soviet government against Kerensky's counterrevolutionary forces. The last third recounts the struggle of the victorious Bolsheviks to get practical and economic control of the country, struggling to gain support, without compromise, from other Socialist parties.

One particularly contentious issue is freedom of the press. Most Socialists, including many Bolskeviks, want an end to censorship now that the counterrevolution has been defeated, but the Lenin faction argues that there can be no real freedom of the press as long as the machinery and paper are affordable only by the bourgeoisie. Carrying the vote in the Council of People's Commissars, the Leninists order all printing equipment seized; from now on it will be withheld from the bourgeois and apportioned among the Socialist parties. Previously loyal Bolsheviks, including Kameniev and Zinoviev, criticize the party and condemn "political terrorism" (Reed 1919, 240). *Ten Days That Shook the World* ends with the peasants' soviets agreeing to support the government proposed and led by the Bolsheviks, thus ensuring the continuation of the "social revolution"—the abolition of private property and the transfer of power to the soviets.

Reed presents the Russian Revolution as a righteous triumph: the workers, peasants, and soldiers take the economic power they have earned by long years of labor and the political power they deserve by strength of number. This righting of a great historical injustice provides the moral framework for the book. (Reed depicts the bourgeoisie as overfed and overdressed; his proletarians eat cabbage soup from wooden spoons and sleep in their clothes.) Within the great sweep of his narrative, other questions of legitimacy tend to get lost: Do the moral claims of the oppressed masses justify abandonment of all constitutional procedures? Is press censorship justified in the struggle? By what right does the Bolshevik Party claim to be the sole representative of the masses? Although Reed never addresses these questions directly, his expressed sympathy with the Bolsheviks implies that their cause justifies their means.

Reed credits the masses not only with moral legitimacy but also with a near-infallible wisdom born of historical agency. It is their moment, and they refuse to be misled by intellectuals. The Bolsheviks, of course, are intellectuals, not proletarians, but for Reed they are the exceptions. David C. Duke, in his biography of John Reed, theorizes that his scorn for intellectuals in *Ten Days* stems from his guilt over the Paterson silk workers' strike in 1913, when he and other intellectuals pressed strikers into appearing in the Pageant of the Paterson Strike in Madison Square Garden in June of that year.[15] The Pageant made good propaganda, serving the goals of Reed and his friends, but it did not give the workers either the money or the political backing they needed to win the strike.

Ten Days That Shook the World was written quickly, in two months in the fall of 1918, while Reed was living in a room on Sheridan Square in the Village. He tells us in the beginning of the book that it is based mostly on his notes but draws also from Russian, French, and English newspapers; the *Bulletin de la Presse*, which was issued daily by the French Information Bureau in St. Petersburg and included a summary of events; reprints of speeches and comments from the Russian press; and the large collection of posters and notices he personally tore from walls. Given the nature of the material, the factual errors he makes are understandable though numerous; they are well documented in the 1967 edition from International Publishers.

In *The Roots of American Communism*, Theodore Draper writes, "John Reed's book undoubtedly made more Soviet sympathizers than did all other Left Wing propaganda combined."[16] When it was reissued in 1922, Lenin wrote the preface, recommending it to workers the world over (Duke, 129). For American Leftists, *Ten Days* was *the* account of the Russian Revolution. Unwilling to accept the political stance of the *New York Times* and other syndicated news sources, they relied on Reed. In light of this fact, the tendency of some segments of the American Left to think that, given economic stress, the American masses might be radicalized quickly and led to power by a small minority party does not seem inexplicable. After all, one of the most compelling impressions to come from Reed's book is that opposition, internal struggle, and feverish ad hoc decision making continued right up to the moment of victory.

═══ Anarchist Reactions ═══

One avid reader of *Ten Days* was Emma Goldman, a Village friend of Reed then serving a two-year term at the Missouri State Penitentiary. She had been found guilty on charges that she misused funds given to the anticonscription campaign, accepted money from the German government, advocated violence against the U.S. government, and conspired to interfere with conscription. The arguments at the trial, however, make it clear that her real offense lay in being an anarchist.[17] The United States had formally entered World War I in April 1917, and the Justice Department moved against the Left soon after.

Goldman's response to the Bolshevik revolution was carried in the November and December issues of the *Mother Earth Bulletin*. Her interpretation of how the revolution was made is particularly interesting: the Russian political activists of the nineteenth and early twentieth centuries (many of them anarchists) prepared the workers *and the peasants;* the army refused to fight any longer; and the Bolshevik Party took as its program the most liberatory yearnings of the people. In short, she sees the revolution as the outcome of an essentially anarchist process—consciousness raising, general strike by the army, general uprising—with the role of the Bolsheviks a bit nebulous. She strongly supports the social revolution (the transference of land to the peasants and of machinery to the workers), and she hails the Russian intention to withdraw from World War I as a response to the people's demand for peace.

What anarchism shared with Marxism was a critique of current governments and a desire to replace them with arrangements that would empower the people. Their disagreement over those "arrangements," however, was fundamental. Thus it is not surprising that most anarchists in Russia and elsewhere generally supported the Bolshevik revolution. Goldman's one criticism of *Ten Days That Shook the World* was that Reed had underplayed the role of the anarchists in bringing down Kerensky's government (Wexler, 256). Nor is it surprising that most anarchists quickly withdrew their support as the Bolsheviks tightened state control in the name of the proletariat. Anarchists were particularly galled by the 1921 decision to use the Red Army against sailors and workers in Kronstadt who were demanding their own soviets, that is, self-government.

When Goldman and Berkman were deported to their Russian homeland in 1919, they soon found reason to be suspicious of the government, but it was Kronstadt that caused them to turn completely against the Bolsheviks. In 1921 they left Russia, and Goldman, in Berlin, wrote an exposé she intended to have published under the title *My Two Years in Russia*. When in 1924 her American publisher cut a number of chapters and gave it the title *My Disillusionment in Russia*, she objected strongly because she had wanted to make clear that she still admired the Russian Revolution even though she felt it had been betrayed by the Bolsheviks. In the preface to the complete (though still mistitled) edition, she stresses this point:

> The *actual* Russian Revolution took place in the summer months of 1917. During that period the peasants possessed themselves of the land, the workers of the factories, thus demonstrating that they knew well the meaning of social revolution. The October change was the finishing touch to the work begun six months previously. In the great

Alexander Berkman addresses a rally in New York City's Union Square on 11 April 1914. From the Baines Collection of the Library of Congress.

uprising, the Bolsheviki assumed the voice of the people. They clothed themselves in the agrarian programme of the Social Revolutionists and the industrial tactics of the Anarchists. But after the high tide of revolutionary enthusiasm had carried them into power, the Bolsheviki discarded their false plumes. . . . Today it is no exaggeration to state that the Bolsheviki stand as the arch enemies of the Russian Revolution.[18]

In the afterword, Goldman gives her political analysis of the Russian Revolution. The Marxists overemphasize industrialization as a prerequisite for revolution; what matters is that the Russian people were *psychologically* ready for social revolution. They were ready to govern themselves, and could have done so through the labor organizations and cooperatives and soviets (councils), supported by the intellectuals. But the Bolsheviks were able to pervert the revolution because the people were politically inexperienced enough to believe that they meant what they said and because the anarchists were not sufficiently organized to counter Bolshevik assertions that the state could be benign. Goldman concludes that the Marxist idea of a revolution that is made by a few and results in the dictatorship of the proletariat is tragically misguided; the only real revolution is one that delivers power to the people themselves and removes government authority altogether.

By 1925, when Goldman's exposé was published in full, the Greenwich Village Left was not as unanimous or sweeping in its praise of the Bolshevik revolution as it had been in 1917. Although Reed's book had been followed by others praising the Bolsheviks, notably those of his wife, Louise Bryant, and of Lincoln Steffens, news of repression, purges, and the Kronstadt massacre had already raised doubts. Reed himself had died of typhus in Moscow in October 1920, and his attitude toward the revolution at the end is the subject of great controversy. As the various parties to this controversy are by no means disinterested—Bryant, Goldman, Eastman, Louis Fraina, Ben Gitlow, Angelica Balabanoff (a Russian anarchist), and Owen Penney (an American anarchist)—it is not too surprising that their accounts, firsthand and secondhand, differ greatly. We will never know whether Reed died an enthusiastic supporter of Bolsheviks; a supporter of the Bolsheviks but angry at Radek and Zinoviev over policy; disillusioned with the Bolsheviks; or disillusioned with Communism itself (Draper 1957, 291–92).

"The Fall of Greenwich Village," the story with which Floyd Dell concludes *Love in Greenwich Village*, is illustrative of both the disillusionment with the Bolsheviks and the breakup of Village life after World War I. One night in 1917, Dell and three friends sit arguing through the night and resume their conversation in the morning at a Village restaurant called the Purple Purp. Julian, the son of a wealthy family, has left his position and his wife and come to the Village to be a poet. Paul, not a son of wealth, has nonetheless quit a well-paying newspaper job to come to the Village and write realistic journalism that will expose the truth about society. Ben is a revolutionist who thinks the artistic and playful life of the Village irrelevant to the real world, where strikes and violence are the overture to class war; but he likes his Village friends nonetheless. The four friends agree that if they had met anywhere but the Village they would never have come to know one another; elsewhere, their social positions would have kept them from admitting their vulnerabilities and trusting one another. Before leaving the Purple Purp, they agree to meet there again in seven years.

The seven years pass, it is 1924, and Dell returns to the restaurant, knowing that Ben is in jail for his politics and Julian has committed suicide. Paul is waiting for him and, after some initial discomfort, tells Dell that he feels no guilt about having become a success and leading a suburban life. At a recent suburban party, he simply enjoyed himself—though he felt contempt for the other party goers—and thought that Ben and Julian had been fools to sacrifice themselves for some greater vision of humankind: "It's a mistake to suppose that one can't be happy in a meaningless world" (Dell 1926, 319). Later that night, as Dell walks through the Village in the December cold, he reflects that all that he loved about it is gone. The Village is now home to a generation that takes it for granted that life is without meaning. Ironically, he thinks of his very anti-Victorian generation as the last to have a late Victorian faith in beauty and goodness.

Dell believed that people should control their own lives, be free from bourgeois values and restrictions, free to be self-expressive and creative in work and in love. But, ironically, the predominant forms of Left political *action* in the late 1920s and 1930s demanded such dedication and involved such risk that the life of a dedicated Left activist looked anything but free.

Indeed, in the story at the middle—one might say the heart—of *Love in Greenwich Village*, "Hallelujah, I'm a Bum!," we have Jasper Weed, a dutiful son who finally rebels against spending his life working off a mortgage and becomes a hobo, riding the rails. He joins the Wobblies and becomes an organizer of miners and lumbermen in the West. He is finally happy, among men whose talk is not about money.

But the authorities are ruthless in persecuting the Wobblies. Jasper, recovering from a wound, allows himself to think a frightening thought: Is he not just another "soldier" even if his war is a righteous class war? Isn't his war as suicidal and destructive as the one being fought in Europe? So he runs off to Greenwich Village, where he becomes a sculptor, teaches his friends Wobbly songs at parties, and falls in love. Then he and more than 100 other Wobblies are indicted, and he is among those found guilty. His lover, Inez, is contemptuous of all political action, telling him his faction would be as ruthless if it were in power. She cannot bring herself to make any commitment to him personally. Back among his fellow Wobbly defendants, he sees her and his Village life as idle, irrelevant to the political struggle that gives life meaning.

So he has come full circle. But the story takes yet another turn. On the evening before he jumps bail and goes to Russia, he goes disguised to a party held by a wealthy benefactor. There he hears a man from the Justice Department describe him as a foreign agent provocateur; his benefactor gives him permission to jump bail; and he and Inez make love one last time before he leaves "to live and die with irrelevant heroism in some strange place" (Dell 1926, 190).

In this story, Dell (who as author invites us to identify the narrators of his stories with himself) presents the dilemma of Jasper sympathetically; he can't be entirely happy either with the role of political "soldier" or with the role of apolitical artist. Nothing in the story refutes Inez's assertion that Jasper loves the IWW because it allows him to combine the life of a tramp with the sense of duty he learned from his bourgeois New England family. But neither does anything in the story suggest that Inez's life of noncommitment is the "answer."

Indeed, the conundrum for Dell, the author, in this era seems to have been that his commitment to personal freedom made him a committed Leftist, but it also limited his Leftism to an anarchism that expressed itself mainly through art and a lifestyle of critique and resistance.[19] As the stories "Green Houses" and "The Fall of Greenwich Village" make clear, his Villagers cannot be truly free as long as they live under a capitalist system in which Village bohemianism becomes a tourist attraction and as long as they are subject to a government that prosecutes Wobblies for free speech. Implicit in *Love in Greenwich Village* is the assumption that only revolutionary change will make them free, but by 1926 Dell presents the Russian Revolution as something of a romantic trap for the "irrelevant heroism" of Jasper Weed and Ben the revolutionist.

Despite Dell's elegiac tone in *Love in Greenwich Village*, radicalism did not desert the Village in the 1920s. The *Liberator*, taking over in March 1918 when the *Masses* was forced out of business, published from offices on West Thirteenth Street and included many alumni of the *Masses*. Max Eastman was its editor and, with his sister Crystal Eastman, owned the controlling interest. Reading his editorials defending the Bolsheviks, one might be tempted to think back with some irony on his early columns in the *Masses* attacking the Socialist Party for dogmatism and faith in scientific Marxism. In "The Russian Dictators" (March 1918) he wrote that "many radical-minded Americans" are outraged that the Constituent Assembly of the Workmen's and Soldiers' Soviets has been dissolved by the Bolsheviks, but they should understand that the assembly, elected before the revolution, when money still determined who would be elected, was not representative of all the people, merely of those with property. He goes on to argue that a bourgeois assembly would never carry out the social revolution; power must be given to "industrial and farmers' unions," which will give land to the peasants and factories to the workers.[20] Eastman continues,

It is never "the people" who will accomplish this—Lenin has been warned against the concept of "the people" in his Bible of Karl Marx from the beginning. It is the working-class who will accomplish it, and they will accomplish it, if they can, by establishing a dictatorship, overt and uncompromising. The truth is that only after a general transfer of land and factories to the workers is accomplished, so that substantially all the people have become workers, and the super-political influence of a capitalist class is removed, can an appeal to the people really *be* an appeal to the people. Only then does the formal justice and democracy of a popular vote become materially just and democratic. (Eastman 1918)

This brief explanation makes clear why Eastman and the *Liberator* and many other American Leftists continued to defend the Bolsheviks.

When Eastman left for Europe in 1922 he gave over the editorship to Mike Gold and Claude McKay. Gold wanted the magazine to be a vehicle for political militancy; McKay wanted it to remain an outlet for artistic self-expression (Aaron, 91–96). Their differences represented no simple dichotomy; both preferred an effective, politically charged literature and art. But, lacking enough of that, would they publish the artistically crude but politically impassioned poem, or the finely wrought apolitical poem? This question was more than one of editorial policy; it is a manifestation of the general question of how politics and culture are—or should be—related. Answers to this question divided not only Gold and McKay but many others on the *Liberator* staff and many other Leftists for decades to come. Finally, in 1922, with Eastman's approval, the *Liberator* was turned over to the Workers' Party. It ceased publication in 1924.

= The Communist Party =

The demise of the Second International brought to the point of crisis the tensions within the Socialist Party in America. Its strategy of working within the electoral system was called into question by the example of European Socialist parties. In Germany, the Socialist leader Karl Bernstein had pursued a revised version of Marxian theory (a "revisionist heresy" to his critics) and urged the value of electoral work in transferring power. He had led the Social Democratic Party to a powerful position in the German parliament. When the SDP did not oppose World War I, some American critics reviled Bernstein's revisionism, claiming that the SDP had chosen to keep its power rather than its Socialist principles. They clamored for the Socialist Party to drop its electoral work and make a revolution.

The war in Europe having reduced emigration, unskilled labor in America saw an opening to push for industrial unions, most notably in the garment industry. The Socialist Party helped organize the unions, and many of the newly organized workers joined the foreign-language sections of the Party. These groups had acquired official status in the Party only in 1912, and by 1916 their numbers were nearly equal to those of its English-speaking segment (P. Buhle, 112). They swelled the ranks of the faction most eager to take the Socialist Party into Communism.

In spite of some internal disagreement, the Socialist Party was staunch in its public opposition to World War I. In the years before U.S. entry into the war, that opposition won them support from the sizeable portion of the American populace that was against the war, and it won them some surprising electoral victories. By 1916, however, the government and the forces that favored U.S. entry into the war were succeeding in their campaigns for "preparedness," and opposition became increasingly costly. Popular sentiment in favor of the war grew. Socialists were demonized and harassed as unpatriotic. The Espionage Act of 1917 and the Sedition Act of 1918, used sweepingly to deny constitutional rights of free speech and freedom of assembly to the anarchists and the IWW, were also used against the Socialist Party. Socialist papers all across the country lost their second-class mailing privileges. The Party's national headquarters were raided. Arrests of Socialists merely for speaking or writing against the war continued, and the American populace raised no great cry for the defense of civil liberties. The arrest of Eugene Debs in June 1918 in Canton, Ohio, for giving an antiwar speech, and his subsequent sentence to 10 years in federal prison, provoked no uprising, even though as the Party's presidential candidate in 1912 Debs had drawn 6 percent of the vote. Seeing that pacifism brought only repression, the militants in the Party, largely situated in the foreign-language groups, pressed for Communism, but without success.

After the Bolshevik revolution of November 1917, Lenin made no secret of his expectation that revolution would soon follow in the industrialized countries. In Hungary, Austria, Germany, and Finland general strikes or revolts did take place, and many other European countries experienced smaller uprisings. All, however, were short-lived. America saw a wave of strikes in 1919. A general strike delivered Seattle into the hands of AFL unions, whose "soviet" managed the city for five days in February.[21] (The AFL, reformist and antiradical, was horrified and denounced the action.) The Party saw no opportunity in the strike, further disappointing its militants.

During World War I, Leftists were harassed and prosecuted on the grounds that their opposition to the war was a threat to national interests and security. The leadership was jailed or deported, and public opinion turned against the Left. The Bolshevik revolution produced an anti-Left weapon that would outlast the war: the Red Scare. It fed on the natural fears of war-weary Americans that their country would be engulfed in a bloody civil war such as that in which the Red and the White armies were then tearing apart Russia, destroying cities and farms and causing thousands of starving people to flee in terror. It also fed on the conviction that the American system of government had shown a capacity to produce reform and was the best available. But fear and resentment of foreigners also played a part. And the direct manipulation of groups like the American Protective League, sponsored by the government, created an atmosphere in which it was considered patriotic to root out "un-Americanism" by any means, including vigilante violence (Georgakas, 11).

In this volatile atmosphere, the Socialist Party met for its national convention in Machinists' Hall in Chicago in late August of 1919. The left wing of the Party—mostly situated in the foreign-language groups but including some native-born militants and the Michigan group (driven by opposition to reformism)—convened its own gathering at the headquarters of the Russian-language group on Blue Island Avenue for the purpose of forming its own Communist party. Another faction of the left wing, led by John Reed and Ben Gitlow, wanted to take over the Socialist Party and convert it to Communism.

The right wing, warned in advance of Reed and Gitlow's intentions, set up guards and a pass system to keep left-wing delegates out of the meeting room in Machinists' Hall. When they broke in and were forcibly removed, they went downstairs to the billiard room and constituted themselves as the Communist Labor Party (Draper 1957, 178).

The next day, 1 September, the remainder of the left wing organized as the Communist Party, under the leadership of Louis C. Fraina, an Italian immigrant who had been a member of the Socialist Labor Party, and Charles Ruthenberg, a Socialist leader from Cleveland. Both Communist parties distinguished themselves from the strategies of the Socialist Party by rejecting reformism in all its guises and rejecting coalitions with other parties (Draper 1957, 185). Unlike the Socialist Party, which taught Marxist theory but blessed a broad spectrum of goals and strategies, both Communist parties were determined to be as single-minded and focused as the Bolsheviks had been. Revolution would be their sole project, pursued through the two strategies of building the parties and building revolutionary unions that would compete with the reformist AFL unions. The Communist Labor Party chose to support the IWW as its vehicle for accomplishing this, while the Communist Party proposed creating a larger union to be composed of the IWW and the more militant AFL unions (Draper 1957, 186). This so-called dual-union strategy would become highly controversial over the coming decades.

One might have expected the Communist Labor Party and the Communist Party to have merged after splitting, each in its own way, from the Socialist Party. Theodore Draper, in *The Roots of American Communism*, argues that they remained separate because the Communist Labor Party did not want American Communism to be dominated by the foreign-language groups (187). This insistence went beyond antiforeign prejudice; it continued the working assumption (later called American exceptionalism) of the Socialist Party that conditions in America were so different from those in Europe that the path to revolution might also be different. So the two parties remained separate, and they competed for recognition by the Third International (the Communist International, often shortened to Comintern), founded in Moscow in March 1919.

The purpose of the Comintern was to promote and coordinate revolution in the industrial countries. And, indeed, both Communist parties in the United States pursued strategies appropriate to the goal of imminent revolution. In 1919 and 1920, they directed their membership to boycott elections. In the midst of the great strikes of 1919, they chose not to support the established unions, believing them reformist and antirevolutionary. When a Labor Party was formed, akin to the British Labour Party, and when it became a Farm-Labor Party, the Communists shunned it too as a reformist diversion. The fevered atmosphere in the country in 1919 convinced them that a small uncompromising party could be the vanguard of a revolution. In opting for revolutionary purity, they were following what they understood to be the Bolshevik pattern; however, as Theodore Draper notes, the Bolshevik revolution was made with slogans like "Bread and Peace," promising immediate improvement in people's lives, not political radicalism (Draper 1957, 218).

In prison in Atlanta, Eugene Debs received word that the Communists wanted him to join them. Debs had earlier proclaimed himself a Bolshevist, but he refused the Communists on the grounds that he could not accept the violence or the dictatorship of the proletariat. He remained with the Socialist Party, upholding the Bolsheviks against their capitalist enemies and applauding their goals, though unable to support their means. His dilemma was and would continue to be a common one for Leftists: how far should one go in defending and supporting the Bolsheviks for the sake of their stated goals? In 1923, giving a speech titled "The Negro Workers" in Harlem, Debs proclaimed, "The reason we [the United States] do not recognize their [the Bolshevik] Republic is because for the first time in history they have set up a government of the working class; and if that experiment succeeds, goodbye to capitalism throughout the world!"[22]

= The African-American Left =

The last years of the 1910s and the early 1920s witnessed a radical change in the lives and the thinking of many African Americans. The Great Migration, begun around 1915, brought thousands from southern farms to northern cities. Jobs there were more available than they had been before the war, when the tide of European immigration flowed unstemmed. By 1919, Harlem in New York and the South Side in Chicago were simply the largest of the new African-American neighborhoods to be found in all the northern cities. The concentration of population that comes with urban living gave African Americans a sense of their collective strength. Fighting with the army in

Europe and fighting for jobs at home created a new militancy and gave rise to what was then called the New Negro movement.[23]

With the end of the war, competition between whites and blacks over scarce jobs led to racial violence on a scale never seen before in this country. The summer of 1919 saw violent confrontations in large and small cities nationwide, begun by whites and often instigated by the Ku Klux Klan, which had come to life again in 1915 and rapidly attracted hundreds of thousands of members (Brisbane, 72).

The increasing militancy and heightened political consciousness among African Americans at this point did not generally lead left. Both the National Association for the Advancement of Colored People (NAACP, founded in 1910 by a group that included Socialists) and the Urban League (founded in 1911) refrained from attacking capitalism.[24] The Urban League, in fact, had functioned as an employment agency, placing African-American workers during the war. When the war ended and jobs became scarce, the national office of the League went on record as opposing the practice of supplying African-American strikebreakers, but it allowed local chapters to go their own way on this issue. Chicago was merely the most flagrant of the locals that cooperated with management against white unions (Brisbane, 67). Given the color bar in force in nearly all the established unions, African Americans' willingness to take work when they could get it is not surprising. Nor is it surprising, with competition over jobs the most volatile racial issue, that class solidarity across the race line did not recommend itself to most African Americans as a political strategy.

W. E. B. Du Bois, a founder of the NAACP, emerged as the chief intellectual opponent of the black political conservatism promoted by Booker T. Washington. Editing the *Crisis,* the NAACP monthly, Du Bois attacked lynching, segregation, and disenfranchisement and created a forum in which black intellectuals could hold an ongoing conversation.[25] He had joined the Socialist Party in 1911 but left the next year, partly in reaction to racism within the Party and to its insufficient commitment to racial justice work, but also because he had decided to endorse Woodrow Wilson for president in 1912. His support for World War I further separated him from the Socialist Party; indeed, his *Crisis* editorial "Close Ranks" has been credited with garnering black support for the war.[26]

His belief in a gradualist road to Socialism prevented him from being fully supportive of the Bolshevik revolution, although he spoke admiringly of its goals. In 1920, he wrote, "Perhaps the finest contribution of current Socialism to the world is neither its light nor its dogma but the idea back of its one mighty word—Comrade!"[27] The next year he summed up his objections, saying, "I do decidedly think that many proposals made by Socialists and Communists and even by the present rulers of Russia would improve the world if they were adopted; but I do not believe that such adoption can successfully come through war or force or murder, and I do not believe that the sudden attempt to impose a new industrial system and new ideas of industrial life can be successful without the long training of human beings."[28] Although he remained an independent Socialist, more radical Socialists and Communists condemned his integrationist and gradualist politics as reactionary. His belief in leadership for change by the "Talented Tenth" of African Americans was likewise criticized as elitist.

The political group that won the greatest and most enthusiastic support was also the most radical: the Garveyites. Marcus Garvey, a Jamaican, came to the United States in 1916 and called on African Americans to ally themselves culturally and politically with others of African descent in all parts of the world. Race, not class, was to be the unifying factor. His Universal Negro Improvement Association (UNIA) was racially separatist and dedicated to pan-Africanism.

Although Garvey spoke positively about the Bolshevik revolution, he praised it as an oppressed people's liberation movement, not a Marxist victory. Garvey was a devoted capitalist, many leaders of the UNIA were owners of small businesses, and the UNIA itself owned a number of businesses, the most famous of which was the Black Star shipping line, intended eventually to return African Americans to their homeland, where they would be self-governing. Garvey's vision of cultural and economic independence and political self-determination was a sweeping vision of social change, and it enlisted from African Americans wider and deeper support than they gave to reformist organizations like the NAACP. By the mid-1920s, however, the UNIA was essentially defunct as a result of Garvey's conviction for fraud and a number of lawsuits against the organization.

The most eloquent voice for the Socialist Party in Harlem belonged to A. Philip Randolph, who did not waver in his support of labor or his opposition to World War I. Editing the *Messenger*, he marshalled considerable electoral support for the Socialist Party and welcomed the literary expressions of the Harlem Renaissance in the 1920s. But, impatient with the inaction of the Party on racial issues, Randolph ended his membership sometime in the early 1920s and, as an independent Socialist, went on to organize the Brotherhood of Sleeping Car Porters. As Philip S. Foner notes in *American Socialism and Black Americans*, the Socialists had begun in 1915 to acknowledge that racism was a separate problem from the general oppression of the masses and required attention in its own right, but further analysis and action were stalled by the split between the right and left wings of the Party in 1919.[29]

Speaking both for black nationalism and for Socialism was the *Crusader* (1918–22), edited by Cyril Briggs, an immigrant from the West Indies. Published in Harlem, the *Crusader* carried reports on cultural events and basketball in the community, essays on African history, and some poetry and fiction. Editorially, it promoted pan-African consciousness, supported the creation of a new free black state either in Africa or somewhere in the Americas, and backed candidates of the Socialist Party. Early in its publication run, the

Crusader had supported Garvey, whose pan-African ideal it shared. But by 1921 it was attacking Garvey and the UNIA as deluded by capitalism and finally as corrupt.

Robert A. Hill, who edited the 1987 book in which reprints of the *Crusader* are collected, thinks March 1919 the likeliest date for Briggs's embrace of Communism.[30] He believes that the declaration of an anti-imperialist policy at the first congress of the Third International was the stroke that won over Briggs; the International had declared that proletarian victory in Europe would be accompanied by anti-imperialist revolution in Africa and Asia. What attracted African Americans like Briggs to Communism in this period was neither its class-based politics nor its economic analysis but its commitment to the liberation of oppressed racial and ethnic groups, what Communists referred to as "the national question" (Hill, xxvi).[31]

The African Blood Brotherhood (ABB), which became the sponsor of the *Crusader*, was founded in fall 1919, at roughly the same time that the Communist parties in the United States were founded, following the 1919 summer of lynchings and racial violence. Briggs later asserted that the Communists did not initiate the ABB, but there is some evidence to suggest that they did. By the early 1920s the Comintern was directing American Communists to enter into what was in effect a "united front" with African Americans, taking the fight against lynching and for racial equality as its own (Hill, xxxvii).

An editorial titled "Bolshevist!!!" in the October 1919 *Crusader* reads, in part, "[W]e would not for a moment hesitate to ally ourselves with any group, if by such an alliance we could compass the liberation of our race and the redemption of our Fatherland. A man pressed to earth by another with murderous intent is not under any obligation to choose his weapons. He would be a fool if he did not use any or whatever weapon was within his reach."[32] Briggs cast his lot with Communism because its program, like Garvey's, promised a radical change in the lives of African Americans but, unlike Garvey's, seemed attainable. The *Crusader* and the ABB were careful after 1919 to give a class analysis and to urge alliances with "other workers," but the felt solidarity resided in race, not class. "Bolshevist!!!" is followed directly by another editorial titled "Negro First!" arguing that the denial of civil rights to African Americans forced them to put race first: "This choice is not voluntary."[33]

When Claude McKay became an associate editor of the *Liberator* in 1921, he had just returned from a two-year stay in London, where he had read Marx and worked for the *Workers' Dreadnought*, a Marxist magazine published by Sylvia Pankhurst. It is in the *Liberator* in the late 1910s and early 1920s that we first find African-American Leftists writing in a magazine with a primarily white readership. Having emigrated to the United States from Jamaica, McKay was among a number of Caribbean theorists and writers who strongly influenced African-American political thinking in the 1910s and 1920s.

It was in the bloody summer of 1919 that McKay published "Roman Holiday," about the unleashing of white violence, and "If We Must Die," in which he declares that "we" will not die like animals, but "fighting back!"[34] More than any other literary work, "If We Must Die" became the signature piece of the New Negro movement. As Tyrone Tillery points out, the poem, so often read as a repudiation of black quietism and the accommodationist politics of Booker T. Washington, never mentions race (Tillery, 35). The lines in the sonnet that come closest to identifying "we" as a racial group are "O kinsmen! we must meet the common foe! / Though far outnumbered let us show us brave." Yet Winston Churchill apparently found in the poem a universal sentiment, for he quoted from it during World War II (Tillery, 35). McKay himself explained in later years that he intended "we" to refer to all the oppressed of any race. The indeterminacy may indeed reflect McKay's own dual allegiance to racial struggle and to class struggle. Nonetheless, African Americans took up "If We Must Die" as speaking their own particular bitterness at having been asked to "close ranks" in supporting the war and then cast aside (Tillery, 36). Black newspapers and magazines all over the country reprinted "If We Must Die," and McKay, rather uncomfortably, found himself regarded as the voice of black resistance (Tillery, 36).

In "Africa" he offers an implicit challenge to Garveyism by describing the glories of Africa as those of the past.[35] The same fate, seeing its glories buried in sand, he envisions for the United States in his sonnet "America," where he speaks of his love for this "cultured hell."[36] In his review of Balieff's *Chauve-Souris* from the Bat Theatre of Moscow (March 1922), he reports his delight in finding again the direct experience of life that he loved in the amateur theaters of Jamaica. He finds in revolutionary Soviet culture respect for the authenticity of "folk" culture.

During his visit to Moscow, McKay was received enthusiastically by the Bolshevik leadership, and he addressed the Comintern. At odds with the majority of the American Communists over the now united Party's remaining underground, he noted in his address that reformist organizations in America had done more than radical Socialists or Communists to improve the lot of African Americans.[37] In his autobiography, *A Long Way from Home* (1937), he recounts his amusement at discovering that Bukharin believed Jack London's novel *The Iron Heel* (1907), a dystopic depiction of a tyrannized America, set in the future, to be an accurate portrayal of contemporary conditions in the United States.[38] Disturbed by the repressive measures of the Soviet government and beginning to lose faith that proletarian victory would mean racial equality, McKay declined the invitation to join the Communist Party. Further, he refused the offered role of proletarian poet. *A Long Way from Home* suggests that he continued to believe in Marxian theory during the years he spent as an emigré in Europe and North Africa, after leaving Russia. But in a 1944 letter to Max Eastman he traced the beginning of his disillusionment to his 1922–23 visit to Moscow.[39]

= Response of the Religious Left =

Eugene Debs, hailing the Russian Revolution in an April 1918 issue of the Socialist paper the *Call,* used the language of Christian triumphalism: "Think of the Ages Russia groaned in the agony of her travail, the deluge of blood and tears poured out in the long night of her persecution and exile, and the costly sacrifices laid by her daughters and sons upon the holy altar of freedom! And now, as if by command of God himself, she rises from her bondage, stands erect in her supreme majesty, and breathes her benediction of peace and love upon the world."[40] In spite of his reservations about the violent means by which the revolution had been made and in spite of his refusal to become a Communist, he could speak of the revolution as a triumph of righteousness.

Christian Socialism as a movement and as a political influence was greatly diminished during World War I, when many adherents of the movement supported the Wilsonian claim that the war would make the world safe for democracy.[41] Support for the war separated the Christian Socialists from many others on the Left, and the Red Scare widened the separation. In spite of the diminishment of the Christian Socialist movement, Christian Socialist thinking continued to be influential within the American Left and mainstream American Protestantism. The native-born tradition was constantly augmented by European Socialist Christian theology, brought by immigrant groups and sometimes translated into English.

World War I, so disruptive of old alliances and animosities, served to integrate the Catholic Church into American society (McShane, 83). The Church joined in the newly formed coalition of reformers, labor unions, and other churches to deal with postwar problems, most pressingly the shortage of jobs for returning soldiers. Father John Augustine Ryan, using the natural rights doctrine that figures prominently in Catholic theology and in the founding documents of the United States, set forth a program based on a full reading of *Rerum Novarum;* it reiterated Pope Leo's call for workers to own the means of production either in producers' cooperatives or through significant stock ownership and a role in management. Ryan consciously crafted his program, issued in 1919 as the *Bishops' Program of Social Reconstruction,* as an alternative to the Bolshevik model of Socialism in which the state owns the means of production (McShane, 168).

The *Bishops' Program* had been signed by only four bishops and therefore was not binding on the faithful. It received wider episcopal and clerical support, and, predictably, also some attacks from inside and outside the

Church. The National Association of Manufacturers demanded its withdrawal, and the National Civic Federation campaigned against it (McShane, 209–11). In the 1920s, the Catholic Church did not continue its move leftward, but the widely publicized *Bishops' Program* gave Catholic Leftists access to the "guild Socialism" of *Rerum Novarum* and one vision of its application to American industrial ills.

= The Red Scare, the IWW, = and the Communists

As the entry of the United States into World War I had become increasingly likely and then after it had become a fact, opposition to the war among the American citizenry had quieted, partly in response to a promotional campaign by prowar forces and partly in response to intimidation. Citizens who did not support the war risked having their houses splattered with yellow paint. Prominent Leftists and organized Left organizations were particular targets. Goldman and Berkman had been deported early on. The IWW, which never organized against the war, was hounded. On 7 September 1917, federal officials raided IWW halls all across the country. Shortly thereafter, nearly all of the leadership was indicted for conspiracy to subvert the war effort. (Their mass trial in Chicago in April 1918 figures in Dell's "Hallelujah, I'm a Bum!")

Local harassment also increased. A U.S. district attorney in Kansas, where the IWW had been organizing oil workers, gave orders for the arrest of anyone in the district belonging to the IWW (Georgakas, 13). Vigilante groups persecuted the Wobblies outside the law. Julia Ruuttila, interviewed for the Oral History of the American Left, remembered "a bunch of farmers in that [Williamite, Oregon] valley with ropes . . . came to lynch my father."[42] Herb Edwards, who joined the IWW in 1917, recalled, "At that time they were searching everybody on the street that looked like a working man— had on overalls—no matter how well he behaved himself. Went out to camps and lined them up against the wall just something like a Valentine's Massacre on a smaller scale, only they didn't kill anybody. Go through their belongings and searched them for [Wobbly membership] cards and so on. And one thing that helped me as a camouflage and beside it kept me warm, I had an army overcoat and an army shirt on." He went on to describe riding on a bus going to Tacoma and realizing that he had been picked out as a Wobbly, so he jumped off at an earlier stop, just as the bus was starting up again. He concluded, "If you were engaged in any organization activity you were a marked man. If the vigilantes didn't get you and beat you up, the police threw you in the can and beat you up. You'd be blacklisted so you couldn't get a job. I changed my name so many times during that time that I didn't remember my own name on some of the jobs" (Edwards, OHAL).

The "Little Red Song Book" could also be used against the Wobblies. Just as the IWW asserted its vision by putting new words to culturally standard songs, so could the new words be quoted and misquoted and the tone distorted to demonize the Wobblies. On 17 August 1917, Senator Henry Fountain Ashurst of Arizona read into the Congressional Record selected lines from John R. Kendrick's "Christians at War," a parody sung to "Onward Christian Soldiers." The poem's speaker—the one being parodied—urges young men to enlist so they can go to Europe and rape and pillage. In Ashurst's quotation, reprinted the following day in the *New York Times,* all references to Europe and World War I are eradicated, and it is made to seem that the IWW is urging its own members to rape and pillage (Stretch).[43]

Such manipulation might go a long way toward explaining public antipathy toward the IWW in the late 1910s. But we might also look for other reasons why there was so much popular cooperation with and so little resistance to the persecution of the Wobblies. Racial and ethnic prejudice are certainly not to be discounted. And any position of privilege, even membership in an AFL union, was threatened by the IWW agenda. The Wobbly strategies of sabotage and direct action no doubt also played a role, associating the IWW with lawlessness, with "not playing by the rules." The breakdown of civil order may have its liberatory aspects, but it sets even relatively poor people to worrying about their personal safety and that of their families. Many Americans knew nothing of the IWW vision of a General Strike initiating a peaceful transfer of power. They knew that when the IWW came to town, violence followed.

Thus occupied in defending itself, the IWW did not react as an organization to the Bolshevik takeover in November 1917. Through the Wobbly press, Harrison George published *Red Dawn,* in praise of Bolshevism, and such important Wobblies as James P. Cannon, Bill Haywood, John Reed, and William Z. Foster were won over to the Bolsheviks (Dubofsky, 462–63). In a *Liberator* article titled "Bill Haywood, Communist," (April 1921), Haywood is quoted as saying, "It is the fact, the example, that has caused any change in me that may seem contradictory. And even now I would hesitate to confirm such a movement if everything that emanates from Moscow did not show that they want to put the workers in control and eventually eliminate the state."[44]

Some IWW periodicals, like *Solidarity,* supported the Communists, while others, such as *One Big Union Monthly,* vehemently opposed them. Much debate followed Moscow's invitation to the IWW to join the Third International, and in 1922 the invitation was refused. The majority of the IWW could not support a revolution that put power into the hands of a centralized government. By the time of its 1924 convention, the IWW was so torn by internal dissension (which may or may not have been helped along by agents provocateurs), so disabled by the jailing of its leadership, and demoralized by the bail-jumping flight of Haywood to Russia that it ceased to be an effective organization.

The emotions and the apparatus supporting the persecution of the Left during the war were continued afterward as part of an ongoing Red Scare. Any Leftist risked being regarded as a Red and hounded as an agent of Russian subversion. On 8 November 1919, Communist offices in New York City were raided under the auspices of a subcommittee of the New York State Senate. Literature was seized, many Party members were arrested, and others in the city went underground. On 2 January 1920, the Palmer Raids, ordered by Attorney General A. Mitchell Palmer, ransacked Communist offices in 33 cities. A second night of raids followed on 5 January. Hundreds of Communists were prosecuted, though few actually served much prison time. The Palmer Raids strengthened the identification of American Communists with the Bolsheviks and drove the entire Communist movement underground (Draper 1957, 207). Now a secret organization, it turned to secret codes, pseudonyms, fronts, and clandestine meetings and was cut off from American political life. Being a secret organization made it all the more terrifying and suspect in the eyes of unsympathetic Americans.

═══ Conclusion ═══

The collapse of the Second International created profound discouragement on the Left. Parliamentary Socialism was judged discredited because internationalism had failed in this one specific historical circumstance. The changes in American society produced by reform and industrialization brought some new constituencies to Socialism and detached others. The Bolshevik revolution, by virtue of its success just when success looked most remote, drew many adherents who might have preferred other Leftist paths had they seemed at that time capable of leading anywhere. Among Leftists, Reed's *Ten Days That Shook the World* was the most influential account of the Bolshevik triumph, and it did much to enlist support and also to establish the "Bolshevik model" of revolution by a small vanguard party, owing success to uncompromising political purity. Some American Leftists became enthusiastic Bolshevists; others were partial in their support; still others turned against the Bolshevik regime and denounced it. In *Love in Greenwich Village*, Floyd Dell illustrates the dilemma of the Leftist who admires the success of the revolution but recognizes that a revolutionist must sacrifice the very self-expression and freedom that anarchists want from a revolution. Likewise, the ambiguity of the "we" in Claude McKay's "If We Must Die" epitomizes the dilemma of African Americans attracted to the Left for its radicalism and its ideal of interracial proletarian solidarity but aware, like McKay, that reformist organizations held more political clout and often did more to improve African-American life.

Wartime persecution and then the Red Scare isolated the Left from the American political mainstream. Thus was American Communism born into a milieu in which the broad spectrum of Leftist discourse had been much reduced and marginalized. The Bolshevik model of political success and the narrow Communist focus on the proletarian class made Communism an unlikely and problematic inheritor of the culturally diverse tradition of American Leftism. Over the next three decades, the united Communist Party met with varying degrees of success in connecting with the needs and ideals that supported Leftism in America, and non-Communist forms of Leftism continued to develop. After 1917, however, a continuing form of attack on the Left was to call all Leftists "Reds," obscuring vital differences among Leftist visions and strategies.

3

From the Jazz Age to the Crash, 1920–1930

DRIVEN UNDERGROUND BY THE RED SCARE, DWINDLING IN NUMBERS, and cut off from the rest of the hard-beset American Left, the Communist parties in 1920 could only hope to follow the pattern of the Bolsheviks as they understood it: to articulate a radical analysis and a radical program and hope to be carried into power by the tide of history. Expecting the economic crisis of 1919, with its attendant violence, to lead to revolution by the workers, Communists of all stripes turned their energies to engaging in factional disputes and theoretical arguments. They were preparing to enter power; they were preparing for a future that never arrived.

In 1920, Lenin recognized that the Russian Revolution would not spark the revolution throughout the industrialized countries that Marx had predicted. Accepting that the historical moment for worldwide revolution had not yet come, Lenin instituted the New Economic Policy in Russia, allowing some sway to market forces, and urged Communist parties in other countries to reenter the political mainstream and work within established trade unions, such as the AFL. At the insistence of the Comintern, the Communist Party (now mostly the foreign-language groups) and the United Communist Party (composed of the old Communist Labor Party and the Ruthenberg faction of the Communist Party) united to form the Communist Party of America in May 1921, after a meeting in Woodstock, New York (Draper 1957, 270–74).

The merger made sense at this time because the theoretical issue that had most divided the two groups—how much to accommodate Communist strategy to American conditions—had itself been reframed. If revolution was not imminent, then the Bolshevik example offered no model. The issue became one of how to be a Communist Party in nonrevolutionary conditions, and for that there was no model (Draper 1957, 249). In coming decades, the Party would be pulled back and forth between the poles of pragmatic politics and uncompromising theoretical purity. Lacking theoretical guidance from Marx for their work under nonrevolutionary conditions, the Communist Party of America looked to the Russian-dominated Comintern. The Russian Communists at least had the authority of having led a successful revolution, though in circumstances different from those prevailing in America. The Comintern spoke with Communist authority and expected to be obeyed. William Weinstone, in an article collected in *Highlights of a Fighting History: Sixty Years of the Communist Party USA*, the Party's own history, accuses Theodore Draper of presenting the Party as a tool of Russia.[1] While it is certainly true, as Weinstone asserts, that the Party spoke to and worked for the real needs of American workers, there is convincing evidence that it took direction from the Comintern.

American Communists did not see their allegiance to the Comintern as allegiance to Russia but to international Socialism, working-class solidarity across all national borders. As James P. Cannon wrote in 1923, "Soviet Russia is not a 'country.' Soviet Russia is a part of the world labor movement. Soviet Russia is a strike—the greatest strike in all history. When the working class in Europe and America join that strike it will be the end of capitalism" (Draper 1957, 265). But to many Americans, sensitized to "un-Americanism" by the Red Scare, Communism simply looked like foreign subversion.

When Lenin and the Comintern directed the American Communists to drop support for the IWW and work within the AFL, they were asking them to make common cause with a group that the American Left had scorned as reformist for most of its history. Of course, their mission was not to support reform unionism but to "bore from within" and try to radicalize the unions, directing them toward revolution rather than reform. Still, many American Communists disliked the strategy and preferred dual unionism. The two strategies generally had appeal to two different political personalities, and the Party's lurching from one strategy to another no doubt contributed to the high turnover rate in its membership.

Lenin's other directive to the American Communist Party was that it come above ground and become a legal political party that could work in a "united front" with other Left parties, such as the Labor Party (later Farm-

Labor). In December 1921, the Workers Party was established as the above-ground wing of the Communist Party. By 1922, government persecution of the Left had ebbed, but many Communists still opposed operating as a legal party; they did not want to give up their outlaw tactics (fomenting revolution, by violence if necessary) in favor of tamer, legal work. They were particularly opposed to membership in a legal party that would omit from its platform any commitment to violent revolution.

In August 1922 the Party convened at summer vacation cabins outside Bridgeman, Michigan. Secrecy precautions included travel orders that omitted a final destination until the last leg of the journey, and a code based on postal money order forms, but a government informer tipped off the location, and the government confiscated Communist documents and made arrests (Draper 1957, 367). The Comintern nevertheless remained insistent that the Party come above ground, and it did so at the end of 1922. The Workers' Party was the Communist Party of America, even though its name wasn't officially changed to Communist Party, U.S.A. (CPUSA), until 1929.

═══   Members Gained and Lost   ═══

The Party in 1923 was very different from the one founded in 1919 in expectation of imminent revolution. No longer an outlaw party, it had been directed to radicalize American institutions by working within them. Draper, in *The Roots of American Communism,* estimates that the membership in 1923 was between 8,000 and 10,000, that at most only 1 in 3 of those had been members in 1919, and that only 1 in 20 had English as their first language (Draper 1957, 391–92).

Still, in spite of being small, marginalized, concentrated in immigrant enclaves, and uncertain in its direction, the Party in the 1920s won some important adherents and reached out to new constituencies. The 1920s didn't roar for everyone. The rising stock market provided the upper and middle classes with more leisure and a panoply of new consumer goods. Unemployment abated, thus reducing the numbers of Americans with nothing to lose, but in each year of the decade, 25,000 Americans died in accidents at work and another 100,000 were so disabled that they could not work again.[2] African Americans were often without work, having lost to returning white veterans the jobs that had drawn them north in the 1910s. The 1920s were desperate years for tenant farmers, itinerant laborers, and immigrant tenement dwellers. Even many unionized workers lost ground as the National Association of Manufacturers assisted employers in undercutting the unions.

Mike Gold's *Jews without Money,*[3] which has been called the first American proletarian novel, gives a fictionalized account of the writer's childhood on Chrystie Steet on New York's Lower East Side. The events take place in the 1900s and 1910s, but the book was published in 1930, when the Great

Depression had begun, and it implicitly invites the millions of newly impoverished Americans to solidarity with the immigrant poor untouched by prosperity. The book has great value in helping us understand what kinds of experiences prompted people like Mike Gold to become a Communist and to emerge as an influential voice within the Party in the 1920s.

Gold's narrative is episodic, beginning with a series of adventures in which childhood exuberance survives despite its encounters with poverty and meanness. The boy Mikey and his gang torment the neighboring prostitutes by chanting their price. He is surprised to find one of the women sobbing and begging his mother to make him stop. He had never before realized that the prostitutes were so ashamed. One girl, Rosie, had worked long years in a sweatshop to save enough money to bring her parents to America; then she became ill with asthma, couldn't work, and lost her savings. Desperate and suicidal, she met one of the pimps who paid their percentage to Tammany Hall, the political machine that controlled the Lower East Side and much of the rest of New York City. He convinced her that being a 50-cent whore was preferable to dying in the East River, and it did allow her to send some money home to her family.

For Mikey, growing up means coming to understand that people are the way they are because they have so few choices. A recurring theme in the book is cruelty to animals. Children's natural desire to nurture stray kittens must be denied because their families cannot afford to keep putting out saucers of milk. Unable to bear the emotional burden of sympathizing with animals they cannot help, the children turn to stoning stray cats. The transformation is one of the most affecting illustrations of the ways in which poverty can corrupt. Work horses, like human workers, are worked to death.

Gold's family and neighbors are not the saintly suffering poor—as a sympathetic writer might imagine them from a distance. They are individuals who react in individual ways to their limited lives. His father, Herman, is a sociable man, a gifted storyteller, who can enthrall his listeners for hours as they sit up on the roof to escape the summer heat. Soon after coming to America, he went into business with his cousin, and they ran a successful shop making cotton suspenders. But when Herman took his bride, Katie, on a wedding trip to Niagara Falls—as befits a successful American businessman—he returned to find that his cousin had cheated him out of his half of the business. His brief taste of success has tantalized him; he works as a house painter but dreams of saving $300 so he can go into business again. He refers to himself as "a man in a trap."

Katie, Mikey's mother, is a religious woman who has only contempt for Christians—except the ones she gets to know. Her generosity and concern extend to the Italian widow and the Irish neighbors with the ill child, and she realizes that they are more like her than different. Religion comforts Katie through the bearable difficulties of life on Chrystie Street, but it is generally discredited in *Jews without Money*. Reb Moishe, Mikey's Hebrew

A family is evicted on the Lower East Side of New York City in 1919. From the Baines Collection of the Library of Congress.

teacher, is a "walking, belching symbol of the decay of orthodox Judaism" (Gold, 65), whose interest in religion seems to stem only from the money it brings him, along with the opportunity to terrorize small boys. In contrast, Reb Samuel, who lives in the neighborhood, is a saintly man whose religious feeling is as deep and sincere as Katie's. He dreams only of leading a righteous life, and he and his small congregation skip meals and save the money to bring to America a respected European rabbi. When the rabbi arrives, he demands a standard of living that far exceeds that of the congregation and leaves them for a wealthier temple. Reb Samuel is so stricken that he is physically destroyed.

When Herman is made a foreman for a painting company, he is over-joyed, sure that he is on the road to success. He dismisses Katie's sympathy for the foreman he replaced, a victim of the "painter's disease," nausea and nervous disorder caused by inhaling lead paint fumes. Herman has been suffering from it too, but he is thinking only of getting out of his "trap." But his is a short-lived euphoria: one day he falls from the paint scaffold and breaks the bones in his feet and legs. He can never work at his trade again. After many months of convalescence, during which Katie supports the family as a cafeteria worker, he works selling bananas from a pushcart, an occupa-tion at the absolute bottom of the scale, even for new immigrants. He is broken and embittered.

During her father's convalescence, Esther, Mikey's sister, has kept the house. She is a sweet, quiet, dreamy girl, who loves fairy tales. One afternoon, she is dragging home a sled full of firewood through a blinding snowstorm when she is caught beneath the wheels of a teamster's wagon. After Esther's death, Katie is reduced to staring into the distance, finally broken. With eviction looming, Mikey gives up all thought of further schooling and takes a series of factory jobs. His life will be as limited as those around him. Then, on the last page of *Jews without Money*, Gold tells his readers that one afternoon Mikey heard "a man on an East Side soap-box" who told of the workers' revolution and hope for an end to poverty. Suddenly his life again had purpose: it would be made meaningful by the struggle for *change*.

In the controversy over what a proletarian novel should be, Mike Gold was the strongest proponent of the primacy of political ideas over artistic polish. Nonetheless, *Jews without Money* remains to this day a powerful novel because it is built on fully realized characters. It is about people and conditions the author knew well, and it rings true. Capitalism is the ultimate cause of the characters' misery and the blightedness of their lives, but its workings are delineated with subtlety. Sometimes the tormentors of the poor are other poor people, like the coworker who lets Mikey burn his hand rather than warn him, like the men who beat their wives, like the workers who take jobs from each other. Gold's analysis is that they have been irretrievably hardened by the meanness and desperation of their lives. Herman blames all of his trouble on his cousin Sam, who stole his business. Sam is no robber baron; he has simply been corrupted by the American success ethic and capitalism at its nakedly Darwinian worst. Capitalism even lies behind apparent accidents: the driver who killed Esther really did not see her; he should not have been driving in that weather, but he needed to feed his children.

Though he meticulously delineates the corruption to which one can be driven by poverty, Gold never gives up faith in the willingness of even the poorest people to reach out to one another. The cruelty he shows us is balanced by compassion and cooperation across ethnic and religious lines and by the willingness of the poorest to drop a penny in the saucer of an evicted family, standing on the street with all their belongings. This balance is extremely effective as a literary strategy. Readers, both the poor and the comfortable, are likely to be moved by Gold's depiction to feel that poverty is an outrage. In his scenes of Chrystie Street, poverty never ennobles, and it never simplifies life. One cannot romanticize it. On the other hand, his depiction of compassion assures the reader that the Leftist dream of a cooperative society is not a Utopian dream.

Gold's announced intention in writing *Jews without Money* was to write a truthful book about poverty. The novel sold well, with 11 printings between February and October 1930 (Rideout, 15) and more than twice that number by 1950.[4] (It was reprinted twice in the 1960s, minus its radical ending; the excision of the paragraphs beginning with "A man on an East Side soap-box . . ." was variously explained.) The immigrant girl forced into prostitution, the disabled father, the little girl crushed by a wagon in a blinding snow-storm—these have become such common symbols of the victimized poor that later writers and critics, dismissive of Gold, have condemned the book as sentimental, full of crude stereotypes intended to play on the readers' emotions.[5] But Michael Folsom, Gold's biographer, argues that the book's popularity was deserved and that its very grounding in the actual experience of the poor raises it above the sentimental, except in a very few passages (Folsom, 244). Similarly, Morris Dickstein has argued that those last few paragraphs, which have proved so detachable, do in fact derive logically and experientially from the rest of the narrative; Mikey's embrace of radical politics fulfills his mother's religious longing, and he hails the workers' revolution as the "true Messiah."[6] The cultural tradition of waiting to embrace the messiah who would uplift the downtrodden made the Jewish community particularly receptive to Communism. According to Folsom, what Gold discovered in revolutionary politics was what he had missed in religious tradition: release from parochialism and faith in the people to solve their own problems.[7]

Gold (born Itshok Isaac Granich) wanted *Jews without Money* sold as nonfiction. If we read it as autobiography, we are struck by the modest role played by Mikey. The book is his story, not individually, but as a representative of the culture of the Lower East Side (Folsom 1968, 246). The absence of a single, individualist protagonist rising above his or her culture, with a story separable from that culture, is a recurring characteristic of Left fiction. To emphasize typicality, Mikey's experience is fictionalized in places. Most notably, Gold underplayed his own political awareness and made the conversion by the soap-box orator more of a turning point than it was. He was not unaware of Leftist ideas as he grew up, and his family had some history of radical involvement. The rhetorical effect of building to a moment of enlightenment is to place his narrative in the long tradition of American religious conversion narratives in which the speaker or writer tells how he or she was once hopeless and wayward (like the audience), felt miserable and trapped (like the audience), but now has found meaning and happiness (as the audience can too). Rhetorically, such a structure is vastly superior to the direct harangue, in which a writer puts forth his or her way of life as right and the reader's as wrong.

Gold also fictionalized his experience in another way: the "man on an East Side soap-box" who moved him to pursue a lifelong political commitment was Elizabeth Gurley Flynn (Folsom 1968, 223). We can only speculate as to the reasons for the gender change. In his journalistic writing for the *New Masses* and the *Daily Worker,* Gold made clear that he saw revolution as manly work, a project for manly men. Perhaps his view is an extension of political logic: "making the revolution" was to be active and communal production, like men's factory work, not like women's reproductive work in "making a baby." Or perhaps he believed that fictional as well as real Party spokespeople should be male, since the culture granted authority to men. Or perhaps he believed that only men were temperamentally suited to revolutionary activity. (Here one recalls *Ten Days That Shook the World,* in which all the major actors are male.) If the last reason is even contributory, then Gold's insistence on gendering political activity suggests that he envisioned revolutionary work as violent confrontation on the Bolshevik model, in spite of the fact that organizing, educating, and persuading were the dominant forms of Communist Party activity during the 1920s.

In that decade the Party and the non-Communist Left attracted many capable women. After the passage of the Nineteenth Amendment in 1920, the feminist movement was divided between those who favored gender-blind equality and those who argued for legislation to protect women from exploitation. No single political issue emerged to keep the "woman question" high on the Left agenda. Nonetheless, gender equality remained a topic of discussion on the Left, and women writing from a Left perspective often—though not always—wrote with a sharp consciousness of gender as a factor influencing one's prospects for self-determination.

Agnes Smedley's fictionalized autobiography *Daughter of Earth,*[8] published in 1929, shows us a woman whose political journey begins with an awareness of gender inequality and also gives us insight into one woman's choice not to join the Communist Party. The book chronicles the radicalization of its protagonist, Marie Rogers, beginning with her realization that having children makes women dependent and, too often, desperate. When

Marie is a child in rural Missouri, she idolizes her handsome father, who is the best dancer and the best storyteller around. But his repeated abandonment of the family in search of "success" turns her sympathy to her mother, whom her father bullies and beats when he is drunk. When he moves the family to the mining region near Trinidad, Colorado, Marie respects his willingness to do backbreaking construction and hauling work and sides with him and the other workers who are cheated of their wages. But brutal treatment drives him to alcohol and violence and gambling, leaving the mother to work herself into premature old age trying to feed the family.

Marie, as an adolescent doing domestic work in the household of a married couple, observes the new wife's boredom. She wants to go back to work, but her husband doesn't want her to have money of her own. Then she becomes pregnant. Unable to return to work and dependent on her husband, she is reduced to placating him with the tearful phrase, "Damn it, kid, you know I love you!" (Smedley, 66). The phrase is chilling to Marie, emblematic of the dependence that marriage and children inflict on women. She resolves that she will never marry. The only alternative she sees to her mother's life of drudgery is her Aunt Helen's life as a prostitute. Because she makes her own money, Helen is never destitute or powerless, and it is to her that the family turns when facing starvation. But prostitution brings its own brand of dependency, and Marie resolves to find another way out of poverty. She turns to the organized Left as a means to overcome the dual oppressions of class and gender, but finds that it will not support her struggle against the latter.

Like Mike Gold, Smedley refuses to romanticize poverty or the poor. Her family's years of relentless work enrich others and leave them destitute and broken in spirit. Her mother is too exhausted to express or even to feel much emotion. Her sister, given a chance for an education, chooses to deny and forget her background. Her father, part Native American, expects to be preferred over the foreign-born workers in the mining towns because he was born in America. Again like Gold, Smedley balances this bleak picture with examples of selfless kindness from people who, though far from being economically secure, have some resources to share and are willing to help others. Marie's education is partly paid for by Aunt Helen and by Big Buck, a cowboy who wants the best for Marie even after she refuses to marry him.

Daughter of Earth is built on the rhetorical principle of plenitude, multiplying its examples of Marie's frustrations and repeating its plot turns. Unlike a Hemingway novel, in which each incident takes the protagonist farther down some path of development or realization, Smedley's novel provides for Marie no linear progression. Her journey from poverty to some measure of self-determination is riddled with stops and starts as again and again she is forced to give up what progress she has made and start over. She quits a teaching job to return to her dying mother. She is asked to leave a teacher's college because her political ideas are unacceptable. She spends all of her savings to buy her younger brothers warm clothes for winter. Marie travels almost in circles across the vast expanse of the West, trapped by poverty and obligation. No doubt the autobiographical basis of the novel predisposed Smedley to include this wealth of incident. But it was also a rhetorically effective choice in that it helps the reader *feel* how trapped Marie is.

Not economic reality alone but also emotional needs and attachments trap Marie Rogers. She has known from adolescence that she does not want to be a wife, but she falls in love with Knut Larsen and agrees to marry him if their marriage can be a partnership. He loves her and tries to keep their agreement, but she resents being called Mrs. Larsen and strikes out against Knut every time she feels anxiety about being pushed into a traditional wifely role. She finally insists that they divorce, for Knut's sake. "There was a merciless war being raged within my own spirit, a war between my need and desire of love, and the perverted idea of love and sex that had been ground into my being from my first breath" (Smedley, 194). Some years later, living in New York, she falls in love with Anand Manvekar, an Indian nationalist, and she marries him because she loves him. But, again, she does not want the traditional domestic role; she remains active in the Indian revolutionary movement, along with Anand. But when another leader of the movement lets Anand know that he has had sexual relations with Marie, Anand is not outraged that she has been raped but tormented that his position in the movement has been compromised: he must defer to the rapist to secure his silence. The novel ends with Marie fleeing the country alone, emotionally devastated.

Smedley allows Marie Rogers to admit that she is not proud of all that she has done. Her awareness of society's injustices often provokes vehement reactions toward those close to her, including those like Knut and Aunt Helen and Knut's sister Karin who try to support her. Always racing against the clock to get some money together to pay for an abortion or for tuition or to send to her sister or younger brothers leaves her little opportunity for relaxed good humor. In fact, one reason she keeps her distance from the Greenwich Village Left after moving to New York is her resentment of their freedom to be less detached.

During her time in the West, Marie sees the Wobblies set upon by police and then accused of initiating the violence. In New York, she becomes a reporter for the *Call*, a Socialist Party daily newspaper. When in *Daughter of Earth* Marie explains her political affiliation, she says that she could not believe in the "gradual progress" agenda of the right wing of the Socialist Party (voting seemed useless). Nor could she follow the left wing, which founded the Communist Party; the authoritarian leadership by intellectuals was repellent to her, as was their insistence that they alone carried the torch of the Russian Revolution in America. Formally, she joins the IWW: "Its ideology and form seemed more natural to me than that of any other organization. It most certainly came closer to expressing my own manner of life and thought" (Smedley, 332). Still, she did not actively participate in the IWW but rather went on working for the *Call*.

Smedley herself was offered membership in both of the newfound Communist parties in 1919, but declined both invitations and continued her association with the *Call*.[9] Later she went on to support and chronicle the Chinese revolution and to be accused and hounded as a Red in the last years before her death in 1950. In fact, she never did join the Communist Party. The reason she gave for Marie Rogers's refusal to join the proto-Communist wing of the Socialist Party was likely her own: its top-down organization meant that the role of most Party members would be to carry out orders. The Party used the term "democratic centralism" to describe its organization; each level of the Party, from the unit to the section to the district to the Central Committee and then to the Comintern, was to contribute its viewpoint to the level above it, and each member was then expected to carry out the policy handed down. In practice, most Party members experienced democratic centralism as far more central than democratic. That the leadership took it upon itself not only to define policies but to decide which issues would get priority was of little appeal to Smedley and others who wanted from their political work an opportunity for self-development and the chance to participate meaningfully in history. Smedley has Marie say, "The Indian work was the first thing I had ever suffered for out of principle, from choice. It was not just living, just reacting to life—it was expression. It gave me a sense of self-respect, of dignity, that nothing else had ever given me" (Smedley, 327).

Politically, too, Smedley was at some distance from the Party, which was focused on preparing the urban working class to lead the revolution. As a woman, and a Westerner, Smedley identified with groups more marginalized than the proletariat: unskilled laborers and farmers and their wives and daughters. She found that the Party, to the extent that it was aware of the concerns of such people, did not give them very high priority. Indeed, Walt Carmon's *New Masses* review of *Daughter of Earth* found the book flawed because of its emphasis on Rogers's suffering as a woman.[10] Smedley's own sense of being culturally excluded from the organized Left is mirrored in *Daughter of Earth* when Marie, having left a gathering at the Greenwich Village home of Karin Larsen feeling both inferior to and resentful of the intellectual Socialists, looks back with some longing at the well-lit windows but walks away through the cold night. So too Smedley, unable to identify with the intellectuals or the urban workers, could not find a satisfying niche within the organized American Left. Rather, it was the revolutionary movements in India and China, both unindustrialized countries with large peasant populations, that won Smedley's commitment. Of course, women and men of a different temperament from Smedley's did cross cultural gulfs of various kinds to join the Communist Party, but *Daughter of Earth* gives us insight into the difficulties involved in the crossing and helps us understand why the Party had limited reach.

Richard Flacks, in *Making History,* asks why the Party specifically and the Left generally failed to enlist the masses but succeeded in eliciting a high degree of commitment from a relatively small and dedicated cadre. He concludes that the American gospel of liberty, or individual rights, predisposes Americans against mass movements of either Left or Right; that protest movements within ethnic, religious, or racial groups seldom move outside those groups if the move would broaden the agenda and lessen the chances of immediate success; and that ethnically organized political machines were effective in delivering jobs, neighborhood improvements, and an entrée into local political offices. He argues that capitalist interests played upon these objective conditions by offering stratified concessions, encouraging each group to benefit itself at the expense of others (Flacks, 106–15). Unlike European countries, where members of the working class shared a culture and had similar training, the United States had a working class divided by ethnic, racial, and religious differences and equipped with different levels of job skills. The metaphor of "going up the ladder of success" suggested stratification as a permanent feature of American society, with each group distinguishing itself from those below it. Flacks concludes that Leftists "were not only in conflict with the status quo and the dominant elites, but also at odds with the patterns of life and consciousness that characterized the subordinated groups they sought to speak for and lead" (Flacks, 116).

He goes on to note, however, that some were drawn to the work of the Left, and in the 1920s and 1930s particularly to the Communist Party, not because it could deliver immediate material improvements but because it offered the opportunity for self-development and because the Party was a sustaining subculture of its own (Flacks, 125–26). Intellectuals, by their choice of vocation, are committed to social improvement, to the use of rationality to influence social development. For many intellectuals—though by no means all—Left political commitments are a natural extension of their vocational commitment (Flacks, 119). Similarly, Left commitment seems to come more easily to groups that have a national or religious tradition of commitment to liberatory struggle: for example, African Americans, with a cultural tradition of struggle for freedom; ethnic groups strongly influenced by nineteenth-century nationalist struggles in Europe; and Jewish Americans, whose scriptures and whose history center on the struggle for freedom from bondage.

Finally, as Flacks emphasizes, Leftist political life offered to working-class men and women the chance for personal growth and self-expression that they were otherwise not likely to have. One thinks of Mike Gold's "Mikey," who found factory work deadening to his mind and heart but found purpose in the struggle for change. In the 1920s and 1930s, the Communist Party offered education, the opportunity to travel and to lead, and, most important, the opportunity to share in the shaping of history—in short, Left political work in itself allowed people to live out the Left ideal. And this living out was done in the company of others similarly dedicated.

Ruth Norrick, interviewed in 1983 for the Oral History of the American Left, said, "My life has been greatly enriched by my association with the radical movement. . . . I feel that these are my kind of people."[11] The writer Malcolm Cowley, interviewed in 1981, said that working in a group for a common future rather than alone for personal concerns constituted a revolution in itself: "It was exciting that so many people should work together for a new society."[12] The strength of this community, of course, varied in different geographical and cultural locations. As Flacks points out, in the Jewish working-class sections of New York one could organize one's entire social life around Party meetings, rallies, and picnics; one could work in Party-organized shops, and read Party newspapers in cafés and cafeterias owned and frequented by Party members (Flacks, 138–39). One could live in, and be important to, an already "liberated" community, one in which Leftist values were constantly articulated and honored—always in theory and sometimes in practice.

In such an atmosphere, one might be inclined to forgive the Party an authoritarian move or an inexplicable policy rather than withdraw from the community. Or one might choose to be a politically active member of the community but not an official Communist Party member. Others, like Smedley, might be supportive of Party goals generally but unable to relate to the Party culturally. Such complicated intersections of culture, community, and politics go some way toward explaining the relationships between the Party, its members, and its nonmember supporters.

═ Sacco and Vanzetti ═

One night in the spring of 1920, Andrea Salsedo jumped or was pushed to his death from the fourteenth-floor window of 15 Park Row, New York City, the offices of the Department of Justice. A typesetter, Salsedo had worked in the shop accused of printing leaflets associated with a bomb attack, and he had been arrested during the Palmer Raids and held by the Department of Justice for eight weeks without arraignment. Nicola Sacco, a shoemaker, and Bartolomeo Vanzetti, a fish peddler, belonged to the same anarchist group in Massachusetts as Salsedo (Lens, 280). They began to organize a protest in Brockton, but before the demonstration could take place, they were arrested and charged with having robbed a payroll shipment and killed the paymaster and a guard the month before, in Braintree, Massachusetts. Vanzetti was also accused of having committed a robbery the previous December in Bridgewater. When arrested, they were carrying guns and lied about their destination.

Neither man had a criminal record, but both had histories of labor and antiwar protest and both were supporters of *Cronaca Sovversiva,* an Italian-language anarchist publication in whose pages violence was considered an acceptable political strategy. And they were "foreign-born radicals" arrested at the height of the Red Scare, when one was at risk for beliefs and for group membership, quite apart from anything one might actually have done. The government was engaging in extrajudicial violence, as the handling of Salsedo illustrates. The Braintree robbery may have been a response in kind from the anarchist group or it may simply have been an apolitical crime, common enough in the "gangster era" of the 1920s. (In *The Case That Will Not Die,* Herbert Ehrmann, a junior defense counsel for Sacco and Vanzetti, points to the Morelli gang, of Providence, as the likely perpetrators.[13])

The status of Sacco and Vanzetti as martyrs rests not on firm evidence of their innocence but on irrefutable evidence that they were executed as the result of a grossly unfair trial. Their politics, not their actions, were the basis for their conviction. (In 1977, the governor of Massachusetts issued a proclamation admitting that they had been denied a fair trial.)

Vanzetti went to trial first for the Bridgewater robbery and was found guilty despite the testimony of many witnesses that he had been elsewhere at the time. He was sentenced to 10–15 years, an unusually long sentence for a first offense. Judge Webster Thayer had instructed the jury, "This man, although he may not have actually committed the crime attributed to him is nevertheless morally culpable, because he is the enemy of our existing institutions" (Lens, 280).

For the second trial, Fred Moore, who had represented the Wobblies in a number of court trials, was brought in as lead defense counsel. He realized that Vanzetti had been convicted for his politics and that the same would happen to both men in the second trial, so he made the deliberate decision to bring the political motivation of the prosecution to light and scrutiny. The defense enlisted public support from labor and political groups and publicized the trial widely in the United States and in Europe.[14] Both men were convicted on 14 July 1921 of the robbery and murder. Judge Thayer, again presiding, would not allow evidence that prosecution witnesses had lied or that the police and Justice Department agents had interfered with investigations; nor would he allow evidence from a known bank robber—Celestino Madeiros, who admitted his involvement—or evidence pointing to the Morelli gang.

In 1924, William Thompson replaced Moore as defense lawyer, after Moore had fallen out with the defense committee and with Sacco, who accused him of exploiting the case for his own ends (Ehrmann, 402). Thompson was an upper-class Boston lawyer who entered the case not because of any political sympathy with the defendants but to try to preserve the American ideal of judicial fairness. He downplayed the political framework of the case, but it remained a lightning rod for political passions, epitomizing the era of the Red Scare. After the two men were sentenced to death, public pressure caused Governor Alvan T. Fuller to put the question of clemency before an advisory committee chaired by A. Lawrence Lowell, president of Harvard University. The committee recommended against clemency.

The day of 23 August 1927 was appointed for the execution of Sacco and Vanzetti. Public protests were staged in Mexico City, Belgrade, Warsaw, Moscow, and other foreign cities, including Paris, where 150,000 people gathered outside the U.S. embassy (Lens, 281). A large crowd waited outside the prison, hoping for a reprieve. When word of their deaths went out, U.S. embassies in Europe were stoned, and 250,000 people marched silently through Boston.[15]

The trial and execution of Sacco and Vanzetti offered a strange counterpoint to the Jazz Age. The Red Scare had driven the Left out of the political mainstream and silenced many of its supporters. Even labor organizing was stalled, not only by Red-baiting but by the relative prosperity of some workers and the vision of a different revolution: in the 1920s, automobiles, radios, vacuum sweepers, and the suburbs beckoned. After the horrors of World War I there was considerable sentiment in favor of ignoring politics altogether and having a good time. With the much publicized trial of Sacco and Vanzetti, the political once again pushed itself into people's field of vision. The long-drawn-out trial became a vehicle for resuming the political conversation. For some, the trial was one more example of the Left getting what it deserved; for Leftists and other cultural critics, it was proof that all was not right in America. The ordeal of Sacco and Vanzetti gave the Left what it has always needed and otherwise lacked in the 1920s: victims conscious of their victimization and possessed of a forum in which to speak about it in political terms. The two men were well aware of the role they had been given: "This is our career, and our triumph!" was their last message (Murray, 267).

The enthusiasm for good times and consumer goods—for *private* life—had in the 1920s reduced the influence of socially conscious writers and intellectuals as it diminished attention to public life. The Sacco and Vanzetti case, with such sensational elements as a payroll robbery, a shoot-out, an anarchist cell, and a dramatic trial, gave them the opportunity once again to raise serious questions before a large and interested audience. Perhaps the best known of the many literary treatments of the Sacco and Vanzetti case is Upton Sinclair's *Boston*.[16] Sinclair had belonged to the wing of the Socialist Party that backed the electoral route to Socialism, that is, the right wing. Christian Socialism had been important in forming his politics, and much of his most successful writing follows a character's coming to consciousness and "conversion." His 1906 novel *The Jungle* was an exposé of foul and exploitive conditions in the meat-packing houses of Chicago. (To his chagrin, its primary effect was not solidarity with the workers but enough public agitation to push through the Pure Food and Drug Act. He is reported to have said that he aimed for the public's heart but hit its stomach.) In 1917 he broke with the Socialist Party over its war policy. He never joined the Communist Party. In 1934 he narrowly lost the election for governor of

California, backed by a group called End Poverty in California and opposed by the Communists. As an independent Socialist, he took the occasion of writing about Sacco and Vanzetti to compare a variety of Leftist perspectives.

The main character in the two volumes of *Boston* is Cornelia Thornwell, the widow of Josiah Quincey Thornwell, former governor of Massachusetts and wealthy mill owner. Though herself of distant Irish ancestry, Cornelia has throughout her long and unhappy marriage learned the way Boston works. She has many times overheard her husband and sons-in-law plotting to ruin upstart business competitors, using their wealth and connections to manipulate the political system to their advantage. As the novel opens, she hears them plotting to get control of Jerry Walker's felt mills by refusing him credit unless he secures the loan with the mills themselves; then, while they control the mills, they will sell off the assets so that he cannot possibly repay the loan. When he defaults, they will own the mills. This business intrigue provides the subplot for *Boston*.

The main plot follows Cornelia's late-blooming career as a Leftist. Widowed at age 60 and determined to have a life of her own, she runs away from her unattractive children and, under the name of Mrs. Cornell, gets a job sewing in a cordage factory. She boards with the Brini family, whose other boarder is Bartolomeo Vanzetti. She adapts to the hard physical work and enjoys listening to the gentle Vanzetti expound his anarchist politics. When the cordage workers go on strike and the police are called in to "restore order," nothing exempts "Mrs. Cornell" from flying nightsticks, and she becomes more sure that the alliance of mill owners, politicians, and bankers that currently wield power in Boston is really a betrayal of the city's rebellious and radical heritage, embodied in the revolutionaries, transcendentalists, and abolitionists.

When Cornelia's family find her, they prevail upon her to "come home." She agrees to return to Boston and live independently in a small apartment. There she is joined by her granddaughter Betty, her only kindred spirit in the family. They engage in protests on behalf of pacifism, trying to prevent U.S. entry into World War I, and are briefly jailed for participating in a woman suffrage protest. The family would like to have their embarrassing matriarch committed to an asylum, but her physician takes her side.

Cornelia, like Sinclair, is an independent Leftist. She begins as a reformer, content to see fair wages, honest business, and a police force that doesn't inflict the will of the rich upon the poor. Ultimately, she thinks of herself as a pacifist, opposed to war (she asks her son-in-law Rupert just how much he will lose if the United States doesn't enter World War I and the Germans win) and to all violence. Vanzetti is explained as an anarchist who will support unions during a strike—as he does when the cordage workers walk out—but ultimately is opposed to any form of political organization. He sees unions as organizations that empower and then corrupt their leadership. He explains to Cornelia and Betty that he became an anarchist only after coming to America and finding his labor so blatantly exploited; he is no "foreign red" (Sinclair, 104). Not opposed to violence philosophically, he carries a gun, but violence is so against his nature that he never learns to shoot it. He is disgusted at the Bolshevik takeover of the Russian Revolution. Betty, eager for change and horrified at capitalist tactics, decides that fire must be fought with fire and becomes an enthusiastic Bolshevik. Her husband, Joe, is a Social Democrat, a believer in electoral politics.

After the Bolshevik revolution of October 1917, pacifists and Social Democrats and anarchists, along with Communists, are persecuted as "Reds." The FBI sifts through Cornelia's trash; old acquaintances are sent by the government to infiltrate her pacifist group. Sinclair does an effective job of using his politically diverse characters to explore some of the central Leftist dilemmas of the time: When the government tramples civil liberties to persecute the Left indiscriminately, how should one defend a Leftist whose politics one opposes? When one has so little access to the media that shape public opinion, how can one make distinctions? When the conflict is framed as the patriots versus the Reds, how can one oppose the government without endorsing or seeming to endorse tactics in which one doesn't believe? Every time a bomb explodes anywhere in the country, one of Cornelia's relatives asks her how she can defend "such people."

But for Cornelia, the true moral dilemma comes when the highly prejudiced trial seems sure to end in conviction and Lee Swenson, a defense attorney, asks Cornelia if she will testify that she met Vanzetti in Plymouth on the day of the robbery. Her alibi, coming from a blue blood, will be unassailable and, according to Swenson, will save Vanzetti. She agonizes over the request, tempted by the fact that the prosecution certainly hasn't been playing by the rules, and her friend's life hangs in the balance. She concludes that she cannot lie for him. This refusal is rhetorically effective in establishing her integrity and commitment to truth.[17]

Anarchism does not come off very well in *Boston*. Vanzetti is painted as a naive idealist, willing to embrace the idea if not the reality of violence as a way to end exploitation. Throughout the novel, exploding bombs create such a fierce anti-Red backlash that one must give a hearing to Vanzetti's theory that private police or hired thugs plant the bombs just to fuel the hysteria. But even if the Italian anarchist cell is innocent, their proclivity for the political uses of dynamite leaves them wide open to the frame-up.

After Sacco and Vanzetti are convicted and while they wait for their appeal, another trial also comes to conclusion. The court finds that Cornelia's sons-in-law have indeed taken Jerry Walker's felt mills fraudulently. While waiting on that appeal, Betty's father puts all of his property in his sister's name so that he can declare bankruptcy without taking a loss if the judgment is upheld. To ensure that it is not, the blue-blooded bankers and mill owners call in all of the favors they are owed and let it be known that the banking system will collapse if the appeals court finds against them. Predictably, "the system" protects itself from all threats: the bankers win their appeal and the anarchists lose theirs. The night before the execution, Cornelia gets a last talk with Vanzetti and asks if he now renounces violence and if he can forgive those who have framed him. He refuses to deny the oppressed the weapon of violence and tells her that he cannot at that moment truthfully say that he forgives the powerful who knowingly destroy the innocent. Later, just before his execution, he says, "I wish to forgive some people for what they are now doing to me" (Sinclair, 742).

In the preface to *Boston,* Sinclair explains that he has attempted to write a true history of the Sacco and Vanzetti case and of the contest between Jerry Walker and the bankers. The figures of the subplot, including Jerry Walker, are fictional, though the court case is real. Many of the 700-plus pages are given over to recounting testimony and motions from the Sacco and Vanzetti trial and the appeal. Sinclair assures us that this material is documentary, and G. Louis Joughin and Edmund M. Morgan, in *The Legacy of Sacco and Vanzetti,* say, "*Boston* contains a thorough review of almost all the important features of the Sacco-Vanzetti case. It is accurate in detail to the degree that one would expect of a scientific study, and it has qualities of proportion in its judgments which indicate careful thinking. This combination of completeness, accuracy, and penetration placed *Boston* in the first rank of historical novels" (Joughin and Morgan, 448). Sinclair's heroines, Cornelia and Betty, are fictional, chosen to represent what he calls the "saving minority" (Sinclair, vi) of proper Bostonians who, throughout its history, have opposed injustice. They, more than the defendants, invite identification and sympathy from the widest readership, as they are native-born, selflessly motivated, and more interested in a fair trial than in making good propaganda. And it is they who vouch to the reader for Sacco and Vanzetti. Thus Sinclair uses considerable rhetorical skill to make the facts of the case and his analysis interesting and credible to the widest audience.

═══ Literature and Politics ═══

A novel like *Boston,* which Sinclair calls a "contemporary historical novel" (v), invites consideration of the role of political literature. Even writing based on personal experience, such as Dell's *Love in Greenwich Village,* is not a reliable guide to "what really happened," but it can tell us how the situation looked to the writer—which is often at least as interesting. Fictionalized autobiographies like those of Gold and Smedley, as well as unfictionalized autobiographies have the same limitation and the same strength. They tell us how the writer wishes his or her life to be seen. Such narratives defend certain political choices and criticize others, and in this way contribute to political debate within the Left. To the non-Left reader they serve as "conversion narratives," invitations to share the writer's discovery of meaning and purpose. And they comfort the converted, in that they assume or proclaim a Left analysis of society's ills. The importance of this last function should not be overlooked: holding onto a minority political analysis when all major media propound the majority analysis can take a good deal of psychological energy. It must have been bolstering simply to hear one's beliefs stated by others. In all of these ways, literature has the capacity to influence history itself.

Boston highlights yet another political function of literature: to influence the way in which an event will be viewed by history. The "historical record" is always a reconstruction and never so simple as "getting the facts straight." There are choices to be made even in deciding where to begin the story, and such choices often have political implications. For example, if one begins the story of Sacco and Vanzetti with the robbery itself, then the story is apt to be a crime story. If one begins with the death of Salsedo (as I have above), one is placing it in the context of the Red Scare, and inviting a focus on political motives.

In a court trial, the defense and the prosecution vie to have their version of events—their narratives—accepted by the jury. In a very real sense, the American public functions as a jury, deciding which political analysis— whose story—to believe. Novels like *Boston*, which recount a historical event, offer the public a reading of the event different from what they might get from the mainstream press or from the Right. In this way, literature from all political perspectives contends to influence the way a given event is understood by history. As our understanding of history affects the way we interpret the present and choose to act in it, such literature influences the course as well as the construction of history. Thus it is far too simple to see literature as "reflecting" history. First, literature is incapable of simple reflection; it cannot help but characterize its materials. Second, literature both arises out of history and participates in the making of history.

Joughin and Morgan in *The Legacy of Sacco and Vanzetti* note that the considerable number of novels, poems, and plays about the case all sympathize with the condemned men (Joughin and Morgan, 233). If, as novelist George Orwell suggested, struggling over the past is a way of struggling over the future, then the multiple retellings of the anarchists' story did much to contravene the jury's verdict in the judgment of history and to impugn the impartiality of American justice. According to Joughin and Morgan, the execution of Sacco and Vanzetti after an unfair trial was interpreted by the public less as an example of class violence and more as an example of justice corrupted and democracy subverted (Joughin and Morgan, 370–72). Their view is consistent with evidence that the case, its publicity, and the literary treatments of it succeeded in influencing public opinion but not in radicalizing it. For many of the writers and intellectuals who had put the weight of their effort and reputation behind the defense committee, to have influenced the historical verdict was not enough; they were profoundly affected by their inability to save the men. In the words of Malcolm Cowley, "[T]he intellectuals had learned that they were powerless by themselves and that they could not accomplish anything unless they made an alliance with the working class."[18] Cowley ascribes the leftward swing of intellectuals in the early 1930s to this experience.

Recognizing the power of literature to shape opinion and to motivate, the Left in the 1920s felt acutely the need for a magazine that would reach a wide audience. The Sacco and Vanzetti case was breathing some new life into political conversation and providing a "respectable" issue around which people from center to Left could come together, but what could be made of it? Mike Gold was keen to find a vehicle for turning any available disillusionment away from cynicism and apathy and into political struggle. But this was one of the least articulate moments for the American Left, discredited, disorganized, divided over Russia, uncertain of its own role. The *Liberator* had been given to the Workers' Party and by 1924 moved to Chicago and merged with other Communist publications. Some of the former editors of the *Masses* began to talk about starting a new magazine, open to constructive debate from all over the Left political spectrum and bringing a Left perspective to intelligent people interested in art, literature, ideas, and modern culture.

In 1926, the *New Masses* began monthly publication. (It became a weekly in 1934). Most of its funding came from the Garland Fund, established by Harvard graduate Charles Garland to support the work of the Left, and its supporters and contributing editors represented a wide spectrum of the liberal and the radical Left (Aaron, 101–2). In the issue of June 1926, Mike Gold wrote that the magazine would "not be a magazine of Communism, or Moscow, but a magazine of American experiment."[19] By 1928, however, lack of financial backing threatened to sink the venture. With a last-chance subsidy from the Garland Fund, Mike Gold became the lead editor. He had the *New Masses* printed on cheaper stock, making it *look* more like a working-class paper, and announced that he wanted to print literature by proletarians (Aaron, 204–5).

It was no simple matter of deduction to assume that literature by proletarians would constitute proletarian literature. According to Marxist theory of the time, proletarians *should*, because of their place in the political economy, have the correct progressive consciousness. They should see things "as they are," while the bourgeoisie would be led by their own self-interest as a class to deny and obscure the central issues of the class struggle. But what if the works produced by proletarians lacked the literary polish to appeal to a wide audience? And could not a writer from a bourgeois background produce proletarian literature by writing from the standpoint of the proletariat? In deciding what kind of cultural work would best foster social change, the Communist Party over the years swung back and forth between pragmatism and theory-driven insistence on proletarian authorship; the swings in its cultural policy generally paralleled the swings in its political strategy. As writers generally resent any attempt to dictate the form or the content of their work, relations between the Party and Leftist writers were often strained and sometimes bitter.

The problem of finding an appropriate cultural expression of Communism was not only an American one. In Russia, Leftist artists and writers had hailed the revolution as the opening of a new cultural era, with a people's culture. In the years between 1917 and 1921, artists who had supported the revolution took it upon themselves to set up new exhibition spaces all over the country, to produce drama in the factories, to paint revolutionary graphics on trains headed for the front during the Russian civil war, so that news of the cultural change would reach even the most remote regions.[20] Olga Rosanova, whose own artistic trajectory was from futurism to abstraction, traveled the countryside in the days when travel was dangerous and transport hard to get, organizing factory production of beautifully designed new fabrics. One faction of revolutionary modernists, the Suprematists, included Malevich and Kandinsky and believed that art should be abstract and spiritual and inspire the people. The "spiritual," however, is problematic for Communists because Marxism is a materialist philosophy, recognizing only the physical world.

By 1921, the Suprematists' view had been overshadowed by that of the Constructivists. *Constructivist* was the term given by one critic to what had been called "production art"; it produced beautiful and functional designs for mass production. In the new Russia, art would not be a luxury for the few; artists would use their talents to design chairs, textiles, and tableware that everyone could afford. Much of what survives of Constructivist art are useful objects like posters, drawings for theater sets, book bindings, and architectural models. Viktor Tatlin, Alexander Rodchenko, and others used a bold new graphic vocabulary emphasizing geometrical forms and portraying the dynamism of workers and machines.

With the end of the civil war in 1921, art was brought more tightly under state control. An organization called Proletcult (Organization for Proletarian Culture), headed by Alexander Bogdanov, asserted that art must be produced by the people themselves with no control by the Party (Gray, 244–45). Anatoly Lunacharsky, commissar of education, was most influential in cultural matters, and he allowed revolutionary modernists like the Constructivists to find their niche during the New Economic Policy of the 1920s by designing for workers' clubs (Gray, 259). Finally, in 1932, under Stalin, Socialist Realism was declared the only appropriate aesthetic expression of Communism. Rejecting the modernist style of the Constructivists, Socialist Realists returned to a prerevolutionary mimeticism but with a heroic presentation of workers, peasants, athletes, and, yes, tractors.

In literature as well as the visual arts, Lenin had resisted the theory of Bogdanov and Proletcult that only factory workers could produce proletarian literature. Addressing the Central Committee in October 1920, he identified proletarian literature as that which is produced from the standpoint of the proletariat, that which furthers the revolution and transformation of society.[21]

Such a definition gave the Party the leading role in directing and promoting such a literature and thus legitimized Lenin's insistence that Proletcult and all other artists and writers submit to Lunacharsky's authority. Lenin further stated his assumption that proletarian literature would make use of what was functional in the bourgeois literary heritage and turn it to Socialist use; such a use presumed a good literary education. In 1925 the Central Committee endorsed again Lenin's definition of proletarian culture, inviting writers to discover a literary style most appropriate to Communism.

The Russian Association of Proletarian Writers (RAPP) looked to Georgy Plekhanov for its aesthetic theory. Plekhanov's ideal is the portrayal of individual people involved in social change movements. Characters must not be stereotypical, not all good or all evil. They must have a complexity that reflects the Marxist theory of dialectical materialism; that is, they must exemplify the incomplete change of consciousness that is to be expected in revolutionary times (Murphy, 29). Aligning itself against RAPP was the Left Front of Art (LEF), which rejected all fiction as antimaterialist and antirevolutionary and wanted a literature of journalism and documentary, thus taking a position to the left even of Proletcult (Murphy, 32–34).

Thus things stood when Mike Gold sent out his call for proletarian writers. To foster their development, supporters of the *New Masses* in 1929 sponsored John Reed Clubs in major cities across the country. The collapse of the stock market in October of that year signaled a dramatic end to rising expectations for most Americans. Many of those who joined the John Reed Clubs were unemployed, a minority were factory workers, and only about a quarter of the members were also members of the Communist Party (Murphy, 57). In a *New Masses* article of January 1930, Gold advised club members to become experts in one industry so that they could write about it as "an insider"; they should also be prepared to write strike publicity and send in periodic reports from their industrial vantage point.[22] Other members of the magazine staff found this an unrealistic program, but the discussion gives us a window into early debates in the American Left, paralleling those in Russia, over the true nature and role of proletarian literature.

In November 1930 the Second World Plenum of the International Bureau of Revolutionary Literature was convened at Kharkov in the Soviet Union. Mike Gold and A. B. Magil were among the official American delegates, and Josephine Herbst attended unofficially. Magil later commented that writers in the John Reed Clubs resented Gold's getting a personal invitation to Kharkov; they thought him an individualist who wrote about the disadvantaged Jews of the Lower East Side, not the proletariat (Magil, OHAL).

The Plenum directed the *New Masses* and the John Reed Clubs to take an interest in writers who, though unaffiliated, were sympathetic to Left thinking and might be enlisted in the revolutionary cause. The number of such writers was growing in America, as the economy spun down into the Great Depression. The Americans were further instructed to create agitprop (agitational propaganda) theater groups that could perform in public or industrial settings; to use cultural work to reach out to African Americans; to strengthen their ties to workers generally, promoting revolutionary writing in the many languages of American workers; and to pay more attention to Marxist literary theory.[23] The John Reed Clubs became the American affiliates of the International Union of Revolutionary Writers and were from then on expected to take their direction from that group (Aaron, 221–22). After Kharkov, the *New Masses* was understood to be a Communist publication.

In Mike Gold's writing for *New Masses* and later in his columns for the *Daily Worker*, we can see him struggling to define, in practical terms, what constituted proletarian literature. James F. Murphy in *The Proletarian Moment* argues persuasively that Gold's views were generally closer to those of RAPP and of the 1925 statement of the Central Committee, endorsing fully realized characters actively engaged in history, than to the views of LEF or Proletcult, though he sometimes took positions associated with those "Leftist" groups (Murphy, 66). Gold praises the effectiveness—especially the complex characterizations—of certain "bourgeois" writers but also urges worker-writers simply to record the truth of their own lives. Murphy also makes the case that the view of Gold and the *New Masses* as promoting a purely propagandist literature owes much to the self-characterization of the *Partisan Review* group, which presented itself as the defender of artistic values and free expression.

Gold's reputation—and by association that of the *New Masses* and the *Daily Worker*—for placing sociological values above literary values rests mostly on his attacks on writers he considered bourgeois for their interest in personal or psychological problems. To Gold, it was simply a betrayal of historical truth to present personal problems in isolation from their social and economic context. He excoriated writers who ignored the determining effect of class on people's lives and presented characters whose problems were made to seem individual or unique to them. Gold criticized American expatriates who wrote about their relationships and their anguish at modern life, all the while moving aimlessly between French cafés and Spanish bodegas.

Perhaps his most famous attack was launched at Thornton Wilder in 1930. In his *New Republic* review of Wilder's *The Woman of Andros*, he ridiculed the "little lavender tragedies" that ignored the growing crisis in America and offered readers an escape into distant settings and the ahistorical morality of "humanism."[24] Gold's pronouncements on literature were always blunt in their forcefulness, and it may have been the rough tone rather than the rough judgment of Wilder that prompted such a vigorous debate that the issue lived on in the letters column of the *New Republic* until the editors simply refused to print any more responses. With this controversial exchange, questions about the politics of literary standards ceased to be simply an interest of Left cultural magazines and moved into the mainstream of American literary conversation just as the Depression was forcing Americans to think once again about large social and economic questions (Aaron, 241).

Worth noting in Gold's attack on Wilder and on humanists generally is his characterization of them as effeminate. He associated bourgeois literary taste with gentility, and both of these with unmanly pseudorefinement. Recurrent in his writing on literature is the contrast between the effeminate bourgeois writer and the manly proletarian worker-writer, who sees things as they are and tells the truth as cleanly and powerfully as he swings a hammer. His oft-quoted characterization appeared in the *New Masses* in October 1926: "Send us a critic. Send a giant who can shame our writers back to their task of civilizing America. Send a soldier who has studied history. Send a strong poet who loves the masses, and their future. . . . Send one who is not a pompous liberal, but a man of the street. . . . Send us a man fit to stand up to skyscrapers. . . . A man of art who can match the purposeful deeds of Henry Ford. . . . Send no saint. Send an artist. Send a scientist. Send a Bolshevik. Send a man."[25] This insistent gendering of the proletarian in Gold's criticism is consistent, of course, with his rendering of Elizabeth Gurley Flynn as "a man on an East Side soap-box" in *Jews without Money*.

Reading Mike Gold's many and contradictory pronouncements about proletarian literature, one gets the sense that he grasped the complexity of the issue, that is, that he recognized the multiplicity of ways in which literature is political—from putting forth a certain description of "reality" to holding out a vision of a desired future. His task of instructing young would-be proletarian writers, however, likely prompted him to try to reduce complex issues to simple directives (Murphy, 68). Influential also may have been the mental habit, common to Communist theorists, of identifying the "correct path" as a narrow one, of believing in a single correct strategy rather than a multiplicity of strategies. Throughout the 1930s, as the Communist Party swung between support for broad Left coalition and strict sectarianism (refusal to compromise purity by making alliances with non-Communists), discarded or disaffected writers would be among its most vocal, and articulate, critics.

═══ Labor and the Communist Party ═══

The economic downturn that had marked the end of World War I had been reversed by 1923, and the next six years saw rising productivity and increasing purchasing power for many Americans—those with steady high-wage jobs. It is generally the case that when a culture is feeling prosperous, labor agitation increases. The 1920s, however, saw little agitation and little gain for organized labor. Among the complex causes of such inactivity, the chilling effects of the Red Scare should not be discounted; nor should the efforts of manufacturers to undercut unions through such mechanisms as the Open Shop Association (Lens, 279). Labor organizing had been seriously disrupted by the virtual destruction of the IWW, and the exit of the Communists from the Socialist Party had opened up new strategic questions.

When the American Communists were directed to "bore from within" the AFL rather than create dual, or parallel, unions, they were set on a course that had been the chosen one of William Z. Foster, who would eventually become one of the most influential Communist leaders. Foster was born in the United States and raised in Philadelphia, making him conspicuously "American" among the many foreign-born Communists. Such a background was an asset in dissociating labor organizing from "foreign subversives." In his early years, he had been a Wobbly syndicalist, urging the IWW to try to work through and win over the AFL to radical rather than reform unionism. In 1920 he formed the Trade Union Educational League (TUEL) to bring together leaders from various unions who shared his radical vision and were committed to pushing their unions to support industrial organizing, unemployment insurance, worker control of unions through a shop delegate system, and a labor party (Lens, 288).

In 1921 Foster was invited by an old syndicalist comrade, Earl Browder, now a Communist, to attend an international labor conference in Moscow. He came home a Communist, convinced that the Party was the most likely means of organizing American workers to take power. The strategy adopted by TUEL to achieve industrial unions was "amalgamation," a coalition of craft unions working together to organize an industry (Lens, 288). It was an effective strategy, but TUEL seems to have overreached itself. Foster later admitted that it had been a mistake to try to tie union organizing to such militant political positions as support of the Red International and recognition of the Soviet Union (Lens, 290). This issue would bedevil the Party throughout its history. It saw its historical role as leading the workers to revolution; to make bread-and-butter issues seem like ends in themselves would then constitute *mis*leading. On the other hand, foisting upon unions political goals that their members did not choose came across as exploitation or an attempt to coopt the unions.

Indeed, it was the latter charge that Samuel Gompers leveled at TUEL when in 1923 he urged that unions expel Reds from their leadership. Although it did manage to lead successful strikes in the textile and the garment industries in the mid-1920s, TUEL was disbanded in 1929, and industrial organizing was again set back. In August 1929, TUEL was superseded by the Trade Union Unity League (TUUL), committed to creating dual unions, that is, explicitly revolutionary unions to compete with the reformist AFL.

The switch from "boring from within" through TUEL to creating competing unions under TUUL was a response not only to the expulsion of radicals from AFL unions in the mid-1920s but also to the 1928 decision of the Comintern that Communists should withdraw from coalitions with reformers and pursue a politics of class confrontation. This decision ushered in the Third Period (following the first, revolutionary, period and the second period, during which the stabilization of capitalism had called for coalition work). Declaration of a Third Period followed from the perception that capitalism was again on the ropes.

After the death of Lenin in 1924, Josef Stalin, Leon Trotsky, and Nicolai Bukharin engaged in a struggle over policy and leadership. James Cannon, who had come to Communism after years in the IWW, was expelled from the Party in 1928 for his support of Trotsky. Jay Lovestone, the secretary of the CPUSA, was expelled in 1928 for backing Bukharin against Stalin and also for coming up with the "Lovestoneite heresy" that revolution in the United States would occur later than in Europe because the United States was a young capitalist country, still enriching itself at the expense of Europe and still holding out to its people the promise of prosperity. This doctrine of "American exceptionalism" was condemned by Stalin, who preached that scientific Marxism did not allow exceptions.

Thus at the end of the decade we find the issue of adapting Marxism to American conditions, one of the thorniest issues for the new Communist parties in 1919, once again coming to the fore. Lovestone's "heresy," if adopted as policy, would have led to a continuation of the coalition and "boring from within" phase in recognition that the American populace was not, in the late 1920s, at all inclined to revolution. The expulsions of Cannon and Lovestone, each of whom went on to found small rival Left parties, fractured the CPUSA and established that the Comintern expected to determine policy and leadership for the American Party.[26]

After the stock market crash of October 1929 and the subsequent economic tailspin, the declaration of the Third Period, the twilight of capitalism, seemed prophetic. Stalin appeared vindicated in refusing to recognize American exceptionalism. Once again expecting a revolution, the Comintern declared Democratic Socialism and other vehicles of mere reform to be the greatest obstacles to worldwide revolution. Comintern leaders believed that economic hardship would drive workers to force change; they were determined that the workers should not be "deluded" into accepting reform instead of revolution. They declared "social-fascism," meaning any reformist politics, to be the greatest class enemy in the Third Period. The preferred strategy was to enter into coalitions with nonrevolutionary Leftist organizations and to try to win the membership over to Communism (Klehr, 13). Thus as the Great Depression began, the Communist Party in America was putting its greatest efforts into subverting "social-fascists" like the Socialist Party, the AFL, and the NAACP. Foster overcame his reluctance about dual unionism and took on the leadership of TUUL.

= Organizing in the South =

As labor organizing and strikes, successful and unsuccessful, had from time to time disrupted manufacturing in the North, a number of owners, particularly in the textile industry, moved their operations to the South, where native-born workers were thought to be less contaminated by—and less open to—"foreign" ideas such as unionization. All the more surprising, then, was the 1929 strike of white textile workers at the Loray Mill in Gastonia, North Carolina. The strike occurred in the springtime, shortly after the arrival of Fred Beal, an organizer for the National Textile Workers Union, a Communist dual union. The chief of police was killed, Communists and strikers were tried for murder, vigilantes attacked strikers and organizers, local strike leader Ella Mae Wiggins was killed, and the strike failed. Communists could hardly point to Gastonia as a model labor action, but the strike had positive symbolic value in that it showed the Party as being able to lead white, southern, native-born workers, even before the stock market crash.[27]

Mary Heaton Vorse's *Strike!* was the most popular of the six novels based on the Gastonia strike. Vorse was a member of the Greenwich Village Left, a founder of the Provincetown Players, an activist for woman suffrage, and a labor journalist, contributing to Left and mainstream newspapers and magazines. She had done publicity for the IWW during their campaign for the unemployed in New York City in 1914. Her thorough familiarity with labor struggles began when she covered the bread and roses strike in Lawrence, Massachusetts, in 1912, the 1916 miners' strike at the Mesabi Iron Range in Minnesota, and the 1919 steel strike. Serving as publicity director for the 1926 textile strike in Pasaic, New Jersey, Vorse developed techniques that became the model in the labor struggles of the 1930s: she enlisted influential liberals to endorse the strike, and she kept material flowing to the mainstream as well as the radical press, particularly emphasizing human-interest stories about strikers and their families.[28] Her influential labor reporting did much to raise awareness of the need for industrial organization and to bring to light the importance of women's work in unionization. Vorse was not impressed by what she saw on her two visits to Moscow, in 1921 and 1933, and she became a critic of Communism. To the end of her long life, however, she remained an active campaigner for Socialism, feminism, and nuclear disarmament.

In *Strike!* she wrote about a strike she witnessed firsthand. For her point-of-view character, however, she chose Roger Hewlett, a reporter new to the labor movement and gradually drawn into firm sympathy with the strikers, thus locating the book in the tradition of political "conversion narratives." Hewlett's unfamiliarity with labor struggles provides an opportunity for Hoskins, a veteran reporter, to tell him and the reader how this strike shares with northern strikes the motivations of the strikers, the response of "comfortable people" of the town, the beginnings of violence, and the way the authorities deal with the organizers. Thus Vorse made of the novel a primer on the dynamics of labor struggle.

Early in the novel, Hewlett goes to visit the Parker family, friends of his mother and definitely among the "comfortable" people in Stonerton, the fictional Gastonia. They are vehement in their claims that the mill workers are better off now than they were before they came down from the hills and that there would be no trouble if it weren't for the organizers from the North, who deserve whatever extrajudicial violence may be visited upon them. In the Parkers' anger and in their endorsement of kidnapping, Hewlett sees the genesis of mob violence. Vorse is careful to note the role of gender norms in promoting vigilante violence: old Mrs. Parker, discussing Fer Deane, the organizer, offers, "Why they didn't tar and feather him and ride him on a rail, I don't know. Men have no courage any more," and later, "If the police and the law act too slowly, I believe in men showing their manhood."[29] "Manliness" is thus defined in such a way that it can be enlisted in the protection of economic privilege.

Strike! is structured by the sequence of events in the actual strike, until the very end. Vorse recounts the insistence of Fer, the organizer, that no one take a weapon to a demonstration or to the picket line; he knows that violence is always cause to railroad the strike leaders into long jail terms. Women therefore make the best pickets, because it is difficult for the police to characterize them as inciting violence. Having taken such risks, they are then reluctant to be entirely submissive to the male organizers. Likewise, when the mill owner evicts strikers' families from mill-owned shacks, it is the women who must somehow keep up "housekeeping" in the open until union-supplied tents finally arrive. The women organizers in charge of "relief" resent Fer's proprietary air about the tent city that they have worked so hard to get set up: "It was an attitude of his of which he was not conscious, but which infuriated the girls. They and not Fer had been responsible for each baby and the safe transportation of each piece of furniture" (131). Yet Vorse is equally critical of Irma, one of the union organizers and a Communist, who criticizes and demeans Fer for deviating from proper strike ideology, just when he needs all the confidence and courage he can muster to continue the strike. Irma becomes a symbol not only of closed-minded ideology but also of a destructive gender battle, restricted to personal sniping and domination.

To present the decisive encounter between the strikers and the mob, Vorse takes the reader inside the strike headquarters, now heavily guarded, since the previous headquarters was raided and looted. The strikers hear footsteps on all sides of the building as they wait in the dark, and they fear for their families in the tent city outside, whom they are supposed to be guarding as well. "A shot came from the direction of the police car. It passed over one of the guard's heads. He fired" (Vorse, 148). More shots are exchanged. When the shooting stops, Sheriff Humphries and two vigilantes are found dead. Fer's prediction is borne out: he and the other guards are arrested and charged with murder, while none of the vigilante mob is charged. The jury of young working men will not find against the union men, so only the organizers and two of the most militant local leaders are retried and found guilty on a lesser charge. This method of disposing of labor organizers was one Vorse had seen in previous labor actions, and in *Strike!* she documents its workings with the detailed rendering of an exposé journalist.

Like Sinclair in *Boston,* Vorse appears to have intended her novel to "tell how it really happened" and, further, "how it really happens," to the extent that the Gastonia strike typifies labor struggles and the response to them. This documentary motive—this attempt to reconstruct a particular history of an event—at the end runs up against the ugly fact of defeat. The strike is lost. What good is it for labor's story to be told if readers are thereby discouraged from labor organizing? As Dee Garrison notes in introducing the 1991 edition of *Strike!* the "strike novel" of the early 1930s typically served the educational function of chronicling the actual walkout and the owners' response in detail, but put those events in the larger framework of developing worker consciousness.[30] The particular strike is lost, but workers and their supporters learn from the experience and become more committed to radical change as the workers' only hope.

Notable in *Strike!* is the diffusion of reader interest among a number of characters—Fer, Roger, Ed, Mamie Lewes, Doris Pond from the relief committee, and more. Novels of the Left are apt to diffuse interest in this way to emphasize community over individualism. The novel is not one person's story because no one's life is lived in isolation from others. Further, the constraints, problems, and opportunities facing a character are apt to be shared in large part by other members of the same class in the same historical circumstances. And the solution to those problems, in a Left analysis, can be found only in working with other members of the class to make change. Alan Bloch, in *Anonymous Toil,* notes that Fer Deane, en route to what he fears will be a violent confrontation, remarks to Roger, "Wouldn't it be great to go fishing?" Bloch points out that going fishing is the favored escape of Hemingway's Jake Barnes: "In *The Sun Also Rises,* one learns to adjust to conditions without having to understand them. Simple personal survival is the goal. . . . But for Fer this escape is not possible: his work must be with the people and their struggle in the world. This effort leads not primarily in the discovery of how to live in it, but, rather, to understand what it is all about."[31] Jake Barnes learns how to survive in the world as it is; Fer Deane works to change it. Barnes's quest is individual; Deane's is necessarily communal. Thus *Strike!* is not his story alone. Similarly, he is not presented as ideally heroic or wise; he has much to contribute because of his experience, but he must draw on the strength and wisdom of the strikers as well.

The ending of *Strike!* is particularly interesting, given Vorse's standpoint as an independent Leftist. Here she departs from the events of the Gastonia strike: Where the actual organizers jumped bail and sailed to Russia, she has Fer Deane murdered on the picket line while awaiting sentencing. She will not end the novel with an action that implies a betrayal of the local strike leaders. But neither does the novel end with a ringing call for revolution. The upbeat note on which it ends is solidarity: at Deane's funeral, "[t]hey were full with an emotion that swept them out into the world of workers, struggling like themselves for freedom" (Vorse, 233). The exact form of that struggle is left unnamed. Perhaps Vorse herself thought the form unknowable in 1930.

Roger Hewlitt, the young journalist who represents a younger Mary Heaton Vorse, at the end knows only that the struggle must go on and that he must be a part of it. In sections of the book, Vorse entrusts the point of view to the older journalist, Ed Hoskins, who seems to represent the older, more seasoned Vorse, educating young Hewlitt—an effective rhetorical device. As Garrison notes in the introduction, however, Vorse must have felt that only male personae would have sufficient authority to give a persuasive account of the strike (Garrison, xv). Having Vorse's own perceptions ascribed to male characters creates difficulty when she wants to communicate an insight that would be unavailable to them. Thus, for example, she shifts awkwardly into omniscient narration to describe conversations between Mamie Lewes (Ella May Wiggins) and Daisy West and to relate the women's resentment of Fer over the tent city.

Further evidence of hasty work, characters are inconsistently named, the dialect is thick and inaccurate, the rivalry between Fer and Irma remains undeveloped and unresolved, and a romance between Mamie and one of the strike leaders is introduced just before her death. It seems likely that Vorse hurried the book to the publisher, without much revision, so that it could reach the public while the strike itself was still fresh in their minds and in time to influence other southern textile strikes that would follow. It enjoyed strong sales. Mainstream reviews were positive, and the Communist press reviewed it favorably, in spite of its deviations from Marxist orthodoxy (Garrison, xviii). Relying on observation rather than theory, Vorse presented the strikers as naive and all too often inclined to helplessness as a result of years of paternalistic treatment by the mill owners (Vorse, 129). The economic deprivation that drives some to strike drives others to remain at the looms for any pay, any hours, especially as the union cannot provide sufficient relief to support the strikers. The Communist Party leadership would have done well to give *Strike!* a careful reading.

=   Conclusion   =

The chilling effect of the Red Scare lasted through the 1920s, lumping together all Leftists as Reds, all Reds as violently un-American. The Communist Party began the decade as the inheritor of many Leftist hopes—and indeed of many Leftists, as the IWW, the anarchist movement, and the Socialist Party fragmented. But the example of Soviet Russia, initially so attractive, continued throughout the 1920s to repel Leftists. Louis Fraina, one of the founders of the Communist Party in America, left the Party in the 1920s. Floyd Dell continued to write positively about Communism when he wrote about politics at all—more often in these years he wrote in praise of marriage—but resigned as contributing editor of the *New Masses* in May 1929 because he disapproved of the narrow editorial interests of Mike Gold. Max Eastman resigned from the executive board of the *New Masses* in January 1928 because his political views were not well received.

Some, like Mary Heaton Vorse, were disillusioned with the Russian example and refused to join the CPUSA. Others, like Agnes Smedley, were put off by Communist authoritarianism and unable to connect culturally to Communist circles. Party membership in spring of 1929 was below 10,000, and a Comintern letter of that year accused the CPUSA of having "been for many years an organization of foreign workers not much connected with the political life of the country" (Klehr, 5). Indeed, the Socialist Party, organizing in the needle trades, had greater drawing power than the Communists and benefited from the upsurge in the Jewish Socialist movement of the 1920s. The labor policy pursued by the Communists throughout most of the decade was ineffective and added to the Party's reputation as subversive and duplicitous, hiding its real agenda so it could use people and organizations.

In spite of these negatives, the Party managed during the 1920s to enlist American-born leaders like William Z. Foster and Earl Browder and to attract a dedicated cadre, whose devotion gave them force beyond their number. As Mike Gold makes clear in *Jews without Money*, the struggle for change itself can give meaning and hope to lives that might otherwise have little of either. Particularly in the immigrant circles of northeastern cities, the Party was a good cultural "fit" and provided real opportunities for belonging and for self-development.

Although the 1920s has entered cultural memory as an era of good times and household gadgets, it also offered plentiful challenges to complacency and even to faith in gradual improvement. The long ordeal of Sacco and Vanzetti showed the American legal system at its worst. Large numbers of the unorganized remained desperately poor even in an era of relative prosperity. Even some unionized workers lost economic ground. Racism was institutionalized and unabashed. How could one take effective action against injustice if one found liberalism insufficient? When the question is "Which Side Are You On?" what choices were there? One might have maintained independence as an anarchist or an adherent of the religious Left. One might have looked to the Socialist Party for a less doctrinaire Leftism than that of the Communist Party, which was the most assertive Leftist voice at the time. One might have joined the Communist Party enthusiastically or joined it despite misgivings about the Soviet example and about particular CPUSA policies, believing it still to be better than acceptance of the status quo and the most likely vehicle for radical social change.

Indeed, one of the currents that runs through a number of novels by independent Leftists in the 1920s is the agony of deciding whom and what one can support. Sinclair's portrait, in *Boston*, of a pacifist, a Social Democrat, a Communist, a Wobbly, and a liberal, all working to save two anarchists, typifies the issue orientation of much political activity in this era. Absent agreement about the desired future, Leftists tried to work together against obvious outrages. It was in this milieu that the Communist Party tried to implement Comintern thinking about the Third Period and embarked on the policy of afflicting its possible coalition partners. Bolshevik theory and the Bolshevik example admitted no coalitions with reformists, no hindrances to revolution. And as the country entered the Great Depression, revolution was not unthinkable.

The search for an effective cultural policy was sent in contradictory directions by the Kharkov conference, which urged the Party to draw in sympathetic intellectuals and to adhere more closely to Marxist literary theory. The tension between these two goals would be lessened, or at least masked, by the willingness of a number of writers in the late 1920s and early 1930s to explore new ways for literature to be political. If, as Malcolm Cowley suggested, the Sacco and Vanzetti case moved writers to look for literary forms that would directly influence not just the historical record but history in the making, then the ongoing struggle to define "proletarian writing" must be viewed as an issue of some urgency.

4

From the Great Depression to the Popular Front, 1931–1935

THE STOCK MARKET CRASH OF OCTOBER 1929 GENERATED A RASH of cartoons and jokes about investors and businessmen standing in line for their turn to jump off the ledge of a skyscraper, but for most working Americans, economic ruin was a more gradual process. Many businesses, without confidence and without capital, either went under or began layoffs. Unemployed workers couldn't buy much; inventories rose; more people were laid off. The cycle drove the economy downward, so that by 1931, nearly half of the textile workers in New England were without work. In August 1931 the Ford Motor Company was employing only 37,000 people, compared with the 128,000 just before the crash (Zinn, 378). By 1933, unemployment had reached 25 percent.

Unemployed working people, who generally had little or no savings, could only turn to family and friends and their own ingenuity. They did day labor, sold homemade bread and garden produce, took cleaning jobs, and often moved wherever there was hope of work. Evictions were common. Bread lines and soup kitchens provided charity for the most desperate. All

Distributing *Art Front*, published monthly by the Artists Union from November 1934 to December 1937. Photo by Lou Block. From the Lou Block Collection, University of Louisville Photographic Archives.

over the country, farm families were unable to repay their bank loans, lost their farms to the auction block, and took to the road. Many went to California, where they did harvesting work for rock-bottom wages and lived in camps. Such camps, like the shanytowns that grew up on the edges of cities, often named themselves Hooverville, after the Republican president who believed that government should not intervene in the economy and that the Depression must simply be endured until the market righted itself. The policy of waiting it out had little appeal; it was not only that times were bad but that they were getting worse.

Howard Zinn, in *A People's History of the United States,* describes the growth of an informal "people's economy" based on barter and co-ops. "In Seattle, the fishermen's union caught fish and exchanged them with people who picked fruit and vegetables, and those who cut wood exchanged that. There were twenty-two locals, each with a commissary where food and firewood were exchanged for other goods and services: barbers, seamstresses, and doctors gave of their skills in return for other things. By the end of 1932, there were 330 self-help organizations in thirty-seven states, with over 300,000 members" (Zinn, 385). Housewives in the city and surrounding farm country played a major role in organizing the Seattle cooperatives; the need to feed their families pushed many into political activity for the first time.[1] The co-op experiments ultimately gave way to early New Deal reforms, but they suggested that the people could imagine an alternative to capitalism. It may have taken a crisis, but people seemed to be heeding the advice of a song from the Wobblies' "Little Red Song Book": "dump the boss off your back." In Pennsylvania, unemployed miners dug their own mines on company land and sold the coal at a discount in the cities; juries refused to convict them (Zinn, 385–86). From restaurants in New York City and a general store in the Ozarks came reports of hungry people demanding or simply taking what they needed. Such incidents, though repeated throughout the country, were isolated and uncoordinated. It was not hard, however, to imagine them sparking a general insurrection, a revolution.

One group that had spent some time imagining just that, the Communist Party, began soon after the crash to organize street demonstrations. On 6 March 1930, it called for unemployment demonstrations across the country, and when the turnout exceeded expectations, some in the Party began to believe that the masses were turning radical (Klehr, 33). But it could not build on that success, and Party leaders were forced to admit that the masses wanted immediate relief and jobs, not control of the state. How then could the Party establish real contact with the masses, so as to exert some genuine influence and direction? The Party plenum in November of that year approved support for "partial demands," that is, immediate relief measures. William Z. Foster explained, "There has been too much reliance on broad political slogans and too little concentration upon questions of the most immediate interest to the workers."[2] Such a policy, at odds with the general analysis

that governed the Third Period, seems to have been dictated by simple pragmatism, a need to have some influence.

The unemployed represented a large and growing group with little or
nothing to lose, and the Party had some success leading them in protests.
From their headquarters in Union Square, the Communists orchestrated a
string of demonstrations and meetings that kept the unemployed visible to
officials in New York and other large cities. Their first demand was for
unemployment insurance, but they went on to link it to a full program,
including worker control of relief and support of the Soviet Union. The strategy of trying to promote both immediate improvements and ultimate revolution was only partly successful; the unemployed generally accepted Party
leadership in the insurance struggle but refused the link to revolution. Likewise, Party-sponsored unemployed councils won respect and gratitude from
the down-and-out for their work in fighting evictions. Party workers organized
rent strikes and, most effectively, simply arrived on the heels of the hired
movers and organized the neighbors to take the evicted family's belongings
back into the apartment. But respect for Party workers and their practical
help did not translate into mass membership.

Salute to Spring, published in 1940, is a collection of fiction and reportage
by Meridel Le Sueur, the rebellious child of middle-class Socialists and well-
known supporters of woman suffrage. Le Sueur met other Left writers, including Jack Conroy and Richard Wright, through the John Reed Clubs,
organized for the Communist Party, and wrote for the *New Masses.*[3] Much
of her fiction deals with women of the northern prairie states, Le Sueur's
home region. Some of her stories describe these women's sexual awakening,
brave subject matter for the time.

A number of the stories in *Salute to Spring* focus on the political awakening of the farm women, and the title reference to spring indicates the new
life that opens up for characters in many of the stories when they embrace
a Left political commitment. "Tonight Is Part of the Struggle" is the story of
Leah, a young mother who lives in one room with her unemployed husband,
Jock, and their infant son. She and Jock snipe at each other, cooped up in
a small space without enough to eat. Leah tries not to worry because worry
dries up her breast milk, but she cannot help it. Jock proposes that they
attend a mass meeting of the unemployed, if only because it will be warm
in the auditorium. Leah agrees because she just wants to be with other
people. So they join the stream of people walking to the meeting through
the blowing snow.

The speaker is Tiala, a Communist organizer who still speaks with the
Finnish accent familiar in the region. Using metaphors of seed bearing fruit
and yeast raising dough, he tells his audience that the hunger marches of
two years ago are now to be built on. Leah thinks, "O Tiala, we are hungry,
we are lonely, we are lonely and hungry. It's dark, and the snow is falling
in March and the night is wide for Jock and me and we might get old without

. . . O Tiala."[4] The thunderous "AYE" with which the audience approves Tiala's speech wakes the baby, who cries above all the noise and makes the crowd laugh. Tiala tells them to march on the capital for workers' security the next Monday. "She and Jock looked at each other. They had something to do now for Monday. She felt close packed with the others as if they were all running forward together" (Le Sueur, 140).

Characteristically, Le Sueur links the experience of hope and solidarity with good relations between husbands and wives. Lack of space, lack of food, lack of purpose have been destroying Leah and Jock's marriage, but on the night that they join the struggle they come together as a couple, with a way to work for a better life for their baby. Leah didn't understand the political vocabulary Tiala used, but she understood what solidarity was. When Tiala told the audience that they were producers using hand and brain, she looked at the baby and knew that production wasn't all by hand and brain. Thus did Le Sueur choose a character to correct the political line of the organizer— an effective rhetorical device, inviting women to write themselves in when Party speeches left them out. By way of explaining the appeal of such Party-sponsored demonstrations to the poor in the 1930s, it would be difficult to imagine more effective lines than Leah's silent prayer to Tiala. Mass demonstrations gave people hope for relief, a sense of solidarity, and a way to help themselves.

But the Party's decision to support "partial demands" did not hasten the revolution, and Communist documents from this period are full of self-reproach, ascribing the failure to insufficient organizing. What the mass demonstrations and meetings did help to accomplish was the characterization of the problem as a national crisis, not simply personal disaster multiplied by millions. It also turned the Party's dedicated cadre to addressing people's immediate needs, such as reversing evictions.

The Party's labor organizing in the early years of the Depression demonstrated much the same pattern of success and failure. In the early summer of 1931, the National Miners Union (NMU) came into Harlan County, Kentucky, after a strike by the United Mine Workers (UMW) had been broken that spring. The NMU was one of the dual unions operating under the Trade Union Unity League. In the Appalachian Mountains, miners and their families lived in poverty, often in company towns, where the shacks and the only store were owned by the mine companies, which could then exert near-complete control over the miners. The NMU—with a program that ran from the practical (use of checkers to make sure miners got credited with the right weight) to the revolutionary (abolition of capitalism)—enlisted thousands, including many of the miners who had been blacklisted for their role in the lost UMW strike.

When the NMU called a strike for 1 January 1932, the number of miners who walked out was much smaller than the union had expected. It had failed to organize well, failed to prepare a large enough strike fund, and failed to counter with its own publicity the propaganda that condemned the union in Biblical terms (Klehr, 46). Calling the strike so prematurely seemed to reflect on the part of the NMU organizers either naivete or the assumption of a revolutionary potential that wasn't there. Jack Stachel, an officer of TUUL, faulted the organizers for "yielding to spontaneity" (Klehr, 46). As in their work with the unemployed, Communists organizing for TUUL unions were inclined to trust that the dynamic of history itself would turn discontent into revolutionary struggle. Just as the Bolsheviks seemed to have succeeded by riding the revolutionary tide (at least in accounts after the fact), American Communists seem to have counted on the same revolutionary "spontaneity." Directives from the Comintern in these years, while berating the CPUSA for its failure to make revolution, contributed to the problem by their assumption that revolutionary conditions existed in America.

The Harlan strikes were exceptional for their level of vigilante violence. With killings and ambushes and a virtual cessation of civil liberties, the area looked more like a war zone than the site of a labor struggle. The novelist Theodore Dreiser in 1931 headed a fact-finding delegation that went to Harlan County under the sponsorship of the National Committee for the Defense of Political Prisoners, a Party satellite group. The delegation included, among others, Mary Heaton Vorse, John Dos Passos, and Malcolm Cowley, who, remembering the experience in a 1981 interview, said, "That kind of brutality was really frightening. We went to a lawyer's office and were told 'better move your chair. There are needle guns pointed this way' " (Cowley, OHAL). Dreiser's committee not only condemned the thuggery but accused the mine companies of the worst exploitation of their workers and the corruption of the justice system (Aaron, 179). Dreiser and Dos Passos were indicted for criminal syndicalism and chose not to return to Harlan County for trial. A second delegation, including writers Edmund Wilson and Waldo Frank, reported from Harlan in the spring of 1932.

The strike itself was broken and the NMU virtually destroyed by the loss. Membership dropped to an insignificant number. Dreiser, Dos Passos, and Wilson, all non-Communist Leftists, much later complained of having been used by the Party, which was not open about its backing of the Committee for the Defense and which, they felt, would have been happy to see them "martyred" in Harlan County just for the publicity (Aaron, 179–80). But on the positive side, the Communist Party succeeded in bringing to national attention the conditions of the miners' lives, which won the miners support in later UMW strikes.

In the fall of 1932, 53 writers and other intellectuals signed a document titled *Culture and Crisis*,[5] which denounced the Republicans and the Democrats as corrupt and the Socialist Party as ineffectual and reformist and asserted that Communism was the only way out of the Depression and the threat of Fascism. The capitalist United States was described as a rotting house, which the incoming Roosevelt administration could perhaps shore up but not restore to soundness. The signers—among them Sherwood Anderson, Newton Arvin, Maurice Becker, Erskine Caldwell, Malcolm Cowley, Countee Cullen, John Dos Passos, Waldo Frank, John Herrmann, Granville Hicks, Sidney Hook, Langston Hughes, Grace Lumpkin, Lincoln Steffens, Edmund Wilson, and Ella Winter—urged support for the Party's presidential ticket of William Z. Foster and James Ford (Aaron, 196, 457). According to Malcolm Cowley, who wrote the introduction to the pamphlet, most of *Culture and Crisis* was composed by Louis Fraina, who signed as Lewis Corey (Cowley, OHAL). Most of the signers were not Party members but were willing to endorse the Party because they believed that conditions in the cities, on the farms, and in the mines (a number of the signers had visited Harlan County) truly represented such a state of decay that only a radical solution could avail. Indicating the identification of intellectuals with the masses, *Culture and Crisis* generated a great deal of attention, largely positive (Cowley, OHAL).

═══ Two Experiments in Left Fiction ═══

For a representation of that segment of labor that had not prospered in the 1920s but in fact lost ground, readers in 1933 could turn to Jack Conroy's autobiographical novel *The Disinherited*. Raised in the coal-mining camps near Moberley, Missouri, Conroy was largely self-educated. By 1928 he was working with Ralph Cheney on the *Rebel Poet* magazine, and in 1933 he went on to found *Anvil,* a magazine for working-class writers that received financial support from the Communist Party. He had originally written *The Disinherited* as autobiography, but at the urging of H. L. Mencken turned it into a novel; still, the experiences of hero Larry Donovan are generally those of Conroy himself. He opens the novel in the Monkey Nest Mine Camp, in Missouri, where Larry's father is a miner and a union leader. The father has been educated in a Roman Catholic seminary in Montreal, where he has family, but aside from the occasional letter, he has little contact with his past. The mine work is perilous, wages buy only salt pork even in the best of times, and when the union goes on strike, scabs take the jobs.

After the father and two brothers are killed by mine work, Larry leaves the Monkey Nest Camp and gets a job in the car department of the Wabash railroad shop. There he meets Ed Warden, who becomes a good friend. Though exhausted by the work in the railyard, Larry, an avowed reader of the Horatio Alger stories, tries to go to night school. "This was the way of escape," he says. "When I saw the broken, apathetic old men about the shops, I told myself that I would study all night, if need be, to save myself from such a fate. The work-dulled old men a few years from the grave, stamped with resignation and defeat. I saw their bleary, leaden eyes before me, their humped backs and gnarled hands which groped for tools even when at rest. After the old men were discharged as unfit for further service at the shops, they sat forlornly on skimpy front porches warming their meagre bodies in the sun, waiting for death."[6]

Townspeople greet World War I with a frenzy of patriotism, and Larry fears that his mother's opposition to the war will attract attention; their house might be one of those that the mob splatters with yellow paint. He watches a Leftist antiwar orator beaten senseless by the mob, who then turns on a neighbor who has tried to stop them. "I decided that everything about the war was cruel. Behind the Liberty Loan posters, I saw the agitator's bloody face," reports Larry (Conroy, 99). His cynicism is only reinforced when government contracts on a cost-plus-profit basis prompt the railroad to hire workers just to sit around: the higher their costs, the greater their profit. His friend Ed Warden returns from the army swearing that nothing will ever get him to go to war again.

On the sly, Larry reads the out-of-town newspapers that the hoboes leave in the boxcars. He wants to understand the world beyond the railyard. But soon he is involved in the great railroad strike of 1922, fervently supporting the union despite Ed's warning that union leaders will sell out the workers. Scab workers take the jobs, Ed goes to Detroit to look for work, and Rollie, the husband of Larry's aunt, remarks, "He *can* go. . . . He's single. But a man with a wife and a mess o' younguns can't traipse off so easy. Larry, lad, don't ever marry, you hear me?" (Conroy, 116). Rollie is later killed in a confrontation with a scab and gets no death benefit from the union because his dues were in arrears.

Larry's Horatio Alger dreams of success through hard work evaporate; he works among the steel cutters and rubber workers, who have been overlooked by the prosperity of the 1920s. They accept pay cuts just to keep their jobs. In the rubber plant, Larry meets Hans, an immigrant Socialist still reeling from the collapse of the Second International. From Hans he gets a reading list that includes Marx, but he puts off the reading until later.

When Ed writes from Detroit that he is making good money in the auto factories, Larry moves there and is lucky enough to get one of the scarce jobs. When he tells Ed that he's taking a correspondence course in accounting, Ed replies, "I know you got ambitious ideas, kid, but it'll only be an accident if you ever get out of your class. You might as well make up your mind that you're a working stiff and that you'll stay one unless lightning happens t' strike you—some kind of luck that hits only one out of a million workin' men. . . . You might as well get used to it and enjoy yourself as much as you can" (Conroy, 195). Detroit has an additional attraction for Larry: Bonnie Fern Haskin, the farmer's daughter from Monkey Nest, is living in Detroit with her family, who have leased the farm and come to the city to try to make money. At home, she was a bit too good for Larry, but in Detroit she befriends him. She is taking college courses and learning about Leftist political theories, but is also being taught that the American worker cannot be radicalized because of a chronic hope for individual success.

The Depression hits, and in the winter of 1930, and Larry and Ed look for work, sleep in flophouses, and eat at soup kitchens. They watch the procession of families moving south again in cars and sometimes on foot. Larry is impressed by the block committees formed to resist evictions, but Ed dismisses such actions as useless gestures and predicts that the radical organizers will get nowhere because they cannot speak people's language: "That's why them soap-boxers never get anywheres. Why don't they talk about beans and potatoes, lard and bacon instead of 'ideology,' 'agrarian crisis' and 'rationalization?' " (Conroy, 239).

The two men buy a near-derelict car and drive home to Monkey Nest, where Larry's mother and his aunt and her children are living in the camp's old barroom, without enough to eat. Work digging a pipeline enables Ed and Larry to sustain them for a while. Bonnie Fern, returned to the farm with her father, seems to regard Larry as her fiancé, but he remembers Rollie's warning. Hans comes to Monkey Nest and reports that he is now an organizer, once again inspired with hope because in the cities the people, black and white together, are marching in the streets. When Ben Haskin's farm is to be auctioned to pay his debts, workmen and farmers surround the farmhouse, bid pennies, and sell it back to him for 99 cents; the crowd prevents any interference by the police. Finally, even Ed is convinced that if farmers are taking things into their own hands, then change is possible. At the auction, Larry gives a speech that makes the old residents of Monkey Nest remember his father. The novel ends as Larry and Ed and other workers leave to do organizing work, committing themselves to the struggle. Bonnie Fern says that she will wait, but Larry makes no promises.

Many are the disinheritances in this novel. Conroy explicitly refers to the unemployed workers as disinherited from their right to a job, the means to support themselves and their families. Larry's father, having put aside religion in favor of union work, is estranged from his family. Larry's own life is marked by the rootlessness of the laboring poor, whose connections to any given place, to friends, to the larger American culture are repeatedly broken. It is only when he gives his first organizing speech that he takes up his true inheritance from his father: resistance. It requires Hans, the European, to restore to American workers their heritage of class struggle.

Conroy's hunger for reading appears to have schooled him in the traditions of American literary realism and naturalism. One of the attractions of his novel, decades after its publication, is the wealth of detail from urban life in the late 1920s and early 1930s; the chrome-legged tables of coffee shops, the slangy flirtations, the Nehi soda signs, the spill of pop music into streets lit by movie marquees bring back the time as effectively as an Edward Hopper painting. Industrial processes, too, are described at a level of detail known only to the worker, and the descriptions hum with a lyrical enthusiasm for the efficient power of the machines and the quick skill of the workers. And in describing the sudden rage of Larry's long-suffering friend Nat, Conroy seems to be consciously applying the "trapped animal" imagery that is the signature of literary naturalism. But in place of naturalism's grim determinism, Conroy envisages purposeful human action that will bring real change. Indeed, *The Disinherited* has its thematic center in the movement from acceptance to struggle.

Conroy's novel received warm critical attention, but, like most proletarian novels, it sold badly—reportedly only 2,700 total, with 1,000 of those at a steep discount (Rideout, 235). One problem might have been that Larry Donovan, least introspective of heroes, has little to distinguish him from the generic worker, except perhaps his rather unkind satisfaction in leaving Bonnie Fern, his once-haughty sweetheart, "on hold" while he assumes the higher task of making the revolution. Indeed, despite Conroy's sympathetic portrayal of his mother, women in *The Disinherited* are not only unrevolutionary in themselves but in general millstones around the neck of working men and revolutionaries. They represent the private sphere of home and family responsibility that impedes a man's participation in the public world and forces him to sell his labor cheap. None of the younger women in the novel is an individualized, developed character.

The character of Larry himself remains an underdeveloped Everyworker for reasons about which it is interesting to speculate. Conroy was not an unpracticed writer when he wrote *The Disinherited,* and simple lack of skill seems too easy an explanation. We might better ask whether in turning the book from autobiography to novel Conroy felt he should remove all self-revelatory material that would keep any worker from seeing himself in Larry. Or, given Mike Gold's 1930 attack on Thornton Wilder's "lavender tragedies," did Conroy feel pressure to suppress the personal even in a radical novel? How does a writer create a character individual enough to seem humanly real and to win our sympathy and interest but still typical enough to represent his or her class? Literary theory has offered answers to this question in the decades since the 1930s, but Conroy had relatively little precedent to draw on. And then, further, if the novel chronicles a character's coming to consciousness, how much attention does the writer wish to give to his reflections while still in a state of false consciousness?

The ending of *The Disinherited* presents an aesthetic problem that is endemic to political conversion narratives but greatly exacerbated by the historical conditions at the time Conroy was writing in 1932. That was the time when the revolution most seemed possible. If it occurred, and succeeded, then the ending would have one meaning: Larry's ultimate commitment to organizing and all of his progress toward it throughout the novel would be justified and given significance by history. If the revolution never occurred or if it failed, then the ending would have a different meaning: the justification of Larry's commitment would have to rest in the assertion—which he and Ed share in the last pages of the novel—that their own lives have been given new dignity and meaning. *Jews without Money,* set earlier, could sustain a positive ending simply from Mikey's embrace of radicalism because the revolution was then a more distant possibility; one could usefully work for a revolution years in the future. But in *The Disinherited,* it is difficult to separate Larry's new sense of empowerment from the possibility of imminent revolution. He and Ed are moved to action by the belief that the masses are awakening, and despite the passage about the discovery of personal dignity, the meaning of the novel is ultimately determined by history itself.

The Forty-second Parallel by John Dos Passos is an experiment in Left fiction very different from that of Conroy.[7] Published in 1930, it is the first volume in the author's *U.S.A.* trilogy. Speaking admiringly, James Farrell would later offer the novel as a positive example of the "collective novel," one which follows not one but a number of characters through parts of their lives.[8] The story that emerges is thus not a personal story but something of a "metastory," a revelation of the way in which class and history shape American lives. It does not, therefore, admit of easy summary. Fainy McCreary (Mac), introduced to Socialism in the Irish-American slums, is cheated by his employer in a book distributing company, tramps across the country, works for an IWW printer in San Francisco, and finally goes to Mexico, leaving behind his wife and children. J. Ward Moorehouse rises from relatively humble origins through his genius for cutthroat trading and dealing. After divorcing his wife and returning from Paris, he marries a steel heiress and promotes a plan for labor-capital cooperation as it becomes clearer that World War I is looming. Eleanor Stoddard, an interior decorator, takes Moorehouse as a lover.

The war begins to seem imminent. Janey Williams is a young woman left on her own when her brother enlists in the navy and her lover becomes a war correspondent. Through her work as a secretary she meets Moorehouse and travels with him to Mexico, where he is trying to coopt Mac. She becomes the lover of G. H. Barrow, a corrupt labor leader. Charley Anderson, a North Dakotan who travels the country, becomes a friend of Ben Compton, the brother of Janey's roommate, Gladys. Charley supports the Wobblies and finally leaves with a friend to join the French ambulance service. Moorehouse departs for Washington to promote both U.S. entry into the war and his scheme for coopting labor. Interspersed among the characters' stories are sections called "Newsreel," which contain clips from popular songs, advertisements, and headlines to link the character's actions to the history and culture of the time. Other sections, called the "The Camera Eye," use stream-of-consciousness narration to comment on the action. A third device for widening the horizon of the novel is the inclusion of biographical sketches of Eugene Debs, William Haywood, William Jennings Bryan, Andrew Carnegie, Thomas Edison, and others. *The Forty-second Parallel* is thus not any one person's story but the story of the United States of America in the first three decades of the twentieth century, and the picture is one of corruption, injustice, and decay. The best values and the kindest impulses are defeated by greed and deceit.

Dos Passos's experiment in the collective novel was hailed by some Left critics and questioned by others who found his use of modernist techniques suspect. James T. Farrell was an enthusiastic supporter. Mike Gold, in a *Daily Worker* review of 26 February 1938, regretted his early hope for Dos Passos and dismissed him as a Trotskyist. "There was such hope Dos Passos was moving up from the bourgeois merde," he wrote. "It was right that we recognised in him a powerful if bewildered talent, tried to help free that talent from the muck of bourgeois nihilism."[9] Granville Hicks's early review in the *New Republic* of 24 June 1931 praised Dos Passos but included an important reservation: "Not even Dos Passos' most fervent admirer is likely to argue that he has yet written the kind of novel of industrial America for which we have waited seventy years. A good many episodes in *Manhattan Transfer* and *Forty-second Parallel* are left on the journalistic level, untouched by any poetic insight, unrelated to any centralizing vision."[10] From Left critics like Gold and Hicks, "bourgeois nihilism" and an absence of "centralizing vision" likely mean that Dos Passos had not built *Forty-second Parallel* around growing support for revolution or evolving proletarian consciousness.

Malcolm Cowley judged Dos Passos's work more sophisticated than novels like *The Disinherited* (Cowley, OHAL), and it has been praised over the decades for its artistic innovations and scope and continues to be read and taught. Modern critics, however, have echoed the critique that it lacks cohesion and have disagreed about what the unifying perspective might be. Barbara Foley finds that history itself unites *Forty-second Parallel* and argues that a radical politics is implied; the reader must come to it through cognition rather than recognition.[11] She notes too that the trilogy is not free from some assumptions—such as the separation of personal and public experience—that arise from liberalism and that contradict the Marxist theory that private life is as much determined by history as public life is (Foley, 207). Michael Clark argues that pragmatism, derived from John Dewey, not any form of systematic radical politics, is the unifying factor.[12] One thing seems likely: the predominance of critique over "program" in *Forty-second Parallel* reflects Dos Passos's own political dilemma. He remained a "fellow-traveler," a non-Communist but in sympathy with many Left political positions.

=   Early Days of the New Deal   =

The elections of 1932 were not encouraging to the Communist Party on any count. William Z. Foster, as the Communist presidential candidate, drew 102,991 votes, better than twice the Party's vote in 1928, but the Socialist

Party's Norman Thomas garnered 918,0000 (Klehr, 88–89). The election of Franklin Delano Roosevelt to replace Herbert Hoover brought little comfort. According to Malcolm Cowley, some thought that Roosevelt would be the American Kerensky, with the revolution soon to follow; "See you at the barricades" was the half-joking greeting of some New York comrades in late 1932 (Cowley, OHAL). True to Third-Period analysis, the Party believed that Roosevelt's promised reforms would simply delay the day of revolution.

Thus the Party found itself arguing against measures like the National Industrial Recovery Act (NIRA), which raised wages and shortened working hours for many Americans and also guaranteed the right of labor to organize. This leading piece of New Deal legislation waived antitrust provisions and established codes for wages and prices. While waiting for basic industries to submit their proposed codes, the administration promoted "blanket codes," calling for a 35-hour week and a minimum hourly wage of 40 cents for factory workers and a 40-hour week and a minimum weekly salary of $12–15 for white-collar workers.[13] Those employers who voluntarily complied were entitled to fly the Blue Eagle symbol, and doing so became a test of patriotism. (The August 1933 issue of *New Masses*, which opposed the NIRA, pictured the eagle with guns in one claw and a worker being crushed in the other; a well-muscled arm is reaching in to strangle the eagle.)

It has been argued that the NIRA boards that set codes for various industries had a disproportionate share of businessmen, who conceded to labor as little as possible. Some African-American textile workers, for example, found that the agreements lowered their wages; others got higher pay but found prices raised at the company store (Bellush, 45, 79). Likewise, Grace Hutchins, writing for the *New Masses* in 1934, objected that approximately a fourth of the codes set by the NRA (the National Recovery Act, which succeeded the NIRA) established lower pay rates for women than for men; some simply set the rates according to the worker's sex, and others had the same effect by specifying lower rates for the kind of work women traditionally did or by allowing historical wage differentials to be continued.[14] Nonetheless, the Party had a difficult job persuading the majority of working people to scorn the legislation, even if, as the Party argued, it bought some off cheaply and harmed others. The Agricultural Adjustment Act (AAA) was similarly problematic for the Party, which argued that it favored large business farms over family farms, though it brought some needed stabilization to farm prices (Zinn, 383).

The Works Progress Administration (WPA), which created public works jobs for the unemployed, building roads and bridges and park buildings and writing local guides and histories and painting murals in public buildings, was also problematic. The intention and the effect of the WPA was to stabilize capitalism, but in the process it enabled the "production for use" that Communism regards as the ideal: in Michigan the WPA leased the building of a defunct underwear factory, paid the workers to go on producing underwear, and gave it to the poor; in the south the WPA paid local women to make mattresses out of surplus cotton and sold them at a price low enough that some people could afford a mattress for the first time (Norrick, OHAL).

Just after the 1932 election, Party membership had jumped to a bit over 18,000, the highest it had been since the Party's earliest days, but by June 1933 it had fallen to just below 15,000. Only slightly more than 20 percent of that number had joined before 1930, but these "old guard" members were disproportionately represented in leadership positions (Klehr, 91–92; the Party's own history, *Highlights of a Fighting History*, gives 14,000 as the 1932 figure, 100). Their disposition was sectarian; that is, they opposed cooperation with non-Communists and were thus comfortable with the Third-Period ideology. In the early 1930s, Communists' relations with other Leftist groups were so bad that the latter formed defense squads in anticipation of Communist brick throwing (Lens, 304).

= The Socialist Party, the Musteites, = and the Trotskyists

The Socialist Party, which had bested the Communists by a wide margin in the presidential election of 1932, was headed by Norman Thomas, a former minister who had come to Socialism through the Social Gospel and through a commitment to pacifism. Through his participation in the antiwar Fellowship of Reconciliation, he knew many on the religious Left. Like his predecessor, Eugene Debs, he spoke positively about the Russian Revolution but could accept neither the doctrine of revolutionary violence nor the controlling impulses of the Comintern. Whereas Debs had been foremost a union man, Thomas, with his ministerial background, attracted intellectuals to the Socialist Party and positioned it as a "people's party" (Lens, 300). As such, it attracted members who were moving left in response to the Great Depression. Socialist Party membership in 1932 was double what it had been in 1928, and it was particularly attractive to young people, on college campuses and in unions. Its nondoctrinaire openness, which had lost it support in the immediate wake of the Russian Revolution, appealed to these young people as well as to many political veterans repelled by the dogmatism of the Communist Party. Under Thomas's respected leadership, the Socialist Party influence extended into the South through the Southern Tenant Farmers Union.

Because it supported the electoral and legislative roads to change, the Socialist Party was in an odd position vis-à-vis the New Deal. Reforms promoted by the Roosevelt administration essentially laid to rest the ethic of rugged individualism and established that government could and should take some responsibility for protecting citizens and regulating business. This was a substantial change in American political life, but it stabilized rather than undercut American capitalism. It generally improved workers' lot, but it left the balance of power and the distribution of resources fundamentally un-changed. And, in allowing business interests to set codes like those of the NRA, the New Deal appeared to Socialists to be promoting economic Fascism. It was thus with a good deal of frustration that the Socialist Party saw its support erode as the New Deal appeared to some to be carrying out the Socialist agenda (Thomas reportedly quipped that it was carried out "on a stretcher").[15]

In the 5 April 1933 issue of the *World Tomorrow*, a Christian Socialist magazine allied to the Socialist Party, Kirby Page wrote that violent revolution is an unacceptable strategy and one likely to lead to prolonged warfare and to failure, given the resources of American capitalism; on the other hand, gradualism can devolve into an acceptance of a snail's pace of change. What Page called for was "rapidly progressive non-warlike revolution. That is to say, reduce to a minimum all entanglements to capitalism, keep eyes eagerly fastened on the goal of socialism, avoid the illusion of utopia-via-violent-cataclysmic-revolution, and step forward vigorously along the pathway of socialist policies."[16] Page went on to agree that relief programs for the poor are clearly necessary, but he warned readers to be wary of the welfare state, which, if it did not transfer ownership of the means of production from private hands to the public (preferably through purchase, not expropriation) could simply add to the power of the state that serves vested interests. In the issue of 31 August 1933, Norman Thomas, in "New Deal or New Day," attempted to sort out whether the New Deal would lead to Socialism or to Fascism. He warned that "the popular temper in America contains plenty of encourage-ment to fascism."[17] The New Deal was doing the right thing with relief and public works programs and labor's right to organize, but these things would not lead to Socialism unless Socialists remained vigilant and energetic. Dis-cussing the right to organize, he wrote, "the organization that moves toward socialism has to be far more zealously eager for the rights of the unskilled and of the Negroes than the official labor movement has yet been" (Thomas, 489).

Within the Socialist Party, 1934 saw a struggle between the Old Guard, mostly from the New York garment trades, and the Militants, the younger element and a group from Milwaukee, a traditional stronghold of the Socialist Party. With the Militants' victory, the Old Guard withdrew from the Party, taking with it control of the Rand School and the *New Leader*, the Socialist weekly, as well as WEVD, the New York radio station. (The call letters stand for Eugene Victor Debs.) The Socialist Party was further weakened when in 1935 the Communist Party embarked on a Popular Front strategy, which greatly increased its appeal, and again after the 1936 election, when the New Deal moved closer to the Left.

In 1936, without the Old Guard to oppose such a move, the Socialist Party accepted into its ranks the membership of the Workers Party (not to be confused with the party of the same name in the 1920s, which became the CPUSA), which was itself a fusion of the American Workers Party, led by A. J. Muste, and the Communist League of America, the Trotskyist party headed by James P. Cannon. Muste, like Norman Thomas, had come to Socialism through the Social Gospel, ministerial work, and the pacifist Fellowship of Reconciliation. He had come to prominence in the labor movement when he led a successful textile strike in Lawrence, Massachusetts, in 1919. He had gone on to chair the faculty at Brookwood Labor College, but his criticism of various union contracts had caused him to fall out with the AFL. To foster a less compliant labor movement, he promoted the Conference for Progressive Labor Action, which in 1933 became the American Workers Party and earned its credentials in industrial organizing by its leadership of the successful Toledo Auto-Lite strike. Muste's scorn for the Comintern provided some ground for the coalition with the Trotskyists.

During the Sixth World Congress of the Comintern in Moscow in 1928, "A Draft Program of the Communist International: A Criticism of Fundamentals," Trotsky's critique of Stalinist policy and bureaucracy, had mistakenly fallen into the hands of James P. Cannon, a delegate of the CPUSA. The Sixth Congress confirmed the 1927 denunciation of Trotsky and the Russian Left Opposition as counterrevolutionary. Cannon, though convinced by Trotsky's arguments, said nothing; he returned to the United States and quietly began recruiting for a Trotskyist faction. Cannon's explanation for his choice not to defend Trotsky publicly at the Sixth Congress is interesting less for his motives in this instance than for what it reveals about the dynamics of critique and of consent by silence: speaking of the professional revolutionist, he writes, "One who takes upon himself the responsibility of calling workers to join a party on the basis of a program to which they are to devote their time, their energy, their means and even their lives, has to take a very serious attitude toward the party. He cannot, in good conscience, call for the overthrow of one program until he has elaborated a new one. Dissatisfaction, doubts, are not a program. You cannot organize people on such a basis."[18] It behooves a professional revolutionist to express no doubts.

Trotsky had accused Stalin of building an authoritarian bureaucracy to support "socialism in one country" (Russia) instead of promoting worldwide revolution. He argued that Stalin should not pretend his transformations of the Russian culture and Russian economy constituted "building socialism"; that the authoritarian imposition of industrialism had no right to call itself Socialism; and that Stalin was making the Comintern an agent of Russian nationalism rather than world revolution. Trotsky ridiculed the idea of proletarian culture, arguing that the period in which the proletariat would destroy capitalism and usher in true Socialism would be too short to allow for the development of any significant cultural forms.

When Cannon, Max Shachtman, and Martin Abern were expelled by the CPUSA, they founded the Communist League, which initially had so few adherents that they were ridiculed as "three generals without an army"

(Cannon, 62). The group's program was both like and unlike the CPUSA's: the League supported the Bolshevik revolution and would continue to support the Soviet Union even though it was in the hands of Stalin; its members would continue to think of themselves as Communists and try to reform the Party and the Comintern; it vehemently opposed dual unionism and committed itself to working within the existing labor movement. True to Trotsky's faith in professional revolutionaries, the League defined its task as winning over the vanguard (that is, converts from CPUSA) rather than trying to organize the masses.[19] The task of the moment was propaganda—educating the few on basic points—rather than agitation—educating the many on a few points (Cannon, 118–19). Because the League, with fewer than 100 members in the early years, had set out to undermine the CPUSA, much of its energy went into printing Trotskyist analyses in its paper, *The Militant,* and distributing the paper around Union Square, right in front of CPUSA headquarters. Fistfights were as common as they were predictable.

After five years of negligible results, the League in 1933 found its fortunes improving. The Russian-directed Comintern was under heavy criticism worldwide when its Third-Period policy of undermining reformers was seen to have given Hitler and the Right an opening in Germany. Trotsky, from exile in France, blamed the Comintern for ordering the German Communists to give over the country to the Fascists without a fight. The prestige of Trotskyism improved noticeably. In the United States, the beginnings of industrial revival brought a wave of strikes in 1934, as workers in the stronger industries were no longer so cowed by fear of unemployment that they were afraid to make demands. The League turned away from propaganda and plunged into labor work. Its leadership of the New York City hotel workers' strike was an embarrassing failure, and the League ended up expelling its chief organizer. But in a Minneapolis strike by truck drivers hauling coal, the League succeeded in taking over the Teamsters' local, no simple feat after Gompers's directive to AFL unions in 1926 to expel Reds. The strike was won, and Cannon credited the victory to his organizers' willingness to stand up to the National Labor Board; they recognized that the New Deal had changed the way settlements were made (Cannon, 147).

While the League was directing the Minneapolis drivers' strike, Trotsky called for a maneuver that came to be known as the "French turn." He directed French Trotskyists to join the French Social Democratic Party and then make a coalition with the left-wing Socialists and win them over to Bolshevism. Trotskyist groups around the world were instructed to implement the "French turn" in their own countries, and the League interpreted this as a mandate to join—and then raid—the American Workers Party. The merger was effected in December 1934 and the new group was called the Workers Party. It was not a happy marriage. By 1936, Muste abandoned the party and returned to the religious Left and pacifist work. His displeasure is not too surprising, as the Trotskyists entered into the merger with the intention of capturing the American Workers' left wing to form with them the core of a new party. During its brief existence, however, Muste's American Workers Party had been notable for its commitment to a Socialist politics grounded in *American* culture and consciously locating itself as a continuation of *American* traditions of freedom, equality, and the refusal of oppression.

One issue that racked the Workers Party was whether to attempt to join with the Socialist Party and thus complete the "French turn." The opposing faction was expelled, and the remnant of the Workers Party (as mentioned earlier in the chapter) was allowed to join the Socialist Party on Socialist Party terms: member by member, not as a body. The Socialists wanted it to be clear that this was not a merger. They correctly perceived that the Trotskyists had takeover on their minds. The Trotskyists shared with the Socialists the critique of the New Deal welfare state: both groups feared that the growth of state control could open the door to Fascism.[20] But Trotskyists opposed pacifism and insisted that the revolution could not be made without violence (Myers, 49–50), while belief in nonviolent change was centrally important to much of the Socialist Party constituency. After several attempts at containment, including the prohibition of Trotskyist publications, the Party expelled the faction in 1937. Taking with them much of the left-wing youth of the Socialist Party, the Trotskyists went on to found the Socialist Workers Party on New Year's Day 1938 and to participate later that year in the founding of the Fourth International, the small Trotskyist rival to the Communist Third International. The weakening of the Socialist Party to near irrelevance in the late 1930s was counted as an accomplishment by Cannon, who wrote, "This was a great achievement because it [the Socialist Party] was an obstacle in the path of building a revolutionary party. The problem is not merely one of building a revolutionary party, but of clearing obstacles in its path. Every other party is a rival. Every other party is an obstacle" (Cannon, 252–53). In the 1930s, it was clearly not only the CPUSA that set about destroying other Left groups in expectation of imminent revolution.

In spite of such intra-Left animosity, one of the most moving accounts of the Minneapolis truckers' strike of 1934 is Meridel Le Sueur's reportage "I Was Marching," which concludes *Salute to Spring* and which was first printed in *New Masses* in September 1934. In it, she describes her experience as a middle-class woman, more accustomed to reflection and analysis than to spontaneous action. For two days she remained a spectator, among the other writers and professionals who stood across the street from the strike headquarters but could not bring themselves to go inside. Having summoned the courage to enter the building, she ignores a request to get a union button because she doesn't want to be known. In 99-degree heat she washes coffee cups and serves coffee to the men coming in off the picket line, while the loudspeaker calls for more men to join the line.

In early afternoon cars come back bringing the men who have been hit with buckshot, and Le Sueur bandages gaping wounds. That night there is a mass labor meeting. She writes, "I have the brightest, most physical feeling with every sense sharpened peculiarly. . . . It is curious, I feel most alive and yet for the first time in my life I do not feel myself as separate . . . and my own fear is not my own alone, nor my hope" (Le Sueur, 187). Like the women working in the kitchen earlier in the day, the men leading cars through the crowd work as part of a group: "They stepped forward to direct a needed action and then fell anonymously back again" (189). Le Sueur suddenly realizes that the cars have been arranged to form a barricade, the traditional signal that a political group has "taken" political space and refuses to let other authority in. Though not a member of the auxiliary—a middle-class outsider, in fact—Le Sueur joins the next day in the march commemorating the slain strikers. "As if an electric charge had passed through me, my hair stood on end, I was marching" (191).

"I Was Marching" is thus the story of the role of the women's auxiliary in the strike and also the story of one middle-class woman slowly coming to join—not just support—the strike. Reportage, or journalism as a first-person account, was a literary form promoted by the Left after the Kharkov conference (Hedges, 10). The form allows the immersion of the narrator in communal events and also demonstrates the effect of communal action on the narrator.

The Religious Left

Begun in 1921 to promote pacifism and published monthly until 1934, the *World Tomorrow* became a voice for one interpretation of Christian Socialism. Over the years, its editors and contributors often had ties to the Fellowship of Reconciliation or to the Socialist Party or both. The magazine became one of the primary vehicles for disseminating in America the ideas of Gandhi. His vision of nonviolent civil disobedience as the most powerful strategy to overturn oppression found a hearing among those repelled by the violence and the subterfuge that the Bolshevists accepted as integral to revolution. It also accorded well with the important strand of anarchist thinking that emphasized nonviolent noncooperation, such as the general strike.

Although World War I had divided the Christian Socialists between those who were staunchly pacifist and those who believed the war a moral crusade, by the late 1920s and early 1930s pacifism was no longer a divisive issue. With Norman Thomas leading the Socialist Party, Christian Socialists became an important part of it. As the Communist Party, the Trotskyists, and the New Deal sapped Socialist Party membership, its defining image increasingly came from its association with pacifism and the moral basis of Socialism.

In 1933, one year before its demise, the *World Tomorrow* reflected concern with the direction of the New Deal, with the rise of Fascism in Germany and its possible rise in the United States, with the possibility of cooperation with Communists, and with pacifism as a strategy not only for change but for resisting a Fascist takeover of the state. In the 26 October issue, in "What Is behind the United Front?" Kirby Page quoted Earl Browder's statement that the purpose of a united front is not cooperation but "boring from within" to destroy the other parties; Page concluded that the Communists' dedication to violent revolution made them unacceptable coalition partners for Socialists dedicated to pacifism.[21] Page had earlier written that Socialists, though pacifists, do not feel bound to work entirely within the framework of legality, especially if confronted with a Fascist threat: "If the German Social Democrats had refused to endorse or rely upon President Hindenburg, and had been prepared to declare a general strike in opposition to a Fascist dictatorship, they might have been successful."[22]

In the July 1933 issue, Reinhold Niebuhr noted with alarm that the enmity between Socialists and Communists in Germany had facilitated the rise of Hitler. He wrote, "America is literally full of radicals and intellectuals who cooperate with communism, even though they have secret doubts about its efficacy, merely because they are unable to find sufficient realism in other quarters."[23] In the 31 August issue he elaborated, "The social struggle is a much more desperate thing than most parliamentary socialism has imagined. The workers who are now facing the full realities of that struggle instinctively feel that a sleepy confidence in constitutionalism is a revelation of the failure to gauge the real character of that struggle. They therefore espouse communism."[24] He argued that parliaments reflect the distribution of power in a society and are therefore suspect as agents of radical change. Socialists must think beyond electoral change, he said; they must go back to theory and think out positions and strategies that will speak to the American people and win them back from Communism (Niebuhr July 1933, 444). Thus, in the pages of the *World Tomorrow* we can watch the pacifists in the Socialist Party debate how to preserve their vision in the face of Fascist threat and Communist appeal.

Within the Roman Catholic Left, the most important development during the early years of the Depression was the founding of the Catholic Worker movement by Dorothy Day and Peter Maurin. Day's autobiography, *The Long Loneliness* (1952), is a literal conversion narrative, proceeding from her earliest attraction to religion, her membership in the Socialist Party, her suffrage work, her life as a reporter for the *Call,* her life in Greenwich Village, and her editorial work for *Masses* to her conversion to Catholicism. Her early reading included Peter Kropotkin, Upton Sinclair, and Eugene Debs. Indeed, she traces her commitment to the poor to her early reading: "Kropotkin especially brought to my mind the plight of the poor, of the workers, and though my only experience of the destitute was in books, the very fact that *The Jungle* was about Chicago, where I lived, whose streets I walked, made me feel that from then on my life was to be linked to theirs, their interests were to be mine; I had received a call, a vocation, a direction to my life."[25]

Her family had been living in San Francisco in 1906 when the earthquake had left so many destitute; Day, a child of nine, had been deeply impressed with the way people took care of those who needed help. That experience, and her reading in Socialism, determined the ideals of her lifetime, as she recounts in *The Long Loneliness*.

Just out of college, she dismissed religion as a "drug" because it offered comfort rather than a spur to action in an unjust world. She associated with Wobblies and Communists and boarded in a tenement on the Lower East Side. Speaking of the *Call,* she says,

> There was no attack on religion because people were generally indif-
> ferent to religion. . . . They were the tepid, the materialistic, who
> hoped that by Sunday churchgoing they would be taking care of the
> afterlife, if there was an afterlife. Meanwhile they would get every-
> thing they could in this. On the other hand, the Marxists, the I.W.W.'s
> who looked upon religion as the opiate of the people, who thought
> they had only this one life to live and then oblivion—they were the
> ones who were eager to sacrifice themselves here and now, thus
> doing without now and for all eternity the good things of the world
> which they were fighting to obtain for their brothers. It was then,
> and still is, a paradox that confounds me. (Day, 63)

Describing the time she spent with the *Masses* and with the group that created the Provincetown Players, she remembers long walks full of political talk: "We took the revolution for granted" (Day, 85).

Living with her lover in a house on the beach at Staten Island, she was happy writing, happy when her baby Tamar was born, but increasingly feeling called to Catholicism. The baby's father, an anarchist opposed to religion, did not want the baby baptized. Although she still greatly loved him, Day left him. Catholicism gave her peace. Still an anarchist at heart, she felt that the solution to the problem of poverty did not lie in organized, impersonal charity or in the welfare state—Day opposed the New Deal—but in building solidarity with the poor and in obtaining the means for the poor to sustain themselves. With her fellow reporter Mary Heaton Vorse, Day traveled to Washington to cover the march for the unemployed and there felt shamed at her withdrawal from political work in the face of such need. She prayed for guidance, and when she returned to New York she found Peter Maurin waiting on her doorstep.

Maurin was a French peasant-intellectual who had been in America for 20 years. The editor of the Catholic magazine *Commonweal* had told him to look up Dorothy Day. His vision was grounded in the social teaching of the Catholic Church, stemming from *Rerum Novarum*. Specifically, he envi-sioned self-sufficient farming communities, a back-to-the-land movement not unlike the ideal of Kropotkin. In such circumstances, with security and dignity, people could truly carry out the commandment to love one another.

To initiate such a movement, he believed, people would have to be taught to farm efficiently (therefore "agronomic universities"), roundtable discussions would be needed to raise consciousness, and houses of hospitality would be needed to meet the immediate needs of the poor.

Thus in 1933, Day and Maurin began the Catholic Worker movement, publishing the first number of their paper, the *Catholic Worker,* on May Day. Some tension emerged between Maurin's emphasis on withdrawal from the capitalist system and Day's faith in unions as solutions to workers' problems. Indeed, although Day traced the intellectual foundation of the Catholic Worker movement to *Rerum Novarum* and later labor encyclicals, her vision and Maurin's were different from and more politically radical than that of the encyclicals or of the Bishops' Program of 1919. Whereas the bishops had put forth the ideal of a guild system that included owners and workers cooperating in the same guilds, Maurin sought an alternative to wage labor, and Day envisioned an end to social hierarchy and, in supporting strikers, implicitly acknowledged that workers must sometimes wrest their rights from management.

The tension between Day's emphasis on political action and Maurin's emphasis on withdrawal from the capitalist system, however, was not disruptive of the Catholic Worker movement, which grew as houses of hospitality opened in a number of cities across the country. In such houses, usually in the slums, Catholic Workers lived and kept the door open to any who needed help. Critically important was the fact that Catholic Workers shared the fate of the poor; theirs was not charity from a distance, but a true solidarity. Day called the movement a "permanent revolution" (Day, 186).

Attempts to get the unemployed interested in self-sufficient farming communities were generally not successful, Day admits in *The Long Loneliness.* The unemployed often returned to the cities to wage-paying jobs as soon as they became available. In Catholic circles, the Catholic Worker movement was regarded with extreme suspicion: "Our insistence on worker-ownership, on the right of private property, on the need to de-proletarianize the worker, all points which had been emphasized by the Popes in their encyclicals, made many Catholics think we were Communists in disguise, wolves in sheeps' clothing" (Day, 188). *Pacifist, anarchist,* and *distributist* are the terms Day used for the political positions taken in her paper.

In the Catholic Worker house of hospitality on Mott Street in the Bowery, Dorothy Day found the love that rescued her from "the long loneliness." Writing on that theme, she explained her integration of sincere Catholicism and a Left vision: "Community—that was the social answer to the long loneliness. That was one of the attractions of the religious life and why couldn't lay people share in it? Not just the basic community of the family, but also a community of families, with a combination of private and communal property" (Day, 224).

Day's autobiography is of literary interest in its own right. Like all who undertake such a project, she looked back on her life from a certain perspective and chose to highlight the experiences that led her to that perspective. She says she wanted to write about what led her to God and to go lightly over the mundane years before her conversion. She seems to want to emphasize "true consciousness" and to downplay "false consciousness." After the founding of the Catholic Worker movement, the book becomes more than her story. It becomes the story of the movement, Day's own life merged into that of the community. True to the philosophical insistence on individual dignity and deproletarianization within the Catholic Worker movement, however, the story of the community is told through a seamless series of vignettes in which one and then another member of the community takes the lead. And her autobiography ends with the death of Peter Maurin and the suggestion that he continues to help the movement through his prayers. Thus death creates no separation in the community. No gulf exists between the physical and the spiritual.

That insistent yoking of spiritual and temporal is the defining characteristic of the Catholic Workers, according to one participant in a conference on the movement in 1983.[26] Whereas social action had marginalized the transcendent in the Social Gospel movement, and whereas A. J. Muste had traveled from the religious Left to the American Workers Party and then back to the religious Left, the Catholic Workers always combine orthodox Roman Catholicism with Leftist politics (Catholic Worker, OHAL). This integration not only determined the literary structure of *The Long Loneliness* but also gave rise to the Association of Catholic Trade Unionists later in the 1930s.

═══ From Harlem to Scottsboro ═══

The Great Depression settled into Harlem with particular vehemence. Throughout most of the Depression years, African Americans in Harlem suffered an unemployment rate one-and-a-half to three times that of white New Yorkers (Naison, 31). Since the mid-1920s, the Comintern had been insisting that the CPUSA make black membership a priority, but the Party in New York City, clothed in immigrant culture and the traditions of antireligious European radicalism, had shown little success by the time the Depression began. Committed black organizers, like Charles Alexander of the International Labor Defense and Cyril Briggs, represented the Party in Harlem and tried to bridge the cultural gap, but the Party remained outside the black churches and even had to concede the best street corners to the Garveyites (Naison, 35–37). Black Communists, conforming to Third-Period thinking, took an antagonistic line toward other black organizations and tried to win for the Party alone the radicalization of Harlem.

Despite the obstacles, the Party enjoyed some success in the early 1930s, with the inclusion of a Harlem contingent in the unemployment demonstration of 6 March 1930 and greater attendance at Communist meetings in Harlem beginning at about the same time. This newfound appeal, modest as it was, seemed to arise from the intersection of economic desperation and Party militancy (Naison, 38). Communists tended to be the most confrontational, and tactics like street demonstrations and mass rallies suited the mood of the times, when so many had nothing to lose. Likewise, in carrying evicted families' furniture back into their apartments, organizers made concrete the rhetoric of "power in the hands of the people."

With continuing pressure from the Comintern to attend to African-American concerns—one strong reason for black Communists to be loyal supporters of the Comintern—the Party began a campaign against white chauvinism. *Chauvinism* was the party's term for an inappropriate group loyalty that interfered with proletarian solidarity. The social as well as the political life of the Party was to be racially integrated. Such a move was radical in itself in the 1930s and was attended by some difficulties.

The most publicized incident involved a Communist named August Yokinen who tried to keep two African Americans from entering the Finnish Workers Club for a social event. The Party staged its own "trial" of Yokinen, with seven black and seven white jurors, Alfred Wagenknecht as judge, Clarence Hathaway as prosecutor, and Richard Moore, a leading black member of the International Labor Defense, as defense attorney. Yokinen was "convicted" and repented his mistake. In the introduction to *Race Hatred on Trial*, the proceedings of the trial published by the Party, James Allen wrote, "Yokinen acknowledged his errors and pledged himself against all forms of race prejudice. As a foreign-born worker he realized that he too was being divided off by the ruling class from other white workers, in the same way as the workers were being divided on race lines."[27] The Party widely publicized the mock trial to educate both black and white workers as to Allen's point. Though all did not go smoothly with the Party's integration policy, many Communists, black and white, seem to have carried it out with the thoroughness of real commitment, and in so doing made connections that would later support the civil rights movement.

A trial with far more serious consequences would soon take place in Alabama. In the spring of 1931, on a freight train going to Memphis, a fight broke out between young white men and young black men, all riding the rails in search of work. As the train pulled into Paint Rock, Alabama, sheriff's deputies removed nine young African Americans in connection with the fight. Later, after authorities discovered that there had been two young white women on the train, they charged the men with rape, even though the physical evidence suggested that no rape had occurred. The nine young men, ages 13 to 21 were arraigned in Scottsboro and pled not guilty. Before two weeks had passed, the "Scottsboro boys"—as they had come to be called—

had been tried and sentenced to death. The atmosphere in the small town was tense, and the National Guard was called in to prevent lynching.

Communists, through the International Labor Defense, made the Scottsboro case their cause. They were sure that only mass action would save the men, that only wide national publicity would make a fair verdict possible. They also saw in the case an opportunity to win black support away from the NAACP, which had been slower to take up the case and preferred a strategy of working quietly through the courts. In March 1932 the convictions of seven of the nine were upheld by the Alabama Supreme Court, and their execution date set for June. The Party in Harlem organized large street demonstrations and a benefit concert by prominent African-American dancers and jazz musicians—this despite the Party's official pronouncement that jazz was a degenerate bourgeois art form (Naison, 70). An announcement by the U.S. Supreme Court in May 1932 that it would review the Scottsboro case during its October term seemed to vindicate the Communist strategy. Up to this point, Harlemites had shown reluctance to support the Communists because of their opposition to the NAACP.

The situation was also eased that summer when the Communists, driven by pragmatism rather than Third-Period thinking, initiated the Scottsboro Unity Defense Committee, a nonsectarian group that was able to enlist broad community support, including that of intellectuals and community leaders. On the other side, the willingness of middle-class Harlem leadership to associate with Communists was aided by the ongoing efforts of Louise Thompson, an African-American college professor turned social worker, whose circle included writers and artists as well as the leadership of the NAACP and the Urban League. The Harlem chapter of Friends of the Soviet Union, which she had formed in December 1931, gathered those interested in Russian artistic experiments and in the gains made by national minorities in the Soviet Union.

Finally, in November 1932, the U.S. Supreme Court overturned the Scottsboro convictions, requiring that the defendants be retried. At the celebratory demonstrations and rallies, a nonsectarian, nonaccusatory spirit prevailed. The high level of commitment demonstrated by the Party, the willingness of black Communists to lead hazardous street demonstrations and of white Communists to follow them in support of the defendants all improved the Party's standing in Harlem. It was no longer a pariah, even if its membership rolls had not grown substantially. The Scottsboro defendants were again convicted by an all-white jury in 1933, but an Alabama Circuit Court judge ordered yet another trial. Finally, in 1937, four defendants were released and five given long prison sentences.

"Party discipline" was a freighted issue when it came to organizing in Harlem. The CPUSA and the Party internationally were overwhelmingly white; could the Party "try" Yokinen for white chauvinism and then send directives telling black organizers what they must do and must not do in organizing their own community? Marxist-Leninism, as "scientific socialism," presumed to describe the road to revolution; Party policy was thus theory driven, in principle. Again, in principle, Party directives came not from individuals but from Marxist-Leninist science, and every revolutionist was bound to support them. In practice, as the Scottsboro campaign developed in the early 1930s, the Party gave its organizers the freedom to win community support through alliances with reformist organizations and even with "bourgeois elements" like the Harlem middle class (Naison, 72).

Communist work in the South went beyond the Scottsboro case. Beginning in 1930, the Communist Party declared itself in favor of "self-determination" in the so-called black belt—the counties, across several deep-south states, with majority black populations. Self-determination most immediately meant equal rights, but the policy also called for the melding of the area into a single state and eventual autonomy of the region, and it held open the possibility of political secession from the United States, with the expropriation of white capitalists' property. This more radical interpretation had little appeal among African Americans in the South, who could foresee only isolation and economic disaster in the policy.

Fortunately, the Party put its practical energies into reversing the evictions of unemployed African Americans, publishing the *Southern Worker,* organizing sharecroppers and tenant farmers, and leading unemployment demonstrations. In 1931, Angelo Herndon, a black Communist, was arrested for leading a biracial unemployment demonstration in Atlanta. He was charged with "inciting to insurrection" and freed only when the insurrection law was ruled unconstitutional. The willingness of black and white Communists to risk their lives for racial justice and workers' rights won them respect from many southern African Americans and from white liberals, just as their courage and militancy won them respect in the street demonstrations and battles against eviction in the North.

One African-American writer profoundly influenced by the ordeal of the Scottsboro boys was Langston Hughes, a signer of the *Culture and Crisis* petition in 1932. His maternal grandfather had dedicated himself to the abolition movement, and his maternal grandmother's first husband had been one of John Brown's men killed at Harper's Ferry.[28] In his Cleveland high school, Hughes had been attracted to Socialist ideas. He completed one year at Columbia University, did manual work for a year, and then in 1923 traveled to Africa, which confirmed his sense of rightness in condemning colonialism (Rampersad, 77).

Back in America, he became one of the leading lights of the Harlem Renaissance, writing fiction and poetry, publishing in the journals of the Urban League and the NAACP and in *The Messenger.* Many of his poems drew on African-American folk themes and rhetorical forms and earned him a reputation as a poet-spokesman for black America.[29] He admired the poetry of Carl Sandburg, who "sang America" and celebrated American folk culture but also wrote poems starkly critical of American elitism and injustice.[30] He was also an admirer of Claude McKay, who wrote love poems and protest poems. In the same way, Hughes wrote lyrics and blues poems about black life and traditions, but also some of the most radical political poetry and stories of the 1930s. In 1930, he accepted the presidency of the League of Struggle for Negro Rights, a Communist front organization, and became more visibly identified with the revolutionary Left (Naison, 42).

In "My Adventures as a Social Poet," Hughes describes the immediate reception of one of his most famous protest poems, "Christ in Alabama."[31] The day he was to read at the University of North Carolina in Chapel Hill, this poem was published on the front page of *Contempo*, a student publication there. At the reading, local citizens protested that he had gone too far in identifying Christ with the African American in the South. One third of his reading fee was missing from his check because one of the sponsoring organizations had pulled out. Grateful to those who continued to support him despite the uproar, he concludes in his essay, "There I began to learn at the University of North Carolina how hard it is to be a white liberal in the South" (Hughes, 210).

A direct response to the Scottsboro trial, "Christ in Alabama" is a short poem identifying the crucified Christ with the whipped and lashed African American, Mary with "Mammy," and God the Father with the white master. It concludes by identifying the "bastard Christ" with the "Nigger Christ on the cross of the South."[32] Biblical references, evoked often enough to support white supremacy, when inverted by Hughes, prompted an outcry. The startling use of the religious analogy was doubly effective in calling attention to the Scottsboro trial and politicizing the image of the suffering Christ who is persecuted on earth but triumphant in heaven—an image traditionally offered to African Americans to promote acceptance of passive suffering and hope of heavenly, not earthly, justice.

In "Brown America in Jail: Kilby," published in *Opportunity* in 1932, Hughes explicitly identifies the Scottsboro boys with Christ: "Daily I watch the guards washing their hands. The world remembers for a long time a certain washing of hands. The world remembers for a long time a certain humble One born in a manger—straw, manure, and the feet of animals—standing before Power washing its hands."[33] In that article and in "Southern Gentlemen, White Prostitutes, Mill-Owners, and Negroes," published in *Contempo* in 1931, Hughes focuses his condemnation on those in the South, in the rest of America, and around the world who stood by and allowed the Scottsboro ordeal to go on. His analysis contextualizes the Scottsboro events in a way that links racial and economic exploitation: "[L]et the South rise up in press and pulpit, home and school, Senate Chambers and Rotary Clubs, and petition the freedom of the dumb young blacks—so indiscreet as to travel unwittingly, on the same freight train with two white prostitutes. . . . And, incidentally, let the mill-owners of Huntsville begin to pay their women decent wages so they won't need to be prostitutes."[34]

In "Good Morning, Revolution," published in *New Masses* in September 1932, Hughes writes,

> Listen, Revolution,
> We're buddies, see—
> Together
> We can take everything.

The speaker of the poem has lost his job and has decided to team up with "Revolution," even though the latter has been branded as a "trouble-maker, an alien-enemy." The speaker, who says his one name is Worker, figures that he has nothing left to lose. He and Revolution will take "All the tools of production, / . . . And turn them over to the people who work." Then they will get on the radio, "Broadcasting that very first morning to USSR: / Another member of the International Soviet's done come."[35] This allegorical poem, spoken in the confidential, even conspiratorial idiom of one down-and-out to another, presents the embrace of Revolution as the same kind of friendly alliance that poor workers have always counted on to help them through hard times. Revolution is somebody you can talk to, somebody who understands your colloquial language, not an exotic foreigner. Thus does Hughes domesticate radical politics for his readers and help to bridge the cultural gap between a European-centered political movement and native-born American workers, black and white.

= Conclusion =

The Great Depression, deepening in the early 1930s, seemed to confirm the Third-Period thinking that capitalism was on the ropes. Desperate economic circumstances certainly made Americans open to new economic arrangements: they ran barter cooperatives, sometimes took what they needed, and finally embraced the New Deal. Communists had great success organizing on bread-and-butter issues but not in building a revolutionary movement. The Depression did prompt many, of various cultures within America, to look more favorably on Communism. This was largely because desperate times seemed to invite radical solutions and because Communists were most aggressive in taking up issues like rent strikes and the defense of the Scottsboro boys.

Culture and Crisis indicated the willingness of some intellectuals to align themselves collectively with Communism. The Party itself struggled to define a cultural policy even as various Left writers experimented with literary techniques and structures to serve a Left analysis or vision. Meridel Le Sueur, author of *Salute to Spring,* developed reportage into an art form. Jack Conroy's *The Disinherited* typifies the novels hailed as "proletarian" for their worker-author and their narrative drive toward revolution. It also typifies the strengths and weaknesses of this kind of book: the fate of the central character is convincingly tied to that of his class in his moment of history, but the story, therefore, tends to be *the* proletarian story, and successive novels risk being repetitions on a theme.

The expulsion of the Trotskyists for opposing Stalin and "socialism in one country" set an ominous precedent for dealing with dissent and criticism from within the Communist Party. Meanwhile, the non-Communist Left continued to fragment and realign. Communist efforts to organize African Americans were hampered by the Party's opposition to equal rights groups like the Urban League and the NAACP, but they finally achieved some credibility when they chose to work in coalition with such groups and when they demonstrated the strength of their commitment in the Scottsboro case. Langston Hughes, responding to the injustices of racism and economic exploitation, used the literary forms of African-American folk poetry in "Christ in Alabama" to name the victimization of the Scottsboro boys in culturally shocking terms, and in "Good Morning, Revolution," to make foreign political ideas culturally familiar.

The religious Left, with ties to the Socialist Party, struggled in the early 1930s with ambivalence over the New Deal, which provided needed economic relief but increased the power of the state in a way that seemed to Leftists especially ominous given the rise of Fascism in Europe. Socialists struggled to define ways in which pacifism, nonviolent resistance, and constitutional means of change could deter Fascism and replace Communism's revolutionary solution. On the Catholic Left, Dorothy Day linked Catholic faith and religion with a vision of social action more radical than *Rerum Novarum* or the Bishops' Program of 1919.

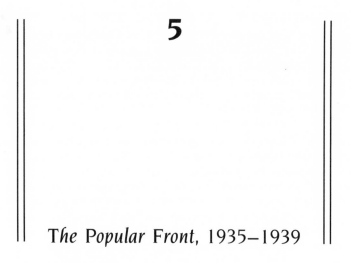

5

The Popular Front, 1935–1939

AS ADOLPH HITLER AND HIS FASCIST FOLLOWERS BECAME AN UNDE-
niable force in Germany, the Comintern was moved to question whether the
"social-fascists," the reformers, truly were the greatest threat to Communist
revolution. At the Twelfth Comintern Plenum in September 1932, policy was
reoriented in recognition of the possible new threat (Klehr, 98). The campaign
against reformist parties and organizations would continue, but there would
also be a renewed attempt to work through such organizations to reach the
masses. Well matched to the cloudy political horizon, this ambiguous policy
was summed up as a "united front from below." Tactically, it was a return to
the days of the Trade Union Educational League and Second-Period "boring
from within," but with greater urgency and the additional emphasis on sacking
the reformists. Communists would infiltrate other organizations, for example,
AFL unions, and work from inside to denounce the reform policies of the
leadership as a betrayal. They would hold rallies jointly with the Socialist Party
and then use the podium to denounce reformist measures. They would create
"front" groups that the Communists controlled by voting as a bloc.

Hitler took power in January 1933, and in March of that year the Comintern called for a "United Front of Struggle." German militarization and expansionist policy directly threatened the Soviet Union. Still, the policy called for Communists to enter coalitions with the intention of destroying their moderate partners. Within this ambiguous formula, there was room for emphasis on coalition or destruction. The latter was never better illustrated than on the February night in 1934 when a group of Communists violently disrupted a meeting that the Socialist Party had called at Madison Square Garden to protest the murder of Viennese Socialists by the Dollfuss government, sympathetic to Nazism. Disrupting an anti-Fascist meeting now seems simply perverse, and Earl Browder, the Communist Party's leader from 1934 to 1945, distanced himself from the action in later years, but at the time it was not out of line with one reading of United Front policy (Klehr, 116–17).

Finally, in 1935, with Rightist parties and armed forces threatening much of Europe, the Comintern called for a Popular Front against Fascism. By the fall of that year, this momentous directional change was noticeable in the CPUSA's softer line on Roosevelt, which put the Party to the right of the Socialist Party—hardly a position any observer would have anticipated in 1934, the year in which Communist Party membership overtook that of the Socialist Party. In a May 1936 rally at Madison Square Garden, Browder announced that Roosevelt, not a Farm-Labor candidate, would have the greatest chance of holding back reactionary forces in America. In the 1936 election, the Party supported Roosevelt even while carrying through with the gesture of running its own ticket of Earl Browder and James Ford. Self-contradictory as the move appears, it accurately reflected the compromise between long-term goals and short-term needs. Sympathetic voters seem to have understood what was wanted of them: local Communist candidates outpolled the Communist Party presidential ticket and, for the first time, the Socialist Party ticket. Furthermore, the election had given Browder a forum in which to expound the new Popular Front face of the Communist Party, and the press gave him respect and serious attention (Klehr, 196). Indeed, Popular Front strategy and an "Americanized" form of Communism seem to have accorded with Browder's personal instincts over much of his career. Quite soon Communists were being welcomed as allies in labor struggles and in issue-oriented coalition work. Pronouncements from the Comintern ceased to appear in Communist Party publications as it downplayed its foreign connections (Klehr, 185).

It would not be surprising if the Party had some difficulty recognizing itself in the mirror at this point. Popular Front strategy called for alliances with other Leftist groups and with sympathetic fellow travelers, without the United Front insistence that they accept Communist positions. In the long term, the Communist Party still intended to triumph over other Leftist groups and be the vanguard party, but in the short term, the Popular Front found the Party genuinely working with other such groups on shared goals, like industrial organizing and the defeat of Hitler. Such work in good faith, with an open agenda, and the experience of having some success in a mass movement seem to have been exhilarating for many rank and file Communists. Party rolls grew during the Popular Front. Communist leaders were quoted in newspapers, giving their opinions on the issues of the day. The Party was a "large evangelical sect" during the Popular Front, according to Malcolm Cowley, and a "small monastic order" before and afterward (Cowley, OHAL).

Sarah Gordon, whose family were active Communists in the Bronx, recalls,

> [E]very day of my life I felt myself both as someone living in a small, coherent community and as part of something global. In the Bronx I knew that wherever I went in the world I would find "my" people, the people who spoke my language, the people who "understood." In a word, my comrades. I was tremendously excited, always, by the thought of taking part daily in something historical. You've got to remember, this was the Thirties. Me, my adored father, all our friends and neighbors, we were turning as the world turned, we were the wave of the future, in us and in all like us lay the exciting, changing world. . . . Imagine the power this politics had! Who were we? We were nothing? And look how we felt about ourselves. . . . Because we were Communists.[1]

But she later explains that that positive sense of identity did not come without sacrifice:

> How I hated selling the *Worker!* I used to stand in front of the neighborhood movie on a Saturday night with sickness and terror in my heart, thrusting the paper at people who'd turn away from me or push me or even spit in my face. I dreaded it. Every week of my life for years I dreaded Saturday night. . . . But I did it, I did it. I did it because if I didn't do it, I couldn't face my comrades the next day. And we all did it for the same reason: we were accountable to each other. . . . You know, people never understand that. They say to us, "The Communist Party held a whip over you." They don't understand. The whip was inside each of us, we held it over ourselves, not over each other. (Gornick, 110)

═ Writing from the Left ═

Among the casualties of the Great Depression were many of the magazines in which young writers could hope to place a short story or a poem. The John Reed Clubs, supported by the Party to encourage proletarian talent, provided a meeting place for aspiring writers to socialize and commiserate and talk shop, and the small journals that some of the clubs were able to publish offered a chance of publication, which was gratifying in itself, and provided the writers with credentials, though the journals didn't pay anything (Cowley, OHAL). Many of the writers who associated with the clubs did not actually join the Party.

The initiation of the Popular Front in 1935 turned emphasis away from proletarian literature and toward connection with progressive elements in the wider culture. At the American Writers Congress in April 1935, the League of American Writers was established; the inclusion of "American" in the name signaled the embrace of American "folk culture" and of sympathetic writers whose interest was in American conditions rather than (or at least more than) worldwide revolution. A literary movement intended to oppose Fascism is necessarily a wider and more permissive movement than one intended to be the voice of the proletariat as it prepares to make the revolution. The John Reed Clubs were left to wither without support, causing resentment among the young proletarians who had been led to think of themselves as standard-bearers.

Alan Rideout, writing in 1956, noted that whatever potential there was for the development of a proletarian aesthetic in American literature was cut off when the Party abandoned the clubs and restricted membership in the League to published writers; the sharp decrease in explicitly proletarian novels in 1936 is a good index of disaffection (Rideout, 244). One could, however, read the evidence a bit differently and say that the narrowly defined proletarian novel, with its emphasis on coming to consciousness, waging a strike, or committing to struggle, was simply tapped out by the mid-1930s. The revolution did not occur; history did not provide proletarian writers with the experiences through which to develop their class literature. Instead, the times called for a literature in which the larger Left movement could search for its bearings. A parallel—absent any idea of revolution—might be found in the literature of the post-Stonewall gay and lesbian movement, which began with "coming-out" stories or "coming-to-consciousness" stories and then moved to greater diversity of theme as writers recognized that history had moved on and given them an already "out" audience with larger concerns. Ample coming-out stories were already available to guide the neophyte through the process. Similarly, by the mid-1930s, Leftist writers could assume a growing sympathetic audience, not for novels about failed strikes or wronged workers, but for books that related Left ideas to a wider spectrum of American life. By the middle of the decade, the changed situation called for a changed literary response—Party policy aside.

American writers in the 1930s generally responded to the conditions of the times by taking up larger social themes in ways that questioned whether the status quo could or should survive. Writers as diverse and "mainstream" as Ernest Hemingway, John Steinbeck, and Dorothy Parker produced work that was socially engaged and critical during this time, as did many, many others. The segregation of some writers from the main narrative of American literary history because they maintained a political focus before and after the 1930s or because they also had activist political lives causes us to tear their work from context and to distort the American literary tradition by their exclusion. Josephine Herbst, writing in the late 1960s to David Madden to explain why she would not write an essay for his *Proletarian Writers of the Thirties,* said, "Who made the demarcations for the works you put into this category? It seems to me arbitrary. I have felt that my own work has been considerably damaged by the category, and that the term since the Second World War has been used more as blackmail than as a definitive term with any valid meaning. I think the whole thing needs a more fundamental approach. Where are the roots to the writing in the Thirties? Was it all political?"[2]

Herbst's last question takes us back again to the relationship of politics to literature: Why would we assume that literary merit must be vitiated by political themes? A novel written to demonstrate the working out of a set of presuppositions, one in which the author mechanically manipulates character and incident to serve the theory, is very apt to fail as literature. But Left politics is surely not the only source from which such presuppositions might come, nor was most Left literature generated in this way. Marxist literary theory at this time, as we have seen, required truthfulness to life, and Mike Gold in his review of *The Disinherited* addressed the following to Jack Conroy: "[I]n avoiding the sickly introspection of the bourgeois autobiographers of youth, the psychological reality often escapes our young authors. They neglect the major problem of all fiction, which is the creation of full-blooded character. Your characters aren't complete."[3]

Thus it was not to any particular kind of novel and certainly not to any certain theme or formula that Gold was committed but to the idea of a developing proletarian aesthetic and to writers of the proletarian class. The term *proletarian literature,* then, is a troubled one, because it refers to what never was. Novels like Conroy's and the several dozen others that Rideout lists (Rideout, 295–300) were first steps in the development of a literary movement that dissipated when the prospect of imminent revolution faded. The term is certainly misused when, as Herbst objects, it is used to reject all Leftist literature as tainted goods.

As Communist Party policy favored the League of American Writers over the John Reed Clubs, Mike Gold, who continued to argue in his *New Masses* and *Daily Worker* columns for proletarian themes and aesthetics, became less influential. The editors of the *Partisan Review* accused him of "Leftism," that is, of being too far out in front of the masses and taking too simplified a view of revolutionary processes. (Lenin had used the term for opposition to his New Economic Policy in the 1920s.) Ironically, the *Partisan Review* began as the publication of the New York John Reed Club in February 1934, but it positioned itself as the defender of writers' creative freedom against politically derived aesthetic strictures such as Gold sometimes called for in his reviews. James F. Murphy, in *The Proletarian Moment,* notes that if Gold's pronouncements were not consistent, neither were they as simple and doctrinaire as William Phillips, Philip Rahv, and James T. Farrell often made them out to be in the *Partisan Review;* nor was the *Review* so consistent a champion of "artistic freedom" as it later made itself out to be (Murphy, 1–2).

Skilled writers resented having literary theory developed by the Party rather than by the writers themselves. It is quite possible that they objected more to this than to any of the particular diverse dictates coming through the *New Masses* and the *Daily Worker.* In 1936, influenced by Leon Trotsky's *Literature and Revolution,* James T. Farrell published *A Note on Literary Criticism.* In it he accuses Gold of "revolutionary sentimentalism," that is, of assuming that proletarian literature would develop naturally out of the proletarian experience and owe nothing to bourgeois literary traditions; he also attacks the idea, which he ascribes to the now-repentant Philip Rahv, that literature should have agitational value, that it should prompt action. Farrell devotes nearly a page to a list of the ways in which a novel can be proletarian, ranging from "written by a member of the industrial proletariat," to "creative literature read by the proletarian vanguard" (Farrell, 86–87).

Particularly interesting is Farrell's discussion of the distinction between "individualistic" and "collective" novels. It should be remembered that Farrell was the author of the Studs Lonigan trilogy, novels about the developing consciousness of a working-class hero. He asserts that it is not politically retrograde to center a novel on one strong central character as long as that character is shown to be influenced by "social pressures and forces" (Farrell, 109). "Even in novels that have taken the individualistic viewpoint of the young man against the world, the writers have always had the world there, standing against the young man" (Farrell, 108). The political error is in portraying the young man as "master of his fate, the captain of his soul" (Farrell, 109). In Farrell's judgment, neither the individualistic nor the collective novel (his example is Dos Passos's *The Forty-second Parallel*) is politically preferable. He believes, however, that fewer collective novels have been successful, because it is more difficult to sustain audience interest without a single strong character with whom to identify.

Thus by the mid-1930s the question of what Left literature should look like was much in dispute. The degree to which various disputants contradict themselves, change their positions, and argue that others have wrongly characterized them suggests a dynamic atmosphere in which the stakes are perceived as high, time as short, and the right direction by no means obvious. Against this background, the production history of Clifford Odets's highly successful *Waiting for Lefty* is especially interesting. The play was inspired by the New York taxi strike of 1934 and was first produced in 1935. Its writing and early productions were done just before the beginning of the Popular Front, but it continued to be produced and reprinted afterward, in slightly different form. The short interval between event and play, and the short writing time—three days—suggest "theatre on the front lines" and recall the Kharkov directive that the Party should sponsor agitprop theater troupes.

In Russia, theater had been at the center of social change. In the last years of the nineteenth century, Konstantin Stanislavsky and Vladimir Nemir-ovich-Danchenko had founded the Moscow Art Theatre, where Stanislavsky oriented acting and the theater to a new realism, which had great influence in the 1930s on the Group Theatre in New York. After the revolution, realism gave way to constructivist theater, with its innovative sets, full of wheels and ladders, founding an aesthetic on the machinery of industrial processes and often being performed in factories. By 1932, there were roughly 200 amateur "workers' theatres" in the United States,[4] most of which were sponsored by Leftist ethnic federations. They performed in the halls of these groups as well as on picket lines and in front of factory gates (Murphy, 106). In 1932, about 100 of these groups formed the New Theatre League, an affiliate of the International Workers' Dramatic Union, based in Moscow. A professional troupe, the Theatre Union, was formed in late 1933.

The whole complex debate over the relative weight to be given to literary values and political values in movement literature often raged the fiercest around theater work. Some of those who were dedicated to the agitprop plays denounced traditional theater pieces as bourgeois in their separation of audience and players, their reliance on sets and props, and their introspective characters. Left dramatists who preferred the traditional theater shot back that the agitprop plays reduced characters to one-dimensional caricatures (for example, the overfed industrialist, the Fascist militarist) and never touched their audiences deeply enough to effect real change.

Waiting for Lefty is a fascinating example because it is agitprop with enough depth to have succeeded in traditional dramatic venues. Written as a series of sketches, it is held together by the ongoing meeting of the taxi drivers' strike council. As the men on the council debate whether to call a walkout, their chairs are arranged so that the audience becomes a part of the meeting; members of the troupe are "planted" in the audience and speak their lines from there. Thus is the audience swept into the debate. As the discussion opens, Harry Fatt, the sellout union leader, is telling the drivers that they would be fools to strike in hard economic times and that they owe it to Roosevelt not to be demanding while he is trying to restore the economy. The lights then dim on the discussion and rise on the side of the stage area to reveal one of the drivers, Joe, and his wife, Edna. She is threatening to leave him for another man unless he can bring home enough money to provide for the family. When he repeats Fatt's arguments about hard times, she says, "He's making a jelly-fish outa you"[5] and further questions his masculinity by asking whether he or she is the man of the family. He tells her she is talking like a "Red."

The drivers' discussion progresses, and the next episode to interrupt it shows us Miller, a lab assistant who turns down better pay for work on poison gas research when he finds out that he is also expected to spy on the head researcher. He decks Mr. Fayette, the boss who offered the deal, and becomes one of the taxi drivers. (In at least one documented production, Fatt and Fayette were played by the same actor, underscoring the links between management and accommodating union officials.) The third episode shows us Sid and his girlfriend, Florrie, who cannot marry because his wages as a driver would not support them. They dance one last dance to a scratchy phonograph and then fall desolate into each other's arms.

Back at the union council, Fatt introduces "Tom Clayton," from Philadelphia, who reports that the taxi drivers' strike in Philly was a mistake, that they had lost ground by going out. But he is interrupted by a member of the audience who declares that "Clayton" is really Clancy, his own brother and a labor spy. Clancy has to flee down the aisle, while the light goes up on Dr. Benjamin, a medical doctor who is protesting that his charity patient has been assigned for surgery to an incompetent physician. Dr. Barnes, his superior, commiserates and has the additional burden of telling Benjamin that he is to lose his post because he is Jewish. They are told that the charity patient has died. Barnes notes that medicine in the United States is not run by doctors but by businessmen. Benjamin praises the socialized medicine of Russia but decides that his place is here; he will drive a cab and educate himself politically.

One further flashback episode was included in the text of the play in 1935 but omitted when Odets edited it for his 1939 collection, *Six Plays of Clifford Odets*. The deleted episode, showing a producer rejecting an actor, includes the most overt reference to Communist revolution in the play: The producer's secretary gives the actor a copy of *The Communist Manifesto* and invites him to become enlightened. Odets explains that the episode was dropped because the problems of cultural workers, like the actor, were not sufficiently representative to merit inclusion. The critic Gerald Weales, however, notes that the episode appears to have been dropped, if the cast list is a reliable guide, when *Waiting for Lefty* opened at the Longacre Theatre on Broadway in September 1935; perhaps the Broadway venue prompted Odets to tone down the agitprop aspects of the play.[6]

The ending of the play is certainly in the agitprop tradition. One of the drivers begins by calling the less militant drivers "ladies" and then refuses to be quiet when Fatt and his henchman tell him to. As they move toward him, the drivers intervene to protect him. He shouts that if it makes you a Red to strike for decent wages then they might as well be Reds, and he gives the Communist salute (described as a right uppercut). Someone rushes in with the news that Lefty has been murdered. The drivers and the audience join in chanting "Strike!"

Waiting for Lefty is well constructed not only to make its didactic points with maximum efficiency but also to motivate the decision to strike. If agit-prop is "the dramatic equivalent of soap-box oratory," as Joseph Wood Krutch notes in his review for the *Nation,* then, according to Krutch, Odets brilliantly turns that limitation into an aesthetic plus by staging a meeting in which various characters directly address the audience from within the dramatic frame.[7] The characters are types, but they are sufficiently fleshed out to elicit sympathy. For this reason, Sid and Florrie's last dance is poignant rather than bathetic. (A sympathetic audience response was no doubt helped along by the fact that the marriage rate declined during the early years of the Great Depression.) The episodes all relate directly to the strike decision, giving the play more unity and dramatic coherence than agitprop plays generally had. The association of labor militancy with masculinity seems cheap and questionable to a latter-day audience, but it too serves to unify the episodes and motivate the decision. All of these evidences of dramatic artistry, along with the temper of the times, help to explain why the play was popular as agitprop, played by amateurs in union halls, and also successful in the professional theater. That it could be both supports the position of those Leftist writers and critics who at the time found the art/politics dichotomy a false choice.

Without undercutting the caliber of *Waiting for Lefty* in the agitprop genre, we can note with Gerald Weales the rather odd relationship it bears to the actual New York taxi strike of 1934. When that strike began on 2 February, the drivers had no union, but the Taxi Drivers Union of Greater New York (TDU) was forged during the walkout. The settlement did not include recognition of the TDU, and it was over this issue that a second strike was begun on 10 March. One review of Odets's play reports that during its second performance, Joseph Gilbert, one of the TDU organizers, appeared before the audience to say that the play faithfully recreated the March meeting at which the strike vote was taken (Weales, 141). It is ironic, given the play's success, that the strike was a failure, unlike the *successful* Philadelphia taxi drivers' strike. In the period of recrimination that followed, organizers were expelled from the TDU on the grounds that they had conducted the strike to promote the goals of the Communist Party and not those of the union membership and were thus responsible for the strike's failure (Weales, 141–44).

Thus *Waiting for Lefty* was agitating for a general labor militancy and a turn to Communism rather than supporting further action by the TDU or presenting the taxi strike as paradigmatic. Indeed, the contradiction between the power of the play to enlist support for the strike and the failure of the strike tells us much about the frustrations of the Communist Party at this time, when it was unable to produce a mass movement out of mass discontent. The play urges the strike on the grounds that the drivers are desperate; it never takes up the question of whether—or how—it might be won. In similar fashion, it links Communism and the decision to strike without examining contradictions between long-term and short-term goals. No literary work can be both agitational and analytical or reflective, and the near hope of revolution privileged the agitational.

═══ The Spanish Revolution ═══

Throughout most of the nineteenth century, the conflict between the land-owning Spanish aristocracy, supported by the Catholic Church, and the peasants, supported by Leftists in the cities, simmered steadily and occasionally roiled, generating moderate land reforms, protests, and the military uprisings called *pronunciamientos*. In February 1936, a Popular Front government, a coalition of Socialists, Communists, and liberals, won an absolute majority of the seats in the Cortez, the Spanish parliament, and seemed poised to carry out a program of political reform that would weaken the control of the aristocracy through land reform and of the Church through a guarantee of religious freedom. The power of the military would be reduced, and social services created. (The willingness of the Spanish Communists to enter into a Popular Front government parallels the willingness of American Communists to support Roosevelt and the New Deal; both are results of the Popular Front policy initiated internationally in 1935.) Throughout the spring of 1936, Spaniards, mindful of the *pronunciamientos* of other years, waited expectantly to see what the army would do. Adding to the fevered condition of the country were rumors that the anarchists and the Socialists each intended to use the Popular Front government as a stepping-stone to revolution. A wave of strikes increased the tension.

In July 1936, Gen. Francisco Franco, supported by much of the high military command, the Falange (the Fascist Party), and some but not all of the political Right, led troops against the Spanish Republic, asserting that only the army could keep order in the country. Their progress was stopped by a popular uprising of unprecedented scope. Peasants took over the land and formed collectives; urban workers took over their factories. The Roman Catholic Church was forced to give over its property. Working-class citizens formed militia bands to defend their towns and villages. Workers' councils, reminiscent of the original soviets in the glory days of the 1917 revolution, did the work of coordination and administration and stood in the place of the government.

The workers were supported by two national general unions, the anarcho-syndicalist Confederacion Nacional del Trabajo (CNT), with roughly a million adherents, mostly in Aragon and Catalonia and the cities of the Mediterranean coast, and the Socialist Union General de Trabajadores (UGT), which numbered more than a million industrial workers and was centered in Andalusia, Castile, and the North. Other supporting groups included the Iberian Anarchist Federation and smaller groups of Trotskyists and independent Marxists. The Communist Party in Spain did not initially support the revolution, believing it to be premature in a preindustrial country, but joined in the fight against Franco after he obtained help from Hitler and Mussolini. Indeed, the war in Spain became internationalized quickly: by early August of 1936, the Fascist governments of Germany and Italy had sent planes to the Insurgents, as Franco's forces were called, and the Popular Front government of France had sent planes to the Loyalists, or the Republicans, as the defenders were called.

The ambiguity over what was being defended was to create tragic conflicts during the course of the war among various groups: those who supported the "bourgeois" Popular Front government, anarchists defending the taking of authority into local hands, and Communists holding a vision of revolution fundamentally at odds with the anarchists' but seeing the war primarily as a struggle against Fascism. The arrival of military equipment and advisers from Russia gave the Spanish Communists influence far in excess of their numbers, and their opposition to the anarchist revolution created deep rifts among the Loyalists.

By September, Franco's troops were marching toward Madrid and seemed likely to take the city, but the decision to rescue a stranded garrison at the Alcazar fortress gave the Madrileños time to prepare. The defense of Madrid by ordinary men and women, who barricaded the streets, fed their army from soup kitchens, and took up the rifles of the dead, inspired songs and poems in praise of their heroism and gave to the Spanish struggle its character as a people's war, calling forth the greatest dignity and self-sacrifice.[8] In early November, several thousand volunteers from the non-Fascist countries of Europe rushed to aid in the defense of the city, beginning the tradition of the International Brigades.

While the democratic nations of Europe were trying to put in place a nonintervention pact, Germany, Italy, and Portugal continued to arm the Insurgents while stalling diplomatically. The Soviet government continued to send aid to the Loyalists. In America, Roosevelt pursued a nonintervention policy. The small but devoted anarchist movement in América formed a coalition called the United Libertarian Organizations. It was composed of the IWW, of Italian, Russian, Spanish, and Jewish anarchist groups, and of the English-speaking group, based in New York, that published and distributed the *Vanguard*. The anarchists that put out the *Vanguard* were a generation removed from Emma Goldman and Sasha Berkman but very much in their tradition. Birth control and "modern schools" (boys and girls together and no religious practice required or taught) were their issues, along with the basic anarchist message of mutual aid and worker control.

Interviewed in 1981, Esther Dolgoff, who had been a member of the group, noted that her comrades joined labor unions, while opposing the AFL, and worked on labor issues; she associated the refusal to join unions (other than the "One Big Union") with an older generation of anarchists.[9] Her husband was an anarchist Wobbly, and in the late 1920s he had traveled and lectured for the IWW. After the near destruction of the IWW in 1924, Wobblies continued to hold forums and sponsor speakers, to hold dances and put on plays. In the 1930s, they responded to the Depression by leafleting and giving soapbox speeches, informing people that the Agricultural Adjustment Act provided for food to be destroyed to buoy prices even while people in the cities went hungry. They preached the Wobbly gospel that the people on their own could make a bounteous country provide for both farmers and city-dwellers. In response to the Spanish Revolution, many American anarchists, including some women, went to join the struggle (Dolgoff, OHAL). This was *their* revolution, and they went not only to defend but also to see for themselves the workers' and peasants' cooperatives and collectives.

In America, the Socialist Party, which had recently accepted into its ranks the Trotskyists, supported the revolution, and sponsored the Debs Column of volunteers. The Communist Party, like its Spanish counterpart, supported the Republic, not the anarchist revolution, but threw itself into the struggle as the first line of defense against Fascism. American Communists formed the Abraham Lincoln Brigade. (Technically, the American contingent formed a number of units of the Fifteenth International Brigade, one of which was called the Abraham Lincoln Battalion; "Abraham Lincoln Brigade," though inaccurate, was the name given in early publicity and it has stuck.) The Lincoln Brigade could boast the first racially integrated unit in American history and the first to have an African-American commander.[10] At least 60 percent of the American brigadistas were Communists, and they changed military culture to reflect their politics: some units elected their commanders, and military protocol was reduced to a minimum (Buckner et al.).

In the part of Spain controlled by the Insurgents, all political parties except the conservative Carlists and the Falangists were outlawed, land reform was reversed, and strikes forbidden. The political opposition, including members of the CNT and the UGT, was destroyed; anyone whose loyalty was doubted was likely to be swept up in the terror and shot. In the Republican zone, the revolution continued, with the collectivization of factories in Catalonia, farmland in many areas, and restaurants and hotels and public utilities everywhere in the zone except the Basque country (Jackson, 11). While support for these changes appears to have been widespread, those who did resist were executed.

As the long siege of Madrid continued into 1937, Insurgent armies captured Malaga and then marched to the Basque country. In April, German planes dropped a variety of experimental explosives that destroyed the town of Guernica, the medieval Basque capital. The destruction of Guernica, far in excess of what any military objective required, came to symbolize Fascist terror and the awesome technological power of impersonal modern warfare, threatening to make human heroism irrelevant. Pablo Picasso's painting, named for the town, has kept fresh the sense of outrage and horror.

Among the Republicans, the difference in political goals began to take its toll. The Communists wanted above all to stop the Fascist advance in Europe, and they were more than willing to stop the social revolution within the Republican zone in hopes of winning the support and military aid of England and France. But social revolution was what the anarchists and Socialists were fighting *for*. Republican military operations were thus made more difficult by a lack of trust and by actual betrayals among the Loyalists. The Soviet purge of Trotskyists was acted out in Spain as Communists moved against Andres Nin, an anti-Stalinist and former secretary to Trotsky. Even Dolores Ibarruri, the Communist leader known as La Pasionaria for her "No Pasaran!" ("they shall not pass") speech, is reported to have approved of the purge of Spanish Trotskyists.[11] In May of 1937 Communists fought anarchists in the streets of Barcelona and brought the replacement of Largo Caballero with Juan Negrin as prime minister. Negrin attempted a compromise, halting the social revolution and making concessions to the Church but also protecting the anarchists and refusing to give complete control to the Communists.

In April of 1938 the Insurgent army drove through to the Mediterranean, splitting the Republican zone in two. Over the summer, Negrin worked to keep his social compromise intact while awaiting the response of the Western democracies to Hitler's invasion of Czechoslovakia; if they declared war, then the Fascist supporters of the Insurgents would no longer be able to keep them well armed (Jackson, 18). With the signing of the Munich Pact, allowing Hitler to take the Czech territory, the Republicans knew that they could not hold out. On 28 March 1939, Madrid opened its gates to the Insurgents, and the war was over.

For Leftists in Europe and the United States, the defeat of the Spanish Revolution was a devastating blow. The sacrifice and bravery of the Spanish people in defense of their freedom had justified for many the idealism inherent in the revolution and in the International Brigades. But the nonintervention of the Western democracies, allowing Spain to fall into Fascist control, seemed unforgivably hypocritical. And the infighting between Communists and anarchists inspired disgust in all but the most committed ideologues.

The Spanish Revolution (or Spanish Civil War, as it is also called), was the best-reported conflict up to that time. Developments in communication technologies made it possible for reporters to send frequent dispatches, and independent newspapers, news services, news magazines, and political papers and journals all had their men and women in Madrid. Free-lance writers from all over Europe and America hurried to Madrid and competed for the scarce transport to the front. Many writers sensed in the Spanish war a foretaste of the coming clash between worldwide forces of Right and Left, or between Fascism and democracy. Politicized by the Great Depression, many of them went to Madrid not as detached observers but as politically committed people, supporters of the Republic. Many of the Left writers invested great hope in the social revolution as well. Often, writing was not enough. Some joined the International Brigades.

Frederick R. Benson, whose *Writers in Arms: The Literary Impact of the Spanish Civil War* focuses on six European and American writers who participated in the war, concludes, "In the democracies, the Spanish conflict ultimately proved to many writers that their political and social theories required closer scrutiny; that a cause which seemed just could nonetheless be corrupted; and that the violence of modern war could not be satisfactorily rationalized in ideological terms" (Benson, xxi). He notes A. J. Muste's opinion that the Spanish war left writers bereft of hope in traditional humanistic or political beliefs, and he goes on to theorize that their Spanish experience turned American writers away from Marxist themes by the end of the decade. What they had seen in Spain made them suspect that Communist revolution would be followed by the dictatorship of the police state, not the proletariat (Benson, 276–78). Benson deals extensively only with Ernest Hemingway among American writers; it will be worthwhile to compare Hemingway's *For Whom the Bell Tolls* with John Dos Passos's *The Adventures of a Young Man* and Josephine Herbst's essay "The Starched Blue Sky of Spain."

In the 1930s the expatriate Hemingway had moved away from depicting enervated and disillusioned characters trying to find something, no matter how small or personal, to admire or believe in after World War I had emptied out all the old verities. His *To Have and Have Not* in 1937 reflected his movement leftward in its exploration of collective action for social change. Experience as a journalist in Spain during the war gave him material for *The Fifth Column*, a play, and for his 1940 novel, *For Whom the Bell Tolls*.[12]

That novel's hero, Robert Jordan, is an American fighting with a Loyalist guerrilla group in the mountains outside Segovia. When he is instructed to blow up a bridge at a strategic moment three days hence, he has time to reflect that he and his companions are unlikely to survive the mission. With the approval of Pilar, an older woman in the group, Robert begins a passionate relationship with Maria, whose earlier treatment at the hands of the Falangists has made her withdrawn and disconnected from life. Pilar's strength and loyalty to the Republic have their opposite in her man, Pablo, whose cowardice endangers the group. Andres, a dedicated member of the group, is sent to the Republican headquarters with a note from Jordan saying that the destruction of the bridge cannot succeed, but he is delayed by Communists who are jealously guarding their own power. The guerrilla band is torn by animosity and suspicion.

Finally, Jordan and the group do blow up the bridge, but he is seriously wounded. Forcing the others to go on without him, he remains alive to shoot the Falangist leader. While he is waiting to take that last shot, he tells himself, "I have fought for what I believed in for a year now. If we win here we will win everywhere. The world is a fine place and worth the fighting for and I hate very much to leave it" (Hemingway, 502). Jordan's belief that a victory in Spain signals a turning of the tide against Fascism in Europe echoes the idea in the novel's title and epigraph from John Donne's "Meditation XVII": "No man is an island . . ." Thus the book is implicitly a reproach to "nonintervention" and a tribute to political commitment, even to the point of giving one's life for a cause.

As many critics have pointed out, however, *For Whom the Bell Tolls* is essentially one man's story. It is compellingly interesting reading and was adapted into a successful movie, starring Gary Cooper, in part because we identify so strongly and easily with the heroic Robert Jordan. At no point in the book does he have to rely on the group to give him courage or to help him decide what course to take. And his last act of heroic self-sacrifice is accomplished alone, without the support of the guerrilla group. Throughout the book, the narration moves quickly and cleanly forward because Jordan's consciousness dominates. For these reasons, Hemingway's Spanish Civil War novel remains curiously individualist. Although its title asserts a shared fate for humankind, the novel focuses on one man's fate and does not deal with the fall of the Republic. The ending is unambiguously heroic; its meaning is unchanged by the fate of the Republic, by history. *For Whom the Bell Tolls* is undoubtedly an aesthetic success, and that success may derive at least in part from the fact that Hemingway set himself the relatively uncomplicated task of asserting the value of personal heroism against Fascism.

Although he was never a member of the Communist Party, John Dos Passos had stronger and older ties to the American Left than Hemingway. He had written about and picketed for Sacco and Vanzetti; he had traveled to Russia and written positively about what he saw there; he was a member of the 1931 delegation to Harlan County. His *The Forty-second Parallel* won some praise from Left critics. In *The Adventures of a Young Man* (1939),[13] he follows Glenn Spotswood through his youthful adventures as a camp counselor, fired for teaching radical songs to the campers, and as a student working his way through Columbia, infatuated with Gladys, who is a faithful Marxist but a faithless lover. The novel consistently juxtaposes personal and political betrayals.

At his father's urging, Glenn accepts a bank job in Texas, where he is involved on the periphery of a strike by the Mexican pecan-shellers. He meets Irving Silverstone, the Communist Party labor organizer, who thinks of the strike as an opportunity to educate American workers in Marxist ideas. Glenn finds him callous toward the fate of the actual strikers. Warned by his brother that vigilantes are planning to run the Reds out of town, Glenn decides to return to New York; the decision is made easier when he is fired by the bank for publicly sympathizing with the strikers.

After Gladys returns to her old boyfriend, Glenn goes to Appalachia to organize for a radical dual union, where he again meets Irving Silverstone. Using the alias Sandy Crockett, Glenn organizes the miners and gets to know them. He and the girl Wheatly are romantically involved. When some of the local miners are arrested on trumped-up charges, Glenn thinks it a high priority to get them a good defense, but Silverstone won't cooperate with the reformist union, and the miners are sentenced to twenty years. After Glenn is beaten by thugs, he goes to New York, where he is taken in by Marice Gulick, a liberal heiress. The Communist Party warns him that it doesn't approve of the liaison. A letter from Wheatly not only reminds him that he has abandoned her but also tells him that prison is hard on the miners; he must do something for them. When the Party abandons the policy of creating dual unions, Glenn hears the news from one of his fellow organizers, who is outraged: "No more dual unions. What the hell had we been getting our blocks knocked off for, and letting the boys get their blocks knocked off for, but our own party union. Now the story was go back and be good little boys and bore from within the good old Mineworkers" (Dos Passos, 257).

The Party decides that it is happy to have the once-untouchable Marice raising money for its causes among her liberal friends. When one of the miners is killed in a supposed escape attempt, Glenn cannot shed the feeling that he has betrayed the miners by getting them to take risks and then abandoning them. Paul, his friend from camp-counseling days, has just returned from working in the Soviet Union as an agricultural expert and reports that Stalin is a murderous autocrat; Paul now supports Roosevelt and the New Deal. In spite of his commitment to the working class, Glenn would withdraw from active political work if it were not that he would be abandoning others, like the miners, whom he has drawn into the struggle. When the Communist Party expels him for failure to follow orders, he and his assistant, Sylvia, put out a small independent labor paper. Marice, meanwhile, has been swept into an embrace by the Popular Front; she keeps company with Irving Silverstone. After sending Sylvia home alone, Glenn volunteers to go to Spain as a mechanic or ambulance driver; he doesn't want to fight. Near Madrid he meets an old friend from the pecan-shellers' strike. But the Party in Spain thinks that this connection brands him as a Trotskyist. He is jailed by the Communists and released only when the prison is being shelled. Ordered to carry water to the lines, he is shot and killed, presumably by the Communists.

Although Dos Passos devotes only the last few pages of the novel to the Spanish war, *The Adventures of a Young Man* is very much *about* that struggle in that it examines the motives of one (fictional) Leftist for going to Spain and connects his experience there with his political life in the United States. For Glenn, who feels not only that he has been betrayed but that he has betrayed others, Spain represents a "clean" commitment; dying for Spain will give him a way out of an intolerable political and personal life and will be a worthwhile sacrifice. Ironically, of course, he does not die for Spain but for the same factionalism he fled at home.

Dos Passos's novel, like Hemingway's *For Whom the Bell Tolls*, follows one man's experience to the death. But it differs in showing Glenn's life as integrally connected to the lives of others. He decides that he cannot abandon political activity because doing so would be a betrayal of those, like the miners, whom he has enlisted. Glenn's heroism consists of continuing to search for a way to be faithful to his ideals, not giving up, not accepting the unacceptable. Hemingway draws Robert Jordan as an individual who interacts with history; Dos Passos draws Glenn Spotswood as an individual member of the working class who makes meaningful choices, both constrained by and affecting history. The ending of *The Adventures of a Young Man* is without dramatic uplift, but its irony does not undercut its hero's life struggle. It simply underscores the difficulty of finding political certainty in the 1930s and indicates why the Spanish Revolution appeared to be a solution but ended up as a replication of the problem.

To get a sense of the tense and partisan atmosphere in which writing about Spain was received in the 1930s, we can turn to "The Starched Blue Sky of Spain," which Josephine Herbst wrote shortly before her death in 1969.[14] Though never a member of the Communist Party, Herbst was a committed Leftist and had attended the Kharkov conference as an observer in the company of her husband, John Herrmann. She was put off by the posturing of the delegates at Kharkov and by the self-promotion of at least one of the American delegates. Throughout the years she was critical of sexism on the part of the Left. A refrain in virtually all of her work is the concern that one's personal conduct be consistent with one's politics; she had a keen eye for hypocrisy and self-deception. Her trilogy of novels about the midwestern Trexler family recalls her Iowa background and was among the most skillful pieces of political fiction to come out of the 1930s.

Herbst went to Spain as a correspondent in 1937. From the distance of 30 years, she recalls, "There was one thing you couldn't do when you came back from Spain. You couldn't begin to talk in terms of contradictions. Everyone I knew wanted an authoritative answer. There were characters who had never left New York who were angry with me because I couldn't say for certain that the Trotskyist leader Nin had been murdered. Other characters raged because I refused to accuse Nin of leading a Fascist plot in complicity with Franco. What was wanted was black or white" (Herbst, 131).

This expectation that writing should be *politically faithful*, or that it should respond to the *need* for political certainty, was repugnant to Herbst. She responds in "The Starched Blue Sky" by focusing on the telling details of personal behavior. In describing her experience of Spain, she likewise reports her concrete sensory impressions and their evocation of parts of her Iowa childhood; it is as if the primacy of the concrete is in itself a protest against theory-driven perception and reporting.

Herbst's memoir of Spain focuses on motives and behavior. She says she went to Spain not in the hope of writing something that would force an end to the policy of nonintervention but chiefly out of her need to find some positive counterweight to the growing strength of Fascism she had witnessed in the 1920s when reporting from Germany. The reasons people went to Spain, she says, were multiple and complex. (Diane Johnson, in her introduction to the 1991 reprint of Herbst's essay in book form, suggests that the author herself was in 1937 still devastated by her divorce from Herrmann, which had occurred in 1935.) She describes Hemingway as living well at the Hotel Florida, with a locked wardrobe full of the kind of food that was hard to come by in Madrid under siege: bacon and jam and butter and eggs. She hears him typing in his room, determined to be the definitive war writer of his era. After she visits the front line at Jarama, she finds that she prefers to spend her time with fighters rather than reporters and novelists. She and Dos Passos take every chance they get in Madrid to talk with the men on leave from the front; she finds an authenticity in their reticence and their concern that fallen comrades be remembered. Writing of Hemingway's work on the film *The Spanish Earth* in 1938 and 1939, she says that he "was entering into some areas that were better known to people like Dos Passos or even myself. He seemed to be naively embracing on the simpler levels the current ideologies at the very moment when Dos Passos was urgently questioning them" (Herbst, 150–51).

In the Spanish villages the will to win the war was strong. On a manor outside Madrid, Herbst observed peasants tending the vineyards of the owner who had fled; from the profits they bought an irrigation pump so that for the first time they could have vegetable gardens. Describing an evening's amateur entertainment by some of the brigadistas, Herbst notes the absolute concentration on the present, the sense of peace that comes to the fighters who have already made all their difficult decisions and whose lives now express their beliefs. That serenity is unavailable to Dos Passos, she writes, who refused to believe that his friend Professor Robles, shot as a spy, could actually have been guilty. Herbst herself, on hearing about the anarchists and Communists fighting each other in Barcelona, is bereft of certainty, and "The Starched Blue Sky of Spain" ends with her telling herself to go on trying to understand.

=== Labor and the CIO ===

Labor militancy, growing under the New Deal, led to a number of strikes in 1934 and suggested that the time was ripe for industrial organization. Although the NRA had been declared unconstitutional in 1935, the Wagner Act of the same year preserved its guarantee of labor's right to organize. Various New Deal Programs like the WPA and the Civilian Conservation Corps provided jobs for the unemployed, reducing the pool of potential strikebreakers and the fear of abject poverty. The AFL, however, was reluctant to admit industrial unions because industrial workers and organizers were generally more radical and further Left than the craft unionists. The very Reds whom Samuel Gompers had turned out of the unions in 1926 would be back to be reckoned with. When the AFL voted against industrial organizing in 1935, eight individual unions formed a caucus within the AFL called the Committee for Industrial Organization, which turned into the Congress of Industrial Organizations (CIO). Communist Popular Front policy encouraged organizing through mainstream labor organizations, and Communists put great energy into CIO work. They were trained organizers, committed and in many cases experienced, and the CIO was glad to have large numbers of Communists at all ranks except the very highest (Lens, 321),

The strike that made it clear that the CIO was here to stay began in November 1936 when General Motors fired four employees of its Atlanta plant for wearing union buttons. Strikers closed that plant, and soon picket lines were going up around General Motors plants across the country. In Flint, Michigan, thousands of strikers remained inside the factory. The sit-down strike was not invented in Flint, but it was there that it proved itself the keenest weapon of the CIO. General Motors, not wanting to endanger its expensive industrial machinery, resorted to court injunction and the National Guard but was reluctant to force the strikers' hand. Finally, on 11 January 1937, the company turned off the heat in the plant and refused to let food be taken in.

In the early morning, police lines were breached. When the tear gas cleared and the morning's battle was over, the strikers still held the plant. Meridel Le Sueur, writing for the *Worker,* describes the excitement of an elderly Polish-American woman, thrilled by the strikers' victory: "I was having a cup of coffee with her the day the Woman's Brigade knocked out the windows so the air could get into the factory to the gassed sit-downers and she told about how they were all singing a song we knew: *'We shall not be moved'* . . . And how they were all leaning out the windows singing this song, hundreds of them probably, with machine guns mounted on the buildings opposite."[15]

Brothers Walter and Victor Reuther, both Socialists, were the most visible union leaders during the strike, but Communists had been heavily involved. General Motors, after some further, minor sit-downs, did settle with the union. Chrysler, after a sit-down strike, also settled. U.S. Steel also decided to do business with the CIO. Industrial organization—a goal since early Wobbly days—was finally established by the late 1930s, though some organizing battles remained.

Battles also were fought over control of the industrial labor movement. Communists, Socialists like the Reuthers, and Trotskyists all contended for power within the movement. In addition, a group constituted in 1937 in New York City as the Association of Catholic Trade Unionists (ACTU; members generally called themselves Actists) intended to bring a Catholic perspective to the CIO to counter the influence of Communists.[16] Organizers of the group, all of them male and, like the association generally, mostly Irish, had come together through the Catholic Worker movement and had studied the Catholic labor encyclicals; they separated themselves, however, from the Catholic Worker's ideal of farming communities and craft production (Seaton, 54–55). More important, they disagreed with Dorothy Day's belief that workers should own the means of production, and they were suspicious of her willingness to support Communist-led strikes (Seaton, 55). In the late 1930s, however, the ACTU discovered that its labor agitation aligned it with Communists and placed it in opposition to conservative Catholic organizations (Seaton, 71). This alignment, a natural outgrowth of the Actists' political values, seemed tolerable to the group at the time, but would later prove untenable.

═══   The Democratic Front   ═══

In spite of the success of the CIO and Communist influence within it, Earl Browder in 1938 was forced to admit that the general tilt of the country toward the Left was not going to give rise to a national Farm-Labor Party. Americans, even many Leftists, were pleased with Roosevelt and the New Deal, which had recently given them not only the Wagner Act but also Social Security. The CPUSA therefore replaced the Popular Front with the Democratic Front, in which the struggle would be primarily one against Fascism worldwide. Liberals, even those of the upper-middle class, would be welcome. The CPUSA, eager to support and strengthen the Democratic Party, reproved Wisconsin governor Philip LaFollette for founding the Progressive Party (Klehr, 209). Unlike the Popular Front, which was backed by Communist policy worldwide, the Democratic Front was declared only in America as a response to the strength of the New Deal. (Despite the change, the period from 1935 to 1939 is generally referred to as the Popular Front.) The Comintern appears to have accepted the Democratic Front as the best means to prevent a split that might put a Republican government in office and swing American foreign policy to the right (Klehr, 210). Within Party leadership, Earl Browder and his protégé Eugene Dennis took up the Democratic Front line with enthusiasm, while William Z. Foster insisted that reformism was a trap. But even the revival of economic problems in the fall of 1937 and Roosevelt's continued policy of nonintervention in Spain did not shake Communist confidence in the Democratic Front. If Americans were not ready for revolution, the Communist Party would support reform.

= Organizing Consumers =

Just as the CIO was organizing that great stronghold of producers, the heavy industries, efforts were going forward to organize another group that had previously been out of reach: consumers. Housewives began to realize that the New Deal had changed the way interests were advanced. The right of labor to organize had been guaranteed, and workers were improving their lot through collective action, so why shouldn't consumers take the same route? (Orleck, 148). Housewives from union families took the lead in organizing women to lobby the government for publicly owned cooperatives and for price controls on staple food items (Orleck, 156). New York, Detroit, and Seattle—all strong union cities—had strong housewives' movements that succeeded in crossing ethnic and racial lines.

In the summer of 1935, the high cost of meat made it hard for housewives to feed their families in the way they were used to doing. (Communists had always objected that the Agricultural Adjustment Act undercut family farms and aided in the formation of huge agribusiness enterprises with monopolistic goals.) In New York, Chicago, Philadelphia, Boston, St. Louis, Paterson, and Kansas City, housewives' councils organized meat boycotts. In Hamtramck, a suburb of Detroit, Polish- and African-American housewives picketed butcher shops and demanded a 20 percent price cut and an end to the practice of price gouging in black neighborhoods (Orleck, 161). An article in the *Party Organizer* explained,

> Party and non-Party women were called to the Section Committee meeting and we planned with them the calling of a mass meeting. A committee of women comrades and non-Party members issued five thousand leaflets calling for a mass meeting on Friday, July 19, 1935, at the Polish Falcons Hall. The leaflets were issued in the name of the Provisional Women's Committee Against the High Cost of Living and were distributed by five women and six men who went from house to house knocking at the door explaining the purpose of the meeting and asking the people how they felt about the high cost of meat.[17]

In the second half of the decade, the movement turned also to electoral politics. A 1936 Washington State ballot measure called for the creation of a distribution system to bring farm produce to the cities at a price fair to both farmers and consumers. The initiative narrowly failed, but it received a good deal of publicity, as newspapers recognized what a challenge it represented to the American economic system (Orleck, 164). Hearst newspapers, always vehemently anti-Left, characterized the housewives' movement as a Red plot. In fact, Communists and independent Leftists in the various cities contributed significantly to the movement, but no attempt was made to manipulate it for Communist purposes. The women doing the organizing seem to have realized, like the African-American organizers in Harlem, that the energy was coming out of particular issues; to exploit it would be to kill it. Popular Front and Democratic Front thinking made it possible for Communists to support the movement and its agenda.

=== African Americans and the Popular Front ===

In the South, where large numbers of African Americans provided a reserve labor pool, the system of racial separation, often written into law, served to keep wages depressed for both black and white workers. The craft unions of the AFL often explicitly excluded black workers from employment and from apprentice programs. In the second half of the 1930s, CIO contracts generally relegated blacks to the worst jobs. Nonetheless, black workers were strong supporters of industrial unionization, and given their numbers, industrial unionization could not have gone forward without them.[18] The preference given to whites in hiring, job assignments, and wages prompted African Americans to see unionization as a possible means of redress. The struggle for the union was a struggle for civil rights (Honey, 56). Earl Browder's report to the Tenth Convention of the CPUSA in 1938 noted that the Party's work was instrumental in creating some movement toward a New South, but that reactionary forces were still firmly in control.[19]

In Harlem, during the Popular Front, Communists integrated themselves into political institutions like the WPA, a number of city unions, the relief bureaus, and the American Labor Party, the party founded as an alternative to the corrupt Democratic Party machine run from Tammany Hall (Naison, 172). Unlike the early 1930s, when Communists were generally restricted to street tactics and mass protests, during the Popular Front years they worked "inside." In May 1935 they were the moving force behind the coalition that initiated the National Negro Congress but chose to let the NAACP and its magazine *Crisis* take the lead in promoting it (Naison, 178). A. Philip Randolph of the Brotherhood of Sleeping Car Porters and several representatives of the Urban League were also influential in establishing the Congress. Fighting against Fascism and lynching and for unionization of blacks were the main items on the agenda (Naison, 178). Unlike its predecessor, the League of Struggle for Negro Rights, the National Negro Congress succeeded in working with churches and cultural organizations and thus integrating itself into the political, cultural, and social life of Harlem, the South Side of Chicago, and, to a lesser extent, other African-American communities.

Despite a good deal of freedom during the Popular Front, Communists in Harlem were still hampered by some Party policies. Their high-profile work for the defense of Ethiopia was undercut, for example, by reports that Russia continued to supply Italy. Likewise, interracial solidarity of the working class was so strong an ideal for the Party that it opposed all-black Party branches; failure to provide a culturally comfortable space for African Americans contributed to the high turnover in black Party membership (Naison, 283). The Party's inability to persuade unions like the Transport Workers Union, in which it exerted considerable influence, to negotiate contracts mandating equality in hiring cost it dearly in credibility (Naison, 265).

Abner Berry, an African-American organizer for the CPUSA in Harlem and after 1934 a member of the Central Committee of the Party, has ascribed the high turnover rate to the fact that blacks seldom had steady work and very seldom had factory work; the conditions for organizing were not generally present.[20] Further, according to Berry, African Americans could not find in the Communist Party a culture that was theirs, even though the Party did promote jazz, which it saw as black folk music, through the *Daily Worker*, and helped to get recording contracts for Josh White and Leadbelly (Berry, OHAL). Generally, the Party during the Popular Front succeeded in entering into the political life of Harlem and won support from a substantial number of black intellectuals, but it did not succeed in winning over a permanent base from the working class and poor (Naison, 283).

The Russian Show Trials

Since the beginning of the Popular Front, the CPUSA had considerable freedom in adapting to American conditions. Roosevelt extended diplomatic recognition to the Soviet Union in November 1933, signaling that the Communist countries were no longer to be international pariahs. Popular Front governments in some European countries and the New Deal in the United States brought Communists into the political mainstream, even if they were never entirely trusted. In Spain, the only government help to the Loyalists came from the U.S.S.R. Ironically, at that point when the Soviet Union was less isolated than at any time since the revolution, Josef Stalin began a purge of his enemies and rivals beginning with a series of highly publicized "show trials" and extending throughout the U.S.S.R. in a reign of terror.

In his so-called pursuit of Socialism, Stalin had resorted to large-scale deportations to establish collective agriculture and had allowed mass starvation in the countryside by having scarce grain shipped to the cities to support industrial development. Rumors of these crimes filtered to the West, but wild and false accusations had been made against the Soviet government from its earliest days, and many Leftists in Europe and America were used to dismissing atrocity stories as the propaganda of right-wing newspapers (Cowley, OHAL). In the mid-1930s, however, the removal of Stalin's political opponents made it clear to many Leftists that his "revolution from above" was just a cover for ruthless tyranny.

The purge began with the assassination of Sergei Mironovich Kirov, the Party leader in Leningrad and a potential rival of Stalin. Kirov was killed in December 1934 inside Party headquarters by a young Party member. The assassin and 13 accused accomplices were shot, and Stalin claimed to have uncovered a conspiracy to assassinate the top Soviet leadership. (In his famous 1956 speech on Stalin's crimes, Nikita Khrushchev came very close to saying that Stalin himself had ordered Kirov's murder.) Then, in a succession of trials, a number of Bolsheviks, including the old revolutionaries Bukharin, Kamenev, and Zinoviev, confessed to having worked to undermine the U.S.S.R. and to having plotted with Trotsky, exiled since 1929. That they should all have been guilty of the crimes to which they confessed seems extremely unlikely. From 1936 to 1938, Stalin used such public trials to legitimize the destruction of his political enemies and to create a climate of paranoia and terror. Bureaucrats, doctors, professors, teachers, scientists, writers—virtually anyone in any position of authority or influence—were liable to accusation and execution. Anatoly Spragovsky, a former KGB agent who has researched the purges, wrote in 1993 that authorities were given quotas of "enemies" to fill. The accused were executed without trial and buried in mass graves. To dissent or refuse cooperation would mean the official's own death, and thus Stalin enlisted widespread complicity.[21] Trotsky himself was killed in August 1940 in Coyoacan, Mexico, and it is generally accepted that the assassin was an agent of Stalin.

=== The Non-Aggression Pact ===

Those who continued to have faith in the Soviet Union, in spite of the show trials of the mid-1930s, had yet more bitter medicine to swallow. On 23 August 1939, Stalin signed a non-aggression pact with Hitler, opening the way for the Germans to invade Poland on 1 September of that year without fear of Russian interference. In return, the U.S.S.R. was able to annex Estonia, Latvia, Lithuania, and eastern Poland. For American Communists, this about-face changed the political terrain in a number of ways. Internationally, it established cooperation between Communists and Fascists, an embarrassing and politically indefensible alliance that could only be explained as a pragmatic move to "preserve peace." It destroyed the Communist Popular Front strategy. It made the Soviet Union an international renegade once again. And, finally, it created a situation that paralleled the one in which the Left had found itself just before World War I: Communists were expected to oppose the coming "imperialist" war just as Socialists had been expected to—and had generally failed to—oppose World War I. Failure in that instance had caused the collapse of the Second International. William Z. Foster is reported to have hoped that Hitler's seizure of power in Germany would lead to proletarian revolution there and Hitler's replacement by a Communist government (Klehr, 392). The old dream of revolution in Europe was revived, but most American Communists found it unconvincing.

Many members left the Party in the late 1930s, disillusioned by the purge trials or the non-aggression pact. Many sympathetic nonmembers, including prominent intellectuals and writers, renounced any affiliation with organizations like the National Lawyers' Guild, the National Negro Congress, or the League of American Writers, in which the Party was the primary influence. Party membership fell from what it had been during the Popular Front, but the Party did not go into a tailspin. Many of its members who were involved in valuable and effective work in the CIO, in neighborhood organizing, in antiracist work, and in support of New Deal social welfare programs seem to have found in the Party a good local support network; its international alignments were less important to them. Some Communists remained with the Party because to have left would have cut them off from friends, neighbors, and workmates.[22] Others no doubt remained with the Party because they continued to have faith in its vision. It appears, too, that the Party's isolationist stand even won it some supporters.

The official Party press worked hard to characterize the polarization of Europe as an imperialist struggle and to rouse sentiment for neutrality with the slogan "The Yanks Aren't Coming!" In 1940, Nazi Germany had not yet begun the mass murder of millions of European Jews, but its anti-Semitic legislation and outbreaks of anti-Jewish violence, as exemplified on *Kristall-nacht* in November 1938, were known in America, raising troubling questions for Jewish Communists (Isserman, 62). The Party publicly argued that anti-Semitism was entrenched in Britain as well. Finally, the German march into France in May 1940 raised the likelihood that Hitler, with the Western Front subdued, would soon turn against the Soviet Union. The French defense had collapsed much more quickly than anyone had anticipated, raising rumors of betrayal from within by a "fifth column," a group of traitors within.

Lillian Hellman was not a member of the Party but supported many of its positions during the late 1930s and was active in support of Loyalist Spain. The immediate motivation to write *Watch on the Rhine*[23] appears to have been the murder of Hellman's friend Julia by the Nazis, an event on which the novella "Julia" in *Pentimento* is loosely based. *Watch on the Rhine* opened at the Martin Beck Theatre in New York City in April 1941, when the Nazi-Soviet alliance was still in effect. In three acts, Hellman tells the story of an American family whose late father was once American ambassador to Germany. The daughter married a German engineer, Kurt Muller, and is now returning with him and their children to the family home outside Washington, D.C., to escape the Nazi regime. Her widowed mother and unmarried brother, David, have also taken in as houseguests a Romanian count and his American wife, a daughter of one of the mother's friends. Teck, the Count, is revealed to be in collaboration with the Nazis, and Kurt Muller is revealed to be an important member of the Resistance. When both receive word that a Resistance leader has been captured in Germany, Teck knows that Muller will be returning to try to free him and that the money in his briefcase will be used for that purpose. He threatens to betray Muller unless he is bought off. Muller knows that he will betray him even if he is paid. They struggle, and Muller kills him. Muller kisses his family good-bye, knowing that he may never return from Germany. The family agrees to help him escape and to cover for the murder of Teck, knowing that it will greatly complicate their pleasant lives. The Countess, finally rid of Teck, is free to marry David, whom she loves.

Watch on the Rhine is interesting not only as a well-crafted theater piece but also for its complicated intersections with Left politics in the 1940s. Kurt Muller, whose character is based on Hellman's friend Julia,[24] is clearly portrayed as a Leftist, though his exact political affiliation is never given. Early drafts of the play made him explicitly a revolutionary Socialist, but the final version emphasized his anti-Fascist stand (Lederer, 55). The CPUSA, however, attacked the play when it opened, because the Party was supporting the non-aggression pact. But as Hellman later noted in *Scoundrel Time*, the Party praised the movie version of *Watch on the Rhine* when it was released, after Hitler's invasion of Russia put an end to the pact. Complicating too was the fact that the play dealt primarily with betrayal. Teck, the Nazi-sympathizing European, attempts to subvert the Resistance. Hellman gives Teck purely personal motives—he has no politics beyond opportunism. Although the Communists clearly had political motives for opposing war against Germany, during the non-aggression pact the role of European-based subverter of anti-Nazism might have fitted them all too well in the eyes of many Americans.

The American public, looking with growing alarm on the Nazi advance, was increasingly willing to support restrictions on the American Left, increasingly willing to see it as a possible fifth column in America. The Smith Act, signed into law by Roosevelt in June 1940, required that aliens over the age of 14 be registered, and it made advocacy of the overthrow of the U.S. government by force a criminal offense; further, it made distribution of literature urging resistance to the draft illegal.

In Minneapolis, the Teamsters local had been under Trotskyist leadership since its inception, and it remained loyal to that leadership and opposed to the war. The AFL pressured the local to repudiate its leaders, but instead the local withdrew from the AFL, and a number of other locals in the Midwest followed its lead (Myers, 180). The Roosevelt administration was eager to have AFL support for war preparedness. A raid on Socialist Workers Party headquarters in Minneapolis and St. Paul on 27 June 1941, authorized by the U.S. attorney general, netted literature judged seditious, and 29 Trotskyists were subsequently indicted under the Smith Act. The jury convicted most of the defendants on some of the counts, and 18 served prison time.

Communists did not protest the prosecution of their old enemies, the Trotsky-ists (Myers, 182).

Communists themselves, however, were most often the target of anti-Left investigations. Congressman Martin Dies was chairing a committee constituted in 1938 to investigate un-American activity, and he stepped up his examination of the Communists after the signing of the non-aggression pact. In October 1939, Eugene Dennis and Jack Stachel both went under-ground, and Dennis was later sent to the Soviet Union; the Party was taking measures to protect its leadership in the event that it was declared an illegal organization. The Voorhis Act, passed in 1940, required any organization controlled by a foreign power to register with the attorney general and provide lists of its officers and information about its meetings, finances, and activities. The Communist Party dodged the Voorhis Act by meeting in November 1940 and hastily disaffiliating from the Comintern.

During 1940 much of the anti-Communist effort was focused on keeping Communist candidates off the ballot. Earl Browder ran for president in 1940 but was prohibited from traveling outside New York after he was convicted of having falsified a passport application in the 1920s. In West Virginia, New York, and Pennsylvania, those who signed petitions to put Communist candidates on the ballot were apt to be visited by vigilantes hoping to "per-suade" them to withdraw their signatures (Isserman, 70).

Within the CIO, Communists were allowed to be unionists first, and they even supported anti-Communist resolutions to avoid being ousted. Labor militancy increased in 1941 as the government poured money into war pre-paredness and labor wanted its share. The Ford Motor Company and the smaller steel companies, all holdouts from the CIO, finally capitulated in the early months of 1941. The wave of strikes, the high number of Communists in the CIO, and Communist opposition to war together created a situation in which claims of Communist conspiracy to subvert war preparedness seemed plausible, although no evidence of such a conspiracy has yet been found (Isserman, 94). Thus the position of the CPUSA was tenuous in several respects in the spring of 1941: its analysis of the European situation was fundamentally flawed, and its justification of the Hitler-Stalin pact once again characterized it as foreign and subversive. Earl Browder was sent to the federal prison in Atlanta in March 1941 to begin serving four years for his passport violation. The Popular Front was over, and the Party was once again suspect.

═ Conclusion ═

The Popular Front brought Communists into the mainstream of American politics and culture more than ever before. Whether that was a positive or negative thing is still debated by American Leftists. The writer Tom McGrath, interviewed in 1977, said that he had opposed the Popular Front because he knew it would mean a loss of militancy.[25] In that same year, at a roundtable discussion of the Popular Front moderated by Paul Buhle, disagreement emerged among veterans of the Old Left not only about the advisability of the Popular Front but also about its goals.[26] One discussant argued that it was a success in that its goal was to halt Fascism in France and other European countries, and it did so by creating Left coalitions. Another answered that the goal was not merely to stop the spread of Fascism but to make a transition to Socialism, contacting the masses where they were and leading them leftward. In the Party's own theoretical justification for the Popular Front, it is possible to read both goals. That those goals were sometimes contradictory is illustrated by the example of the Communists who achieved leadership in CIO unions and did not want to jeopardize their positions by expressing radical political ideas (Popular Front, OHAL). Another member of the roundtable said that the Party reached workers on bread-and-butter issues but never succeeded in giving them an attractive *American* vision of Socialism.

On the question of whether the Popular Front, by its support for reform, blunted the possibility of revolution—a judgment often made by the New Left—the discussants again disagreed. One man repeated that there never was a possibility of revolution. A woman answered that during the Popular Front, bread-and-butter goals were allowed to appear to be ultimate goals. Another man noted that the Party could never connect culturally with Americans and so could never lead them politically. Bad leadership decisions were also blamed, especially for the policy of trying to control front organizations: "How would you like to go to a meeting where a certain bloc of people vote a certain way no matter what's said or discussed? This is the way it was done. And the Party leaders insisted on it" (Popular Front, OHAL). Finally, one speaker suggested that the Popular Front really ended because the country had gone as far left as it was inclined to go after the mass industries had been unionized and economic conditions much improved over what they were at the beginning of the 1930s.

Thus, although Left magazines like the *Guardian* and *Monthly Review* have generally judged the Popular Front a misguided failure, the participants in the OHAL discussion, with their divergent views, probably represent more accurately the response of Leftists who participated: some judge it a success; some blame it for failing to lead the masses leftward; some judge that the potential for leftward movement never existed. Whatever potential had existed and whatever hope the Party had of leading were essentially lost when it defended the non-aggression pact of 1939.

Under the aegis of the Popular Front, writers experimented with the relationship between literature and politics, writing what James T. Farrell referred to as "individualistic" and "collective" novels, plays that were traditional drama or agitprop, or—as in the case of *Waiting for Lefty*—both.

(Indeed, the move of that play from workers' theaters to Broadway in September 1935 parallels the movement of the CPUSA from margin to near mainstream after the Popular Front was declared in the summer of 1935.) The Spanish Civil War in particular called forth a rich literary response, perhaps because it epitomized in a concrete way the struggle of the Left against Fascism and also the difficulties of the Left, divided against itself, not always comfortable with the means to its ends. Just as surely as the Great Depression and the Popular Front had drawn American writers generally to the Left, the non-aggression pact and the authoritarianism it revealed provoked an exodus. According to Malcolm Cowley, those who tried to maintain the League of American Writers after the pact were jokingly referred to as the "lonely hearts club" (Cowley, OHAL).

6

From World War II to the Demise of the Movement

COMMUNISTS AWOKE ON THE MORNING OF 22 JUNE 1941 TO READ what their leadership had learned only hours before: that the German army had invaded Russia. This turn of events rescued the CPUSA from an increasingly indefensible political line but confronted it with the threat that the Soviet Union might be overtaken by Fascist forces. Opposing Fascism came naturally to the Communists, and they executed a 180-degree turn with maximum speed. Most of the old Popular Front organizations, like the League of American Writers, were beyond resuscitation, but the Party soon involved itself surreptitiously in organizations with agendas so impeccable—like Russian War Relief—that liberals would again join (Isserman, 111). Enthusiastically supporting Roosevelt and war preparedness, the Party again came in from the cold, though it would never again regain the modicum of trust it had enjoyed during the Popular Front. Within the CIO unions it generally managed to retain the leadership positions held before the pact.

When the Japanese bombed Pearl Harbor on 7 December 1941, pushing the United States into the war, Communists volunteered for the armed services in great numbers. And as the Soviet Union continued, at great cost, to resist the German invasion, it came to be seen as a heroic ally. Its respectability was further enhanced with the publication of *Mission to Moscow,* by Joseph E. Davies (Isserman, 128). A well-connected corporate lawyer and not a Leftist, Davies praised the efficiency of the Soviet Union, rationalized the purges, and assured readers that Stalin's Russia was no longer guided by Communist ideology.

In their heartfelt desire to defeat Fascism and defend Russia, Communists committed themselves to the war effort with the fervor and dedication for which they had become famous in labor organizing. The successful defense of the Soviet Union depended directly on war materiel sent from America to Russia. Communists therefore found themselves in the unaccustomed position of urging maximum industrial production and opposing strikes and slowdowns. And the government found itself in the unaccustomed position of wanting the support of the CPUSA because of its influence in the CIO. In May 1942, Roosevelt commuted Earl Browder's sentence to time already served, and Browder took back the reins of the Party from Robert Minor's "caretaker" administration.

Shortly after Pearl Harbor, union leaders had agreed to a no-strike policy for the duration of the war. A War Labor Board was created in January 1942 to settle wage disputes and also to find ways to guarantee that unions would not lose ground as a result of Board mediation. (Early in the New Deal, some workers had seen NIRA codes as doing away with the need for a union; the establishment of the War Labor Board posed the same threat.) The agreement that was reached tied wage increases to the cost of living and gave union members only the most limited opportunities to resign their membership. During the war years strikes did occur, and Communist support for the no-strike pledge became a political liability.[1] But at the time it was by no means clear that an alliance between labor and New Deal government would be a deadend. Remembering the antiunion activity that followed World War I and noting that each congressional election after 1938 brought in more antilabor votes, Communists saw in the alliance with Roosevelt and the more Leftist elements of the New Deal a chance to guarantee labor's gains (Isserman, 138).

In *Which Side Were You On? The American Communist Party during the Second World War,* Maurice Isserman argues convincingly that while the Party focused its energy on support for war production, it did not abandon its interest in the rights of women and African Americans but rather attempted to promote those rights through its labor policy. Communists argued that Jim Crow laws deprived the war effort of the contributions of blacks. A parallel argument was made on behalf of women. The United Electrical, Radio and Machine Workers established apprenticeship programs for women and urged equal pay, and the National Maritime Union, another Party-led

CIO union, bargained for contracts that prohibited racial discrimination (Isserman, 140–42). The Party's inability to influence the Transport Workers Union to negotiate an end to racial discrimination, however, illustrates the limited success of the Party's approach. As the war took men away from civilian life and simultaneously beckoned women out of the home, nearly half of CPUSA membership was female by 1944. The occupants of the famous "ninth floor," the area of the Party's Union Square headquarters where the leadership had its offices, were still overwhelmingly male.

To read Rose Pesotta's *Bread upon the Waters*,[2] published in 1945, is to get a visceral sense of the frustrations of a woman labor organizer a decade into the New Deal and in the early years of the war. Her perspective is especially interesting because her politics are anarchist, and she looks on Communist work in the labor field with a critical eye. Born in Russia, Pesotta emigrated in 1913 and found work in a garment factory. Between 1881 and 1924, 2 million Jews from cities and villages in eastern Europe came to America.[3] Many settled on New York's Lower East Side, where the young women found that their skills as seamstresses earned them jobs in sweatshops. In Russia and Poland, the prevalence of radical political ideas and groups, and the precarious position of the Jews, had all fostered political awareness and created a tradition in which women were allowed to be politically active. In America, many involved themselves in political groups and union work, at least until they married (Weinberg, 93).

Pesotta heard Emma Goldman speak in 1914, and the two exchanged letters after Goldman was deported in 1919. Pesotta's lover, Theodore Kushnarev, was deported along with Goldman on the *Buford*.[4] During the 1920s, Pesotta worked with great passion in defense of fellow anarchists Sacco and Vanzetti. The anarchist movement itself was in decline after the Red-Scare deportations and the near destruction of the IWW, but Pesotta's convictions remained firm. While some anarchists opposed unions and especially reformist unions, Pesotta accepted a more syndicalist line and reasoned that if workers were ever to stage the General Strike that would put an end to government, they would have to be organized in some way or other.[5] Her philosophical opposition to Communism was no doubt strengthened by news of her father's execution by the Communists in Russia (Schofield, vii).

Thus Pesotta cast her lot with the International Ladies Garment Workers Union (ILGWU), which had been founded in 1901. Her Local 25, based in the Socialist radical circles of New York, was often in conflict with a less radical national leadership. The *Jewish Daily Forward* and the Socialist Party—especially the Party's women—were strong supporters of the union. After the great garment industry strikes of 1909–10, the ILGWU emerged as the third largest union in the AFL, but many members, especially those from the more radical locals, felt that the contracts allowed too many concessions.[6] Already pulled between AFL reformism and Socialist Party radicalism,

LIN-50

Workers demonstrating for union rights in Louisville, Kentucky, in 1945. Photo by Lin Caufield. From the Lin Caufield Collection, University of Louisville Photographic Archives.

the union was further torn apart by Communists, who in the 1920s were "boring from within" established unions, under the tutelage of the Trade Union Educational League. The Communist faction itself split in 1928 when the CPUSA expelled Jay Lovestone, and the ILGWU became a base for the otherwise inconsequential Lovestoneite group. Most "orthodox" Communists abandoned the ILGWU to set up a dual union, the Needle Trades Workers Industrial Union, but returned in 1934 when the dual union movement folded. Throughout the 1930s, David Dubinsky, ILGWU president, moved gradually from Socialism toward the center and in 1940 took the union out of the CIO and back to the AFL. In 1944 the union lost power within the American Labor Party, the left-wing alternative to Tammany Hall Democrats in New York, and ceased to be a political force as the country moved rightward.

Bread upon the Waters defies easy classification; it is too impersonal to be a memoir, too personal to be a history. Pesotta never tells us exactly why she wrote the book, saying in the foreword only that after her years as a field organizer she realized that she had accumulated a great deal of documentary material. Though we cannot know her unstated motives, we might get some clue from that part of her history that she chose to leave out of the book.

As a union vice president, she was the only woman on the general executive board—this in a union in which the membership was overwhelmingly female and in which many of those women had finely honed political skills. Resigning her vice presidency in 1944, she objected that having one woman on the board was mere tokenism. Ann Schofield, writing the introduction to the 1987 reprint of *Bread upon the Waters,* speculates that Pesotta declined to relate this incident—as well as her critique of sexism in ILGWU leadership—out of loyalty to the union, out of a belief that there was no audience for such issues, or perhaps out of a belief that such issues were on hold for the duration of World War II (Schofield, ix–x).

Pesotta's biographer, Elaine Leeder, suggests that one of Pesotta's motives in writing the book was to tell her story after her disastrous clash with Louis Levy, the Pacific Coast ILGWU director, over the handling of a Los Angeles strike in 1940 (Leeder, 153). Pesotta remained angry with Levy and with Dubinsky, who may have suggested that she resign, and they remained angry enough with her to refuse to include her book in ILGWU libraries (Leeder, 152). Among her charges against Levy was that he used ILGWU funds to recruit Communists and that Communists were allowed more than their share of power at union meetings (Leeder, 87).

Primarily, however, *Bread upon the Waters* is a *record* of what worked for Pesotta as a field organizer and an analysis of why organizing failed when it did. It reads as if Pesotta, unable to get the leadership to see things from an organizer's viewpoint, finally resorted to writing down what she had learned from her years in the field so that it would not be lost, even as she went back to working as a dressmaker. As such it demonstrates yet another role for literature in relation to political movements: to preserve political insights for another time, in the hope that they will again be relevant and useful. If such a time comes, then the author will have struggled meaningfully and contributed to the making of history after all, thus realizing the ultimate Leftist ideal.

Much of what Pesotta learned was how to organize women workers of different cultures and ethnic backgrounds. Her emphasis on taking care of details (teaching her strikers not to touch their eyes when teargassed, providing good meals at the union hall, quoting the prolabor encyclical *Rerum Novarum* to Polish recruits) bespeaks her anarchist belief in the efficacy of human initiative. Some feminists had accused Emma Goldman of overemphasizing the *decision* to be free; Pesotta, an anarchist of the next generation, demonstrated just what kind of action it would take to bring that freedom about. In *Bread upon the Waters,* we see her first on her way to Los Angeles in September 1933, at the very beginning of the New Deal, to organize for the ILGWU in a city where she was once blacklisted—refused employment—because she was recruiting for the union while working in a factory there a few years earlier. She then tells the story of her initial involvement in union work, professes her admiration for Emma Goldman, and relates the facts of her attendance at the Bryn Mawr Summer School for Women Workers in 1922 and then Brookwood Labor College.[7] She calls the Bolshevik government of the U.S.S.R. a dictatorship and blames TUEL for the factional fighting that so weakened the ILGWU in the 1920s.

Organizing the Mexican-American women garment workers in Los Angeles is described as a particular challenge by Pesotta; most are Spanish speaking and have to rush home from their jobs to cook for their families. Pesotta realizes that inviting them to meetings is not the way to reach them. She distributes the paper the *Organizer* and leaflets geared to specific shops, both in Spanish and in English, and she joins a local Mexican-American cultural association that runs a radio station. Because she pays six months' dues in advance, the station manager allows her to broadcast messages about the union, giving her the opportunity to reach all of the families that own a radio every night. She reports proudly how little overhead the ILGWU has; its dues money is there for strike benefits. When the rent on possible union halls near the garment district in Los Angeles is prohibitively high, she rents a vacant loft and furnishes it with second-hand equipment. She is especially keen on defending ILGWU leadership and organizers, who have been, as she reports, targets of a smear campaign by the Communist dual union:

> In the period between 1925 and 1933, the Needle Trades Workers' Industrial Union succeeded in demoralizing our International, among others, and tearing down every important gain we had made in three decades. Stock tactics of the dual union were to sow distrust in their chosen leadership among the rank and file. Derogatory epithets

hurled at decent officials in widely distributed newspapers in various
languages were picked up by labor's enemies and used as weapons
against unions generally. Discouraged members dropped out of both
organizations, crying: "A plague on both your houses!" The employers
reaped vast benefit from all this internal dissension. (Pesotta, 35)

During the Los Angeles strike, Pesotta guards her unionists not only from
the disruptive tactics of the employers but also from those of the Needle
Trades Union.

In Chinatown, she makes personal contacts to hear why Chinese women
are afraid to join the union; she also discovers that conservative unions do
not welcome Chinese members and writes an article for a labor paper dis-
cussing why and how the Chinese women in the garment industry should
be organized. In Puerto Rico, she charters ILGWU locals, and those locals
set up educational programs in child care and birth control. Throughout
Bread upon the Waters, Pesotta begins her organizing by reaching the workers where they are, and this choice seems not merely tactical but rather a
natural outgrowth of her belief that unions exist to meet workers' needs and
foster worker empowerment. Shorter hours, better pay, better lighting in the
factories—these are real goals to her. In keeping with the anarchist tradition,
she does not imagine the proletarian revolution or even the General Strike
occurring until workers have more confidence, more organization, and a
greater sense of their own dignity and potential.

Pesotta welcomes the NIRA precisely because it changes the way workers see themselves: "Unorganized workers who had never before raised the
question of their rights as human beings, and who had accepted whatever
they were given as inevitable, suddenly awakened to the fact that they were
part of a great democratic nation. With a new sense of their own value in
production, they began to clamor for organization" (Pesotta, 97). Her union
enlists many new members in the early years of the New Deal, as unions
prove their worth in policing NIRA code enforcement. Sent to organize in
Seattle, Pesotta prefaces her story there with a history of radicalism in Seattle
and a brief general history of the IWW. She notes among the many reasons
for the decline of the IWW its tactical mistakes, particularly its refusal to
sign labor contracts. "Its attitude toward the future, though idealistic, was
visionary and not practical" (Pesotta, 148), she writes, and adds that the CIO
has learned much from the Wobbly experience.

In a fast-paced narrative, Pesotta relives her experience in the Akron rubber
workers' strike and in the auto workers' strike that built the CIO. At a United
Auto Workers convention she speaks against the expulsion of Communists,
noting that Leftists must end factional fighting and form a solid line against
exploitative capitalists; in urging political tolerance, she cites the examples of
the IWW and the Haymarket martyrs. Her pragmatism (in this case combined
with disingenuousness) also reveals itself when, organizing in Montreal, she

does not distribute copies of her own union's paper if it praises actions taken by the Loyalists in Spain against the Catholic Church; the Church was powerful in Montreal and the potential unionists were Catholic.

Bread upon the Waters describes the return of the ILGWU to the AFL, from which it had been expelled for supporting the CIO; that return, signifying the acceptance of industrial unionization, completes one era of labor organizing. Pesotta is driving across the desert back to Los Angeles when she hears the radio broadcast reporting the bombing of Pearl Harbor. She concludes, "[I]n light of the tragedy that had plunged us into a world holocaust, my job was no longer important" (Pesotta, 392). In the last chapter, however, she warns that the task of unions is now to protect workers from exploitation during the war. She criticizes the terms of the no-strike pledge and warns that the enmity between the AFL and CIO will compound labor's vulnerability when the war ends.

Her silence about her reasons for leaving full-time union work gives the book a curiously ambiguous feeling at the end. It has been structured as a "success story," following the growth of unionization, once the NIRA opens the door, and the acceptance and development of industrial organization. But instead of ending on a triumphant note, the book conveys an unexpressed dissatisfaction, an odd emptiness. We can only speculate on the sources of ambivalence that at once prompted Pesotta to withdraw from union leadership *and* to write a memoir/history that is virtually a "how to" book on multicultural women's organizing.

Perhaps some clue can be found in her presentation of self in the book. She describes her family background and her journey to political consciousness, and the book is entirely a recounting of her experience, but she is present only as a political person. She never mentions her personal life or romantic relationships. Her steadfast commitment to the value of labor organizing calls her to be an uncritical supporter and a gung-ho recruiter; that persona is the one we meet in *Bread upon the Waters*. Whatever doubts and frustrations she had about the treatment of women or about internal union politics, these belong to the private Rose Pesotta. When the commitment to noble "ends" calls her to be one person and her criticism of the "means" calls her to be another, how can the conflict be resolved? This dilemma is not an uncommon one. Rose Pesotta appears to have resolved it by withdrawing personally from organizing but writing *Bread upon the Waters* as a way of continuing to uphold the ideal and preserving for a later time the lessons she learned as an organizer. Narrative is one field in which the good can easily be separated from the bad.

Writers and Communist Cultural Policy

Once the director of the Harlem bureau for the *Daily Worker,* Richard Wright was one of the best-known African-American writers of the Old Left. Though his job was to report on the Harlem section of the Party, he himself belonged to a "downtown" section because he was a cultural worker (Berry, OHAL). That situation in itself symbolized Wright's conflict as an African American, a writer, and a Leftist. He had joined the Party in 1932 through the John Reed Club in Chicago, drawn by the opportunity to publish his work and by the ideal of racial justice. In his highly acclaimed novel *Native Son* (1940), however, he presents the Communists as unable to influence race relations in any significant way. And in the autobiographical *Black Boy* (1945), he represents the Communists as duplicitous and heavy-handed. Abner Berry has objected that the "American Hunger" section of *Black Boy* is so exaggerated a portrayal of the Party as to be a caricature (Berry, OHAL). He speculates that Wright's anger at the Party and his resignation in 1944 stem from resentment of the directives from white members in the cultural section (Berry, OHAL). Moving to Paris in 1947, Wright became a friend of Jean Paul Sartre and published *The Outsider* (1953), a novel in which he again focused on the relationship between the Party and an African-American Chicagoan, this time from the perspective of existentialism. Whereas Marxism theorized individuals as members of a class, interacting with the dynamic of history, existentialism theorized individuals as free to make their own history, to create their own essence.

Wright's nonfiction account of his experience with the Party was published in a collection of such pieces, *The God That Failed*.[8] As the title suggests, the theme of the book is disillusionment with Communism, and Wright joined Arthur Koestler, Ignazio Silone, André Gide, Louis Fischer, and Stephen Spender in providing an account of his attraction to Communism and his loss of faith in it. Wright begins by telling how he, though skeptical, followed up an invitation to the Chicago John Reed Club, which met on the upper floor of an old building in the Loop. Given an armful of old copies of *Masses* and *International Literature*, he reads them and is interested: "It was not the economics of Communism, nor the great power of trade unions, nor the excitement of underground politics that claimed me; my attention was caught by the similarity of the experiences of workers in other lands, by the possibility of uniting scattered but kindred peoples into a whole. It seemed to me that here at last, in the realm of revolutionary expression, Negro experience could find a home, a functioning value and role" (Wright, 118). The art and the writing in the magazines, however, strikes him as naive and ineffective, and he realizes that the Party needs writers.

The John Reed Club welcomes him. Indeed, he is elected executive secretary. Later he finds out that the writers in the club wanted to seize control from the painters, so they nominated Wright, knowing that the members would be reluctant to vote against an African American. Not all club members are Communists, but the Communists, some of whom do not reveal that they are Communists, have a "fraction" within it, that is, they control it by voting as a bloc. The non-Communists resent this. In particular they resent the Party's pressure to cease publication of *Left Front*, the magazine that drew many of them to the club. Wright is told that he must join the Party if he is going to lead the club. He asserts that writers and artists must be given artistic freedom. The Party doesn't object, so he signs his membership card. But when he tries to interview another black Communist, "Ross" (the only name he's given), for a biographical sketch, Communists warn him off and remind him that he should take orders. Black Communists on the South Side distrust him for being an intellectual.

Disturbed and angered to hear that the Party is dropping the John Reed Clubs because its People's Front strategy calls for a more inclusive organization, Wright argues against the move and is further disturbed to realize that even those who share his viewpoint are going along with the Party line, because that is what the Party expects. Sent as a delegate to New York for the 1935 writers' congress, he cannot find a hotel that will admit blacks, and when the vote on the fate of the John Reed Clubs is taken, his is the only vote against dissolution. Wright decides to leave the Party and stops attending meetings. But then a comrade tells him that the Party has "decided" that he should head a committee. "I knew the meaning of what he had said," Wright remarks. "A decision was the highest injunction that a Communist could receive from his Party, and to break a decision was to break the effectiveness of the Party's ability to act. In principle I heartily agreed with this, for I knew that it was impossible for working people to forge instruments of political power until they had achieved unity of action" (Wright, 145). He grudgingly accepts the committee appointment and then refuses an assignment to go as a delegate to Switzerland and the Soviet Union. When he resigns from the Party at a unit meeting, he is told that if he goes through with his resignation, he will be called a Trotskyist and a subversive.

Given WPA work as a publicist for the Federal Negro Theater in Chicago, Wright angers the black actors by promoting realistic plays about conditions of black American life. The troupe doesn't want to anger audiences. Wright asks to be given another job and is sent to a white troupe. At this point he is invited by the Communists to attend the Party trial of Ross, his old comrade, who is accused of Negro nationalism, among other things. At the trial he is stunned when Ross stands and says that he is guilty. Instead of breaking with the Party, Ross endures his ordeal, and Wright concludes, "The vision of a communal world had sunk down into his soul and it would never leave him until life left him" (Wright, 156). The trial and confession are the price of his return to the fold. Wright recognizes that his South Side Party unit is so deeply distrustful of him, as an intellectual, that it would one day exact the same price from him, if he remained, and would execute him if it were the state. (Constance Webb, Wright's biographer, interprets this comment as a reference to the political trials just beginning in Moscow.[9])

When Wright is transferred to the Federal Writers' Project, fellow employees who are Communists do not speak to him because it is Party policy not to speak to enemies of the working class. The same excomrades try to have him fired as incompetent, and he hears that the Party was behind the animosity toward him at the Federal Negro Theater. At the May Day parade in 1936, he misses his union's step-off time, is invited by a black Communist to march with the South Side Party unit, begins to do so, and then is forcibly removed by two white Communists as a Trotskyist. He concludes the last section of this brief memoir with the words, "I headed toward home alone, really alone now" (Wright, 162).

This potent image of separation does not, however, mark the end of Wright's association with the Party. In 1937 he went to New York to begin his job with the *Daily Worker*. His continuing ambivalence about the Party is indicated by a comment he hoped would be quoted in the Book-of-the-Month-Club review of *Black Boy*, even after the "American Hunger" section was mysteriously cut (Webb, 206): "I am as collectivist and proletarian in my outlook as when I belonged to the Communist Party, and the Negroes are my people. But there is a need to think and feel honestly, and that comes first" (Webb, 208).

As Richard Wright was distancing himself from the Party in the mid-1940s, poet Thomas McGrath was moving toward it. Raised in North Dakota in a family sympathetic to the IWW, McGrath served in World War II and then studied with Cleanth Brooks at Louisiana State University. In 1949 he published *Longshot O'Leary's Garland of Practical Poesy*, which deals with the plight of workers and the corruption of unions by organized crime. Of all his work, this book is the most closely tied to political events of the moment, and he called it "tactical poetry," being couched in accessible forms and dealing with immediate issues (McGrath, OHAL). He contrasted it with "strategic poetry," which is more removed from the immediate political situation and is intended to raise consciousness. McGrath believed in the need for both kinds of political poetry and expressed this belief, even though it wasn't always well received by Left critics in the 1940s. *New Masses* didn't publish many of his poems, and he didn't like much of what they were publishing: "It seemed to me very thin, and the politics seemed to me undigested, and it seemed full of slogans rather than poetic images" (McGrath, OHAL). In McGrath's judgment, most of the influential Left writers and critics in the 1940s had a limited experience of American life; they knew the cities on the coast, but knew little about the heartland. And they knew too little about American literature, which they dismissed as bourgeois. Wider knowledge of American literature would have made them wiser about the "dark side" of the American character (McGrath, OHAL).

Among McGrath's strategic poetry, *To Walk a Crooked Mile*,[10] published in 1947, is particularly interesting. In "The Heroes of Childhood" he looks back nostalgically on the unmixed admiration he had for the older generations of revolutionaries, "Big Bill Haywood or Two Gun Marx." They championed the poor against the bankers and never had second thoughts. "But we in our time are not so sure," he writes; we have begun to doubt our direction, "For the saint is the man most likely to do wrong" (McGrath, 40). He concludes that we must trust the heart to lead us forward in spite of our uncertainties. In a 1977 interview, McGrath explained his attitude toward the Party in the 1940s: "I think that what we felt probably was that all battles would be lost except the last. I think that most of us had a certain amount of irreverence for leadership, and a sense that any organization was likely to be wrong more than it was going to be right. As a result of that, I think, we weren't thrown by a lot of difficulties one time or another—ideological differences or splits or whatever. We managed to get past these without losing a sense of the importance of the revolution" (McGrath, OHAL). The image in "The Heroes of Childhood" of persevering on the journey despite the absence of landmarks seems an especially apt one for Communists in the years after World War II.[11]

= The Communist Political Association =

When in February 1943 the German Sixth Army surrendered at Stalingrad, American respect for the Soviet Union soared; the tough and successful struggle of the Russians seemed even more heroic after the frighteningly swift collapse of France and Belgium earlier in the war. Mainstream American magazines praised the Russian people (Isserman, 158). For those looking toward the end of the war, it was not difficult to see that the United States and the U.S.S.R. would emerge as the two world powers. Whether the relationship between them would be cooperative or antagonistic remained to be seen. In June 1943 the Comintern—the Third International—was officially disbanded; the reason given was that conditions varied so much from country to country that centralized direction of the path to Socialism was no longer effective. Communists in each country were now to work for the ascendancy of the working class by engaging in the political process in their particular countries—at least, that was the publicly announced policy. (*Polycentrism* was the term that came to denote this decentralized policy.)

In late November 1943, Roosevelt, Churchill, and Stalin met for the first time in Teheran, Iran, the headquarters of the U.S. Army's Persian Gulf Command and a hub on the route by which American war matériel was shipped to the Soviet Union. The main item on the agenda was setting the date for the Allied invasion of France, but already the three world leaders were discussing the spheres of influence in the postwar world. Stalin understood that he could install a Communist regime in Poland. The Teheran Declaration pledged cooperation among the United States, Great Britain, and the U.S.S.R. after the war.

Earl Browder's reading of the Teheran Declaration led him to envision a postwar world in which American-Soviet cooperation continued, class struggle in western Europe would be waged through parliamentary means, and developed countries would cooperate because they needed peace to sell their goods in unindustrialized countries (Isserman, 188). In America, he envisioned a continued alliance between Communists and New Deal Democrats in moving the country toward the Left through constitutional means; capitalists would recognize that their best interests lay in cooperating with government and with labor in opening new international markets. Joseph Starobin, in *American Communism in Crisis, 1943–1957*, theorizes that Browder was powerfully motivated by a desire to forestall a rightward turn in the United States and by the recognition that the New Deal had strengthened capitalism.[12]

In keeping with this fundamental change in the role of the Communist Party in America, Browder proposed, over the objections of William Z. Foster, that the CPUSA cease to be a revolutionary party and become instead a player within American democratic politics. Overthrowing the government and replacing capitalism with state Socialism was no longer the Party's goal. At the CPUSA convention in New York in May 1944, the assembled delegates followed Browder's lead and voted to disband the CPUSA and replace it with the Communist Political Association (CPA). Browder directed that Communist groups should be based in neighborhood and community rather than in labor settings, and he instructed Communists to become active, open, and respectable participants in the political life of their communities. The strategy appears to have been an attractive one: In 1944 CPA membership was roughly equal to that of the CPUSA just before the signing of the non-aggression pact—about 70,000 (Isserman, 205).

The CPUSA had seen itself as a Leninist party, that is, a vanguard party making contacts among the masses in order to lead them in revolution. A Leninist, or revolutionary, party required near-military discipline and a top-down command structure to be quick and decisive in revolutionary conditions. When the CPUSA gave way to the CPA, discussion naturally arose about changing the structure and the process of making policy. In proposing the CPA, Browder had hailed the idea of greater internal democracy but had maintained the importance of strong central control (Isserman, 191). Joseph Starobin interprets this contradiction as a reflection of Browder's belief that the Party, officially disbanded, would really continue to be a Leninist revolutionary party and simply bide its time (Starobin, 61); Maurice Isserman is less skeptical of Browder's announced faith in the Teheran Declaration and postwar cooperation. Whatever his motives, Browder did not choose to democratize the workings of the CPA, and the continued centralization, now more than ever at odds with the CPA's announced goals, no doubt contributed to the high turnover in membership.

═ The Duclos Letter ═

When the Allied armies triumphed over Nazi Germany in spring of 1945, the United States and the Soviet Union faced each other in a new light. No longer united by the need to oppose a common enemy, would they be united in pursuit of peace and progress, as Browder envisioned, or would they settle into enmity and a struggle for world domination? While the outcome of Browder's gamble was still in doubt, Jacques Duclos, one of the leaders of the French Communist Party, published in his Party's journal, *Cahiers de Communisme,* an article titled "On the Dissolution of the American Communist Party." Appearing in April 1945, the article purported to be a response to questions asked by French Communists about the American move. Quoting from unpublished documents, it explained Browder's line and condemned it as revisionism (Isserman, 218). Comrade Browder had erred in thinking that the Teheran Declaration portended class peace in western Europe, and he further erred by depriving America of a revolutionary party.

When the article reached Browder in May, he realized that only Moscow could have sent Duclos the unpublished documents he had used, and therefore the condemnation was coming from Moscow. When the CPUSA had been dissolved, every signal from Moscow had indicated support for Browder. Now the Duclos letter must have left him wondering how and why things had changed—and what he was supposed to do about it. The purpose of the letter remains unclear, but Isserman speculates that Stalin, knowing that it would be read by the U.S. State Department, intended it as a reminder of Communist power in western Europe; mindful of that, the United States should not interfere in his takeover of eastern Europe (Isserman, 219).

The *Daily Worker* printed the Duclos letter on 24 May, with an introduction by Browder, playing down its significance. But in June his leadership became purely nominal, as the power passed to a triumvirate of William Foster, Eugene Dennis, and John Williamson. In an emergency convention the next month, the CPA was disbanded and the CPUSA reconstituted. Browder was widely repudiated, not only for his mistaken foray into revisionism but also for suppressing any dissent when the move was made. Foster once again emerged as the leader of American Communists, and he looked at the mounting waves of strikes and the increasingly antilabor Congress and concluded that thwarted labor militancy would provide fertile ground for organizing.

═ The Cold War ═

When Roosevelt died in April 1945, the presidency passed to Harry Truman, whom Roosevelt had chosen as his vice president in 1944 to replace Henry Wallace, his previous running mate, deemed too far to the left. Indeed, Roosevelt's reelection in 1944 had been by a slight margin, compared with the landslides of 1932 and 1936, and the 1946 congressional elections moved the legislature significantly to the right. Republicans could find few issues on which to run, given widespread support for the New Deal, but they made the most of the charge that Democrats were "soft on Communism" at home and abroad. As the war was winding down, most Americans were hoping for stability and a chance to concentrate on their private lives after the disruption and sacrifices of World War II. They did not welcome the unrest in labor relations and race relations that accompanied the transition to peacetime.

As it became clearer that the Allies were indeed going to defeat Hitler and Japan as well, American workers who had accepted the codes set by the War Labor Board became restive. They pointed out that wage controls were well enforced, but price controls were not nearly so well policed. Strike succeeded strike in the headlines of 1944 and again in 1946. Race relations, too, were unsettled. African Americans had understood that their contributions during the war, in the military and in industry, would be rewarded after the war by civil rights guarantees and improved opportunities for employment.

As had happened in World War I, black workers had come north during the war to take factory jobs left open by the military draft. In many northern cities, a significant sector of the labor force, both black and white, was drawn from the rural South. As wartime production called for additional shifts, more workers flooded into the cities, competing for the best jobs, for housing, for seats on the buses (Isserman, 168). Detroit in June 1943 had been the scene of a race riot, sparked by an interracial fistfight; federal troops imposed order after three days of looting, arson, and gang attacks that left 34 people dead and caused $2 million in property damage (Isserman, 168). Later that summer, a riot erupted in Harlem on the rumor that a black soldier had been killed by a white policeman. (A Catholic Worker house was conspicuously left untouched.)

Communists were actively helpful in putting down the false rumor and quelling the riot, but their approach to African-American and women's rights during the war—we need everyone's contribution to the war effort—left something of a vacuum as the war was ending. Browder, in his revisionist way, had seen racial integration as the way forward for African Americans, and that, of course, was the path later chosen by the civil rights movement. After Browder's downfall, the Party returned to saying that racial inequalities could not be eradicated under capitalism; this left them with no practical policy, since separatism had little appeal at the time (Starobin, 200). Despite the change in the theoretical line, individual Communists continued to work with dedication for civil rights. In Alabama, where poor blacks had traditionally formed the core of the Party, Communists ignored the reemphasis on separatism and continued to work for voting rights, civil rights, jobs, and housing.[13]

No general consensus exists about the point at which East and West decided that wartime cooperation would be replaced by Cold War. Perhaps wartime cooperation was only a pragmatic device. Seeing Stalin squelch free elections in Poland and institute dictatorial Communist regimes there and in Bulgaria and Rumania, Americans concluded that the Soviets were deceitful and dangerous aggressors. As Richard M. Fried notes, however, in *Nightmare in Red,* some historians also point out that the United States had not left the shape of the postwar Italian government entirely to the Italians.[14] If the Duclos letter was Stalin's way of reminding the U.S. government of his power in Europe, then the explosion of two atomic bombs over Japan in August of 1945 gave evidence of overwhelming U.S. military superiority. Very soon after the war, East and West settled into mutual distrust, in which each explained its own actions as defensive responses to the other's aggression. In February 1948, Czech Communists, backed by the U.S.S.R., seized control of the Czech government. The United States responded with the Marshall Plan to rebuild Europe and with the North Atlantic Treaty Organization (NATO) to keep Communism "contained."

The term *liberal* in the late 1940s and 1950s usually referred to those who supported a continuation of the New Deal domestic agenda but also an aggressive Cold War stance toward the Soviet Union. Liberals believed that visibly separating the New Deal program from any toleration of Communist regimes was the only way to save it. Communists, who linked the two, were perceived as a serious threat, giving conservatives the ammunition they needed to discredit the welfare state. As a result, liberals in this era worked hard to distance themselves from Communists, not only shunning coalition but also, in many cases, failing to uphold the civil rights of Communists when they came under attack.

= The Progressive Party =

To oppose the rightward turn in both foreign and domestic policies, many supporters of the New Deal joined in forming the Progressive Party in 1948, running Henry Wallace as a presidential candidate in opposition to Democrat Harry Truman and Republican Thomas Dewey. Backers of the Party hoped to tap into continuing faith in the New Deal agenda of support for labor, support for internationalism through the United Nations, and use of the federal government to guarantee the rights and the welfare of citizens. Two events in 1947 suggested that the Truman administration would not protect the New Deal. In March, Truman signed an executive order requiring civil service employees to sign a loyalty oath. Then, shortly after that, the Taft-Hartley bill was introduced, requiring an 80-day cooling-off period, outlawing secondary strikes, and requiring unions to file affidavits saying that their leaders were not Communists before they could make use of the Labor Board to certify union elections.

After some initial resistance to the affidavits, the CIO adopted a policy of letting each of its member unions decide for itself whether it would comply. In consequence, there began a purge of Communists from the CIO, which they had been so influential in founding and which had formed so much of their political base during the New Deal. The Association of Catholic Trade Unionists, strongest between 1946 and 1950, strongly opposed the Leftist influence within the CIO (Seaton, 187). The split between the Party and the CIO was widened irrevocably when the Communist Party ordered its people in the CIO to support Wallace against Truman. Some refused and quit the Party; others complied and were removed from union leadership. International events also motivated the Party to press for a third-party campaign: In October 1947, the Communist Information Bureau (Cominform) had been established, and it urged a militant line (Starobin, 170).

Certifying bodies in various states put up obstacles to keep the Progressive Party off the ballot. A Gallup poll revealed that 51 percent of Americans thought the Progressive Party to be under Communist control; another 28 percent were undecided.[15] The press made much of the fact that at the Party's founding convention, the so-called "Vermont resolution" failed: offered by three delegates from Vermont, it had stated that the Party was critical of current U.S. foreign policy but did not "give blanket endorsement to the foreign policy of any nation" (Starobin, 193). Claims, made then and now, that the Progressive Party was simply a Communist front are not supported by the evidence, though Communist influence increased during the campaign to a point where Communists had a largely determining role.

The poor showing of the Progressive Party in the 1948 election no doubt reflected the effects of Red-baiting but was also an indication that Wallace's conciliatory approach toward the Soviet Union had lost credibility. By November 1948, the American public perceived Stalin as an aggressor. Even in losing, the Progressive Party had succeeded in moving Truman's platform slightly to the left, so that it included a civil rights plank and repeal of Taft-Hartley. The adjectives most often applied to the Wallace campaign, however, are "disastrous" and "ill-advised." Truman's victory proved that he could win without the Left. The influence the Left had enjoyed in the Roosevelt administration was at an end. Any politics to the left of liberal were effectively marginalized.

= The McCarthy Era =

The era in American political life from the late 1940s into the mid-1950s, characterized by severe measures to restrict Communist influence, takes its name from Sen. Joseph McCarthy. The junior senator from Wisconsin epitomized that time when anti-Communist feeling in the United States ran so high that civil liberties were sacrificed in the desire to ferret out and remove the Reds. (One indicator of how deeply anti-Communist sentiment ran in the culture in those years is provided by the example of the Cincinnati Reds professional baseball team, which from 1955 through 1958 changed its name to the Cincinnati Redlegs.) McCarthy stood out as the most aggressive and highly placed Red-hunter, but his campaign against the Communists could never have had the effect it did if it had not fed on the fears and political passions created by complex forces of the time.

We cannot know with certainty all of the factors contributing to the rise of McCarthyism, but many historians have speculated about the source of such vehement feeling. Surely the Cold War, in which Russia replaced Germany as our prime enemy, provided the grounding. Some historians have looked for motives in the immediate political struggles of the time. Robert Griffith, in *The Politics of Fear,* argued that anti-Communism was pushed into the spotlight by conservative Republicans seeking to discredit the New Deal, turn the Democrats from office, and move the country to the right.[16] Mary Sperling McAuliffe, in *Crisis on the Left: Cold War Politics and American Liberals, 1947–1954,* is one of a number of historians who note the anti-Communist themes used by Truman and the Democrats to generate support for the Marshall Plan and a foreign policy of "containment."[17]

Most recently, the search for causes has turned to culture. Americans were justly proud of their efforts, sacrifices, and victories in World War II, and many seemed comfortable, some even eager, to carry on as warriors as long as it was a Cold War. Fearing and distrusting Russia were familiar mental habits, going back to 1917, and accounts of the purge trials, mass deportations and starvations, and finally Soviet aggression in eastern Europe only confirmed the original judgment. The more brutal and authoritarian the Russian regime was revealed to be, the more we felt justified in opposing it; if it represented the forces of evil, then America must represent the forces of light. And the stakes were high indeed. The next world war would be an atomic war, not confined to Europe and the Pacific, but bringing massive destruction to America as well.

Uneasy with the disruptive strikes in the mid-1940s, Americans could blame Communist influence within the CIO—in spite of the fact that Communists had been the staunchest supporters of the no-strike pledge until the war ended. When postwar prosperity created jobs and raised wages, reformist unions like the AFL were able to satisfy workers' demands, and a more radical brand of unionism seemed more threatening than welcome. Because Communists had been visibly in support of the most militant expressions of African-American discontent, those who opposed any change in the racial arrangements could check the civil rights movement by labeling it a Communist plot. Indeed, *any* challenge to the status quo could be headed off in that way.[18] But, ultimately, Richard Fried argues, "anti-Communism derived its persistence from a deeply rooted cluster of values shared by American society, a set of views antithetical to Communist doctrines and friendly to private property and political democracy (albeit sometimes oblivious to imperfections in the latter)" (Fried, 9).

Americans believed that Communists threatened their way of life not only because they advocated revolution in America but more immediately because they were perceived as agents of Stalin. The directing hand of the Comintern could be read in Party policy shifts throughout its history, and the return to CPUSA after the sojourn as CPA was merely the most recent confirming example. In 1945, Louis Budenz, once a member of Muste's Workers Party and most recently an editor of the *Daily Worker,* abandoned the CPUSA and testified before the House Un-American Activities Committee, where he said that "the Communist Party in the United States is a direct arm of the Soviet Foreign Department"; he added that every Party member "is a potential spy against the United States" (quoted in Isserman, 239). Budenz would be followed by a long line of ex-Communists repudiating the Party and condemning it as an agent of Stalinist subversion.

When in September 1949 it became known that Russia, too, had the atomic bomb, Americans suspected that only espionage could have enabled the Soviets to obtain nuclear capability so quickly and to deprive the United States of its one great advantage in the Cold War. When in October of that same year the Communists gained control in China, Americans suspected that U.S. policy was being made in such a way as to undercut American interests and benefit the Communists. In June 1950, the United States sent troops to aid South Korea against the Communist North, and in August of that year 57 percent of Americans surveyed told the Gallup pollster they believed the Korean conflict to be the beginning of World War III.[19]

Given the fear of espionage and betrayal felt by Americans in 1950, we should not be surprised that "Communist" came to be synonymous with "spy" or "policy saboteur." Nor should we be surprised, then, that the question of Moscow's direction of the American Party came to be *the* central issue for the generation of historians who wrote about the Party in the 1950s and 1960s.

In 1946, the House Committee on Un-American Activities (HUAC, because it was popularly referred to as the House Un-American Activities Committee) became a permanent standing committee of the Congress. In 1950, the Senate Internal Security Subcommittee (SISS) of the Judiciary Committee was created. Also in 1950, the McCarran Act, known as the Internal Security Act, acknowledged that membership in the CPUSA was not a crime but asserted that it represented a "clear and present danger" to national security; therefore, leaders of Communist front organizations were required to register with the attorney general.

Determining which groups were front groups rested with the Subversive Activities Control Board. Individuals tainted by association with such fronts could not hold government jobs or passports or work in defense. Communists from abroad would not be allowed into the United States. Further, if the president declared a national security emergency, those individuals associated with Communism could be preemptively detained. No such emergency was ever invoked, and no group actually registered under the McCarran Act. (In 1963 a U.S. Appeals Court ruled that those who registered would be laying themselves open to prosecution under the Smith Act and thus were being illegally required to incriminate themselves.)

Though the McCarran Act was chiefly used to deny Leftist foreigners entry to the country, its power over Americans should not be underestimated; with old POW camps and military bases being readied to accept "detainees," Communists, other Leftists, and even liberals could foresee dire consequences for taking a Leftist line (Fried, 118). In February 1950, fear of Communist spies had been ratcheted up a peg when Senator McCarthy, giving a speech in Wheeling, West Virginia, claimed to have a list of 205 Communists working in the State Department. The number changed in subsequent speeches; such a list never existed. The claim of hard evidence, however, energized the Red-baiting campaign and put the investigations in the national spotlight.

That same year, 1950, saw important developments in three of the most famous investigations, those of Alger Hiss, of Julius and Ethel Rosenberg, and the "Hollywood Ten." Hiss had joined the State Department in 1936, one of the enthusiastic supporters of the New Deal, and had worked in the office of the assistant secretary of state for the Far East. In 1945, he had been a junior member of Roosevelt's delegation to the Yalta Conference, and he served as secretary general of the conference that had created the United Nations. He was thus in a position to have roused suspicion on three counts: he was, in his accusers' eyes, in a position to have sabotaged U.S.-China policy and to have influenced American-Soviet negotiations, and he promoted the UN, which to conservatives seemed always to work against American interests and advance those of the U.S.S.R. Questions were raised about Hiss's loyalty as early as 1939, when Whittaker Chambers, a repentant Communist, claimed to the FBI that Hiss had passed documents to the Soviets through him.

By 1945, allegations about Hiss were mounting sufficiently for him to be blocked in his government career, and he resigned to become executive director of the Carnegie Endowment for International Peace. (Hiss, in a letter to the *Wall Street Journal* on 29 November 1993, asserted that he left the State Department not because of allegations but simply to take the job at Carnegie at the request of John Foster Dulles.) That might have been the end of it, if Whittaker Chambers had not been summoned to testify before the HUAC in 1948 in connection with the case of Elizabeth Bentley, the "spy queen," who admitted having been the lover of a Soviet spy master who "ran" several New Dealers (Fried, 62),

Chambers named Hiss as a Communist who promoted Communist policy through his influence on the New Deal. Hiss denied ever being a Communist, ever knowing Chambers. He assumed that he had exonerated himself. But Chambers was able to describe details of the Hisses' private lives, including home furnishings. Recalled before the HUAC, Hiss said he remembered knowing Chambers under the name of George Crosley. He still denied ever having been a Communist. Chambers repeated the charge and produced a packet of documents that he had hidden in the unused dumbwaiter of an apartment in Brooklyn. In December 1948, he produced additional evidence from its hiding place on his farm in a hollowed-out pumpkin. These famous "pumpkin papers" consisted of five rolls of microfilmed documents, including some rather unimportant information originating in the State Department office where Hiss had worked (Fried, 20). Someone had microfilmed typed copies of documents, but there was no indication of who had typed the copies. They might have been produced after the fact specifically to incriminate Hiss. The case against Hiss began to mount, however, when he did not immediately lead federal agents to the whereabouts of his old Woodstock typewriter (Fried, 21). Evidence that it was the typewriter used for the documents was convincing but not conclusive, and nothing else tied Hiss himself to the actual copying.

In July 1949, a trial of Hiss on charges that he had perjured himself before the HUAC resulted in a hung jury. At a second perjury trial in January 1950, he was convicted and served almost four years in federal prison. Those who had opposed or resented the New Deal made much of Hiss's conviction to discredit Roosevelt's policies. Supporters of the New Deal and those who opposed the abrogation of civil rights by the Communist-hunters wanted to believe that Hiss had been framed. The case has not yet been resolved in the court of public opinion. In the summer of 1992, after Glasnost had opened some Soviet archives and thawed relations somewhat, Soviet General Volkogonov reported that his search of Soviet intelligence files revealed that Chambers had indeed been a Communist but never a spy or a courier.[20] Those who refuse to accept Volkogovov's evidence, however, insist that in the time he had he could never have searched *all* the Soviet intelligence files.

One month after Hiss's conviction, Klaus Fuchs, a British physicist who had worked on the development of the atomic bomb in America during the war, was arrested by the British as a Soviet spy. He confessed and was sentenced to 14 years in prison. Soon, the FBI began arrests of Americans, charged with aiding in the transfer of atomic secrets to the U.S.S.R. Among these were David Greenglass, his sister Ethel Rosenberg, her husband, Julius Rosenberg, and Morton Sobell, who had attended City College of New York with Julius Rosenberg. Greenglass pled guilty and testified against the Rosenbergs, saying that he had given Julius sketches of the Los Alamos reactor, to which he had access while working as a machinist in the army, and information about the making of the bomb. Greenglass, with the corroboration of his wife, Ruth, further told how Julius had cut the side of a Jello box in two and given one to Ruth. Later, Harry Gold, a confessed accomplice of

Klaus Fuchs's, arrived at the Greenglass apartment in Albuquerque with the other half,[21] which they believed he had received from Julius. (Gold said that he had been given his half of the identifying Jello box by Anatoli Yakovlev, a Soviet diplomat.) The famous Elizabeth Bentley testified that as part of her espionage activities she received phone calls from a man called Julius.

The Rosenbergs pled not guilty and refused to make any statements about their political beliefs or activities except to deny that they had ever engaged in espionage. They were convicted and sentenced to death. Greenglass was sentenced to 15 years in prison, Sobell to 30 years, as he was judged to have been a spy but not to have assisted in passing atomic secrets. The Rosenbergs were repeatedly invited to recommend themselves for clemency by confessing and naming others, but they refused. They were executed at Sing Sing prison on 19 June 1953, while crowds massed in protest outside the prison and in Union Square. As with Sacco and Vanzetti, no consensus exists even now about their guilt or innocence but there is a widespread recognition that their trial became a political struggle in itself.[22] The severity of their sentences compared with those of Fuchs and Greenglass suggests that their refusal to confess and "cooperate" was particularly objectionable.

The year that began with Hiss's conviction and the arrest of the Rosenbergs, 1950, also saw most of the Hollywood Ten—all screenwriters accused of contempt of Congress for failure to cooperate with the HUAC—begin serving their prison terms. The HUAC had begun as early as 1947 to investigate Communist influence in the motion picture industry in the 1930s and 1940s. Although a number of writers and performers had at one time been Communists or left leaning, evidence that the movies were used for Communist propaganda was notably unconvincing. The Reddest example found was *Mission to Moscow,* produced in 1943 at the request of the Roosevelt administration to foster public support for aid to Russia in the war against Fascism.[23] Initially, Hollywood responded uncooperatively to the HUAC, asserting that the government had no right to meddle in the movie industry. Some of the first screenwriters called to testify took this position and were cited for contempt. Very quickly, Hollywood solidarity collapsed. Two days after the contempt citations were issued, producers met and pledged never to hire a Communist or a subversive. An industry as sensitive to public opinion as the movie industry was very vulnerable. The appeals of the screenwriters were denied, and most of them went to prison.

The intention of the movie industry to steer clear of trouble by purging Leftists resulted in a blacklist, a list of those who would not be hired because of their politics. Those in positions to do the hiring denied the existence of such a list: writers and actors and other performers simply found that their services were not wanted. Screenwriters could sometimes continue to work if they could get another writer to "front" for them, that is, to say that the work was theirs. In recent years, the Writers Guild of America has recredited—given credit to the real writer—a number of films including *Gun Crazy* (1950, by Dalton Trumbo), *Broken Arrow* (1950, by Albert Maltz), *Roman Holiday* and *The Brave One* (1953 and 1956, story credits to Trumbo), *The Bridge on the River Kwai* (1957, by Carl Foreman and Michael Wilson), and *The Defiant Ones* (1958, cowritten by Nedrick Young).[24] Only in 1960, when actor Kirk Douglas insisted that Trumbo receive screen credit for *Spartacus,* was the blacklist defied, and then over the objections of the American Legion.[25]

Actors and performers, unable to work through fronts, simply found their careers had ended. In 1951, the HUAC decided to look further into Communist influence in the entertainment industry. The committee summoned those who had been Communists or members of Communist front organizations and asked them the famous question, "Are you now or have you ever been a member of the Communist Party?" Some, like Elia Kazan, who once played a driver in *Waiting for Lefty* for the Group Theatre, asserted (and continue to assert) that they believed there to be a Communist conspiracy which they had a patriotic duty to expose and destroy.[26] For others, the question created an excruciating dilemma. If they admitted to having once been a Communist or member of a front group, they would be given a chance to abase themselves by claiming that they had been "duped" into joining and now repented the association. They would then be invited to "name names," that is, to name others in the industry who were also members. If they cooperated in this way, they might be kept off the blacklist. Some agreed to talk about their own pasts but refused to name others. Some compromised and named only people who had already been named by others. Some chose to give new names and testimony about others' involvement.

Given the swings and reversals of policy, as well as the high turnover rate of the CPUSA, one can imagine that some of the HUAC witnesses did genuinely believe that they had been duped. Perhaps they had joined a front group or the Party itself to support unionization or unemployment insurance or Loyalist Spain or fairness for the Scottsboro boys; they might reasonably feel duped or used when they discovered that the Party saw those causes as means and not ends. Other witnesses might have felt that the question itself was a misleading one. The Party had, at various times since 1919, stood for revolution, reform, opposition to the war, cooperation with the New Deal— what, then, did it mean to say that one had once been a Communist?

In spite of the pressure to "cooperate," most witnesses chose not to name names. Even among those who had repudiated the Party long before, there were many who felt that the hearings made a travesty of the Bill of Rights, or that the real agenda of the HUAC was to attack Left-liberal values in which they still believed, or simply that they had no right to save themselves from the blacklist by implicating others. For the "unfriendly" witnesses, the common strategy was to invoke the Fifth Amendment, which shielded the witness from a contempt citation but generally landed him or her on the blacklist.

The fate of the Weavers is illustrative of the power and the character of the blacklist. The members of the quartet—Pete Seeger, Lee Hays, Ronnie Gilbert, and Fred Hellerman—had all been supportive of Left causes in and around the New York area in the 1940s. Their recording of "Goodnight Irene" was the top seller of 1950, and they followed it with hits like "On Top of Old Smokey" and "Kisses Sweeter Than Wine"—not the stuff of which revolutions are made. Their play list included some Woody Guthrie Depression-era protest songs and a song or two from the Spanish Civil War, but was mostly drawn from American folk traditions. They were in demand at all the best clubs across the country in 1950 and 1951 and were offered a regular show on the new medium of television.

With publication in June 1950 of *Red Channels: Communist Influence on Radio and Television*, the Weavers began to be dogged by their political pasts. *Red Channels*, published anonymously, listed entertainers suspected of being Communist, generally based on their having been mentioned in the *Daily Worker*.[27] Seeger was the only Weaver listed. Enough damage had been done so that the group's TV offer disappeared, as did an appearance on the Dave Garroway Show. The Weavers were removed from the entertainment program at the Ohio State Fair in August 1951, after Gov. Frank Lausche requested and was shown their FBI files (Dunaway, 40). Then, in February 1952, all four members of the group were "named" by government informer Harvey Matusow in testimony before the HUAC. Bookings dried up quickly after that, and the group was forced to disband.

Seeger appeared before the committee and invoked the First Amendment, saying that he would not cooperate because the HUAC proceedings were unconstitutional (Navasky, 421). Not until the 1960s was his contempt citation reversed on appeal. The subpoena for Lee Hays was first sent to an actor with the same name; when Hays testified, he took the Fifth. Hellerman was not scheduled to testify until later. Subpoena-servers never found Ronnie Gilbert because they did not know her married name.[28] Matusow, meanwhile, eventually confessed to perjury.

The Weavers didn't perform together again until their Christmas Eve concert of 1955 in Carnegie Hall. By that point, the anti-Red fervor had died down enough for the group to appear, but mere attendance at the concert was considered a political act, a protest against McCarthyism not undertaken without fear by those in vulnerable positions.[29]

The HUAC investigations sent a deep and long-lasting shiver through the entertainment industry. The second edition of the *Time Out* film guide lists a dozen films made about McCarthyism since it became a safe topic, reflecting the industry's effort to come to terms with what it did and what was done to it. Victor Navasky in *Naming Names* argues that the act of naming names shattered the trust, the sense of community that had existed before the investigations (Navasky, 370). The question of self-censorship, too, is raised. Did the industry, having once had its products investigated for ideology, then shy away from political topics? We can only speculate about whether and how American movies, for example, would have been different if there had never been a blacklist.

Many besides the famous were caught up in the net of McCarthyism. Ruth Norrick, who had quit the Party in 1935, was called before a grand jury and then before SISS, both investigating an alleged Communist conspiracy at the United Nations. Norrick, who says she didn't know anything about such a conspiracy and doesn't think there was one, lost her job in the Children's Bureau (Norrick, OHAL). Many others lost jobs at the UN, in the U.S. government, in research labs and defense plants, and in private businesses.

University professors, presumed to have influence over the young, were under particular scrutiny, even though there had been virtually no organized Communist activity on American campuses since the end of the war.[30] Overwhelmingly, they were accused not of teaching or promoting Communism or of carrying out any Communist agenda but of being Communists. In 32 states the legislatures passed laws requiring professors to sign loyalty oaths, which sometimes were rather vague statements of patriotism but sometimes a sworn statement that one was not a Communist; the California oath also required the individual to swear off having been a member of any group advocating violent overthrow of the government *in the last five years* (Schrecker, 116, 122). In some cases, even professors without radical ties or pasts refused to sign the oaths because they objected to professors being given a political test that was not imposed on citizens generally.

A debate arose over the meaning of academic freedom: Some argued that it protected the professoriat from tests for ideological purity; others argued that it meant only that the professoriat was responsible for policing itself. Central to the debate was the issue of whether Communism was in itself antithetical to academic freedom and thus undeserving of protection. Those who thought it so characterized it as an ideology that forbade independent thinking and required strict submission to the Party line; accused professors more than once argued that such could not be the case because they had freely chosen to resign from the Party and thus demonstrated that their will and ability to make independent judgments were still operable (Schrecker, 107–8).

Ultimately, the charge against many professors was that they had hidden their Communist affiliation and that such dishonesty was at odds with the academic life. Ellen W. Schrecker, in *No Ivory Tower: McCarthyism and the Universities,* estimates that nearly 20 percent of those called before national and state investigating committees were professors or graduate students, and most of those lost their jobs even if they took the Fifth Amendment (Schrecker, 10).

As the Korean conflict ended with a stalemate and the Cold War became a familiar backdrop to American politics, much of the energy behind McCarthyism dissipated. Americans were not accepting of Communists or of Communism, but without an immediate sense of threat, the impetus for Red-baiting at the cost of civil liberties was much reduced. Sen. Joseph McCarthy himself fell from power in 1954 when he held hearings investigating Communist influence in the army. The hearings were televised over several months in the spring of that year, and public approval of the senator fell from 50 percent favorable in January to 34 percent at the end of the hearings (Fried, 138). The public seems not to have liked what it saw of McCarthy in action, bullying, accusing, and insulting. Finally, he was censured by the Senate in December 1954 for having insulted other Senators and a Senate committee. That verdict, however, was read as a referendum on the witch-hunts.

May Sarton's 1955 novel, *Faithful Are the Wounds*,[31] looks at McCarthyism from an oblique angle, as the family and friends of Edward Cavan attempt to understand the passionate political commitment and the political despair that led to his suicide. Cavan, an English professor at Harvard, is described as having been a Christian Socialist, profoundly upset by the Communist takeover of the Czechoslovakian government in 1948. His Harvard colleagues and even his sister, Isabel, found his participation in the Wallace campaign and his active Leftist politics generally to be an embarrassment in the postwar years. Isabel, a surgeon's wife, talks about wanting "safety," finding it in her husband Henry, and feeling it threatened most powerfully by Edward.

Edward Cavan himself prefers the working-class coffee shops and bars in Cambridge, places that his earnest and sympathetic student George Hastings finds merely gloomy. Hastings, courting Pen Wallace and writing his dissertation, responds lyrically to the academic village of Cambridge and cannot understand why Cavan finds the world such a depressing place in 1949. Cavan cannot explain—indeed, the impossibility of communication even between friends is a recurrent theme in the novel—how the repudiation of the New Deal, which had brought intellectuals into government, the political disinterest of his students, the beginning of the Cold War, and the political repression of McCarthyism have made him become what he has most dreaded: an outsider, marginalized.

At the October meeting of the Civil Liberties Union, a letter is read from the national organization requesting each branch to certify that it has no Communists on its board. The majority, including Damon Phillips, a friend of Edward, votes to comply; a minority protests that to do so is to undermine all that they stand for, even though there are no Communists on the board. After the vote, Edward walks out, feeling betrayed by the majority and especially by Phillips, whom he describes scornfully as a liberal, willing to compromise anything. His friends, including Phillips, who is having self-doubts, worry that Edward is being destroyed by the seriousness with which he takes political matters. Edward is unable to forgive Damon or Ivan Goldberg, the colleague who has refused to come to the defense of a Professor Lode, at another university, who has been dismissed for working in the Wallace campaign.

Remembering the summer of 1937, spent with his friends in Europe helping refugees, Edward finds the apolitical tenor of 1949 an unbearable betrayal: "In Europe the intellectual is still part of life itself. I'm tired of being a kind of governess without real responsibility, without dignity, someone who may be turned out like Lode at any moment at the whim of the employer— and who is only considered responsible as long as he is *not* responsible" (Sarton, 121). The friend to whom he says this thinks that Edward no longer even feels so passionately about the matter but only wishes that he did.

After Edward's suicide, his friends agonize over what they might have done to save him, over the possibility that their political positions are as cowardly and expedient as Edward thought. Ultimately, they decide that their present opposition to Communism is a principled choice even though it leaves them no ideology in which to believe. They identify themselves as liberals, sure only that oppression from the Right or the Left must be resisted, and fully admitting how hard it is to break with the radical Left. When Isabel comes for her brother's funeral, her attempts to understand Edward's political passion help to break barriers and get his friends genuinely talking to one another again. *Faithful Are the Wounds* emphasizes the importance of a forgiving human community and suggests that it is a necessary basis for a decent politics. Asked by Isabel what Edward was seeking, his clergyman friend says that it was solidarity, "the communion of saints on earth" (Sarton, 181). The cruel irony of Edward's uncompromising politics, lived within the historical moment of the late 1940s, is that they cut him off from his friends. "Intolerant" is Isabel's word.

Isabel comes to explain Edward's politics as a working out of his early childhood emotions. As he hated watching his mother being stifled by family life, with him unable to help her, so he cannot tolerate merely being a witness to history. This explanation recurs often enough in the novel to suggest that Sarton herself saw psychological explanations of politics as persuasive. But, as Isabel comes to admit at least briefly the shallowness of her own apolitical life, Sarton upholds politics as more than an expression of neuroses.

Throughout the novel, characters affirm the value and rightness of Edward's refusal to be an intellectual without a political life. In the epilogue, set in 1954, we see the effect of Edward's example. Damon Phillips has been called to testify before a government committee investigating Communists on campus. Asked about his former association with Edward Cavan, Phillips becomes calm and sure and tells the committee that Edward was wrong to think that Socialists could trust Communists, but right to think that intellectuals must defend freedom of thought from the likes of the committee. His friends—Edward's friends—including George and Pen, now married, are buoyed up by his statement, even though they know he will face a contempt citation. One old friend, an old Bostonian radical spinster, finally admits that liberals may be fine and generous.

Faithful Are the Wounds conveys effectively the agonies and self-doubts of former radicals who in 1949 had honestly come to see Communism as a threat. They doubt their own political judgment. They long for the solace of an ideology. Finally, they know at least that they must stand up to McCarthyism.

Only in rather recent years have blacklisted writers and moviemakers generally been willing to take McCarthyism and the blacklist for their subject matter or even to discuss their experience. The relatively open political climate of the late 1960s and the 1970s prompted the beginning of a reexamination of the period. We can speculate, too, that only recently have those actually involved felt it safe to remind the public that they were once of interest to the HUAC. Moving into retirement, they are finally out of the reach of any blacklist and seem to have a desire to come to terms with their experience. Important moral and ethical questions are examined and debated even among those who were blacklisted: Albert Maltz strongly disagreed, for example, with the judgment of fellow screenwriter Dalton Trumbo that even those who named names were victims (Navasky, 388–401).

In 1976, Lillian Hellman published *Scoundrel Time,* an account of her experience of the blacklist, which became a best-seller. Hellman had been a supporter of Henry Wallace in the 1948 election and had been a high-profile supporter of the Cultural and Scientific Conference for World Peace, held at New York's Waldorf-Astoria hotel in 1949. In *Scoundrel Time* (1976) she describes having gone with Dashiell Hammett to several Communist Party meetings in the late 1930s, though she was not a Party member.[32] She had watched the growth of Fascism and anti-Semitism in Germany and had seen the Great Depression take its toll on America. She believed then that the Soviet Union would respect human rights once it was no longer threatened with counterrevolution and had securely instituted state Socialism.

Given her background, she could expect to be called before the HUAC. On 21 February 1952 she walked out of her apartment to meet the man who had rung to be admitted; he handed her a subpoena from the HUAC. Then began the torturous period of deciding how she would respond. As she describes in *Scoundrel Time,* her friend Abe Fortas tells her he thinks the time is right for someone to take a moral stand, agreeing to answer questions about oneself but refusing to discuss others. He admits that he could not advise this if he were her lawyer, as it would risk a contempt citation and a jail term. Hammett tells her she would be a fool to do as Fortas suggested; he has already served his jail time and knows that prison would be a horrific experience for someone of her temperament. Joseph Rauh, her lawyer, suggests reminding the committee that the Communists once attacked her play *Watch on the Rhine,* but she refuses to defend herself by making the Communists look worse.

While she is preparing for her appearance, she is surprised to receive a dinner invitation from Clifford Odets. He asks what she will tell the committee, and she simply says that she hopes she does the right thing. He tells her that he will declare his radical sentiments and defy the committee. (He testifies one day before she does, denies his radical beliefs, and repents his past.) Elia Kazan tells her that he has been warned that if he is not a friendly witness he will never direct another film. She sends a letter to the chair of HUAC, saying that she will testify about her own activities but take the Fifth Amendment if asked about others. Going to Washington early, she is nervous and aimless, starts to go home to New York, turns around before getting to the airport. When she hears that the committee has rejected her letter, she goes to the hearing prepared to take the Fifth: "I remember saying to myself, 'Just make sure you come out unashamed. That will be enough'" (Hellman, 99).

The committee asks her about people she has known slightly. She takes the Fifth. Then the committee chair criticizes her phrasing of her refusal. As she describes it, "Wood's correction of me, the irritation in his voice, was making me nervous, and I began to move my right hand as if I had a tic, unexpected, and couldn't stop it. I told myself that if a word irritated him the insults would begin to come very soon. So I sat up straight, made my left hand hold my right hand, and hoped that it would work. But I felt the sweat on my face and arms and knew that something was going to happen to me, something out of control" (Hellman, 105). She realizes that refusing to answer questions about known Communists will be interpreted as an admission of guilt. When she explains again why she will not cooperate and refers to her earlier letter, the chair agrees to have the letter entered into the record. Her lawyer takes that as permission to distribute the letter to the large press corps in attendance. As she persists in her strategy, she hears an unknown voice from the press gallery thank God that "somebody finally had the guts to do it" (Hellman, 106). Soon afterward, the committee dismisses her.

Blacklisted, she cannot make enough money to live on and to pay an IRS judgment against her. She sells her beloved farm and goes to live in Rome to write a screenplay for a fraction of what she used to get paid. While there, she reads that McCarthy himself has subpoenaed her, but it turns out to be a false story, planted by a CIA agent, apparently just to see what she would do. Back in New York, she works part-time as a department store clerk, under an assumed name, until an inheritance gives her some financial security once again. Some effects of her experience, however, are more subtle than her financial problems. She has an affair with a man she knows is a liar and a cheat; she explains, "punished by what I thought was a group of political villains, I was evidently driven to find another kind of villain and another kind of punishment" (Hellman, 129).

Hellman tells us more than once in *Scoundrel Time* that her encounter with the HUAC disillusioned her about intellectuals. She writes,

> I have written before that my shock and my anger came against what
> I thought had been the people of my world, although in many cases,
> of course, I did not know the men and women of that world except
> by name. I had, up to the late 1940s, believed that the educated, the
> intellectual, lived by what they claimed to believe: freedom of thought
> and speech, the right of each man to his own convictions, a more
> than implied promise, therefore, of aid to those who might be perse-
> cuted. But only a very few raised a finger when McCarthy and the
> boys appeared. Almost all, either by what they did or did not do,
> contributed to McCarthyism, running after a bandwagon which
> hadn't bothered to stop to pick them up. (Hellman, 38)

Hellman more than implies that those who might have opposed McCarthyism but did not were still thinking like immigrants, accustomed to dealing
with cossacks, or the children of immigrants, unwilling to give up newfound
affluence. She asks why intellectuals condemned radicals as a threat, both
in the McCarthy era and when Woodrow Wilson allowed the persecution of
the IWW, but failed to condemn the government for its violations of civil
liberties. Why, she asks, did the *Partisan Review* condemn repressive Communist regimes but never take an editorial position against McCarthyism?
Her one-dimensional answer is that radicals threaten the status quo, which
serves intellectuals well. Her judgment on the Communists themselves is
that most were sincerely trying to bring into being a better world, and their
error was in following Russia.

On sleepless nights, Hellman says in *Scoundrel Time*, she gets up and
writes the fully condemnatory statement she wishes she had had the courage
to deliver before the HUAC. Indeed, for Hellman and for many others, the
desire to write about one's encounter with McCarthyism seems motivated by
a desire to tell the other side of the story, to have one's say after being silenced
by the blacklist. Hellman's decision to revisit the era in *Scoundrel Time* also
seems motivated by the desire to have it all to do over again. Reviews of
Scoundrel Time in 1976 were largely positive. Murray Kempton, writing in
the *New York Review of Books*, praises Hellman's memoir and her courage
before the committee, although he disagrees with her recollection of some
small factual matters.[33] Admitting that Hellman was correct to be afraid at
the time, he nonetheless notes that Joseph Rauh's clients were not in much
danger of going to jail because he was known to accept only non-Communists
as clients.

Sidney Hook, reviewing for the *Encounter*,[34] strongly objects to Hellman's reconstruction of events and to her moral judgments. He insists that
Communists posed a real threat to America, that Hellman assisted the Communists, and that liberals and non-Communist Socialists did, in fact, object
to McCarthy's tactics. Hook himself was once regarded as the first Marxist
professor in the United States, in the early 1930s when he taught philosophy
at New York University. Disillusioned with the Communist Party, he was

influential in the Trotskyist American Workers Party, defined himself as a member of the anti-Stalinist Left, and then moved rightward from the 1950s onward.[35] The emergence of Hellman and others who defied McCarthyism as heroes was infuriating to Hook, who had come by the late 1940s to regard Communism as an evil and a genuine totalitarian threat. The critical position of the anti-Stalinist Left is virtually erased by the heroic stature given the HUAC martyrs, according to Hook, but, as Alan Wald notes, such might not be the case if the anti-Stalinists had been more forceful in their criticism of McCarthyism (Wald, 311–12).

= The Twentieth Party Congress: = Denunciation and Disillusionment

The CPUSA, cause célèbre of the postwar years, had been bereft of its top leadership in 1949, when Eugene Dennis and 10 others were convicted under the Smith Act of having conspired to teach and advocate the overthrow of the government. The replacement of the CPA with the CPUSA loomed large in the case against the defendants as evidence that the Party was revolutionary and not reformist. True to their belief that American justice always operates in the interests of the propertied class, the defendants regarded it as a waste of time to make arguments based on constitutionality or the rules of evidence; instead, they used the trial as a forum for Marxist argument (Fried, 94). All were found guilty, even though none was shown personally to have planned or promoted any violence against the government.

If early events of the Cold War prompted Americans generally to fear imminent conflict between East and West and domestic upheavals as well, they prompted Communist leaders to the same kind of apocalyptic thinking, and they adopted what came to be known as the "five minutes to midnight" strategy (Isserman, 246). Four of the 11 convicted leaders evaded federal marshals rather than surrender and begin their prison terms after their convictions were upheld in 1951. The Party went underground and dropped from its rolls any member whose loyalty was not demonstrable. Though understandable, the decision to go underground simply reinforced the image of the Party as a lawless and secret conspiracy. Only in 1954 did the Party begin to operate in the open again.

The national committee of the CPUSA was meeting in April 1956 for the first time in five years when it heard Eugene Dennis, just released from prison in January, argue that the Party had been wrong in thinking that conflict was imminent. His speech was no endorsement of Browderism, but it represented an admission that Browder's analysis had been no further from the truth than Foster's. Then he read to the committee the speech that Nikita Khrushchev had delivered to the Twentieth Party Congress in closed session back in February. In it, Khrushchev details Stalin's crimes: mass executions, phony trials, torture, the elimination of dissent by any means. Thus did the Soviet premier admit that the accusations against which Communists had for years been loyally defending Stalin were, in fact, true. In November 1956, Soviet tanks moved into Hungary to bring that country back in line with Soviet policies.

To American Communists, who had borne so much in the name of their political ideals, the Khrushchev revelations were profoundly disturbing because they showed undeniably that Stalin had made a travesty of those ideals. To feel revulsion even at *some* of what had been done in the name of Communism was to admit the falsity of a simple dichotomy in which the HUAC stood for duplicity and corruption and the Party stood for righteousness and for the people. By the summer of 1958, the Party is estimated to have had no more than 3,000 members (Isserman, 254). Those who left between 1956 and 1958 included most who had tried in that time and failed to reorient the CPUSA away from Moscow.

Why would someone at this point remain loyal to an organization that had more than once changed its line, required uncritical support of the Soviet Union, proved ineffective in leading the masses toward revolution, and finally become the object of a witch-hunt? The answers must be various. Some might have stayed because their Party work gave them some authority, and they were reluctant to give up whatever power they had in the organization. Some may have stayed because they had already invested in the Party so much of their lives, their energies, and their hopes that to give up on it would be to condemn their own pasts. Still others may have stayed because they still found the CPUSA more attractive than the HUAC. Others may have remained because they found the Party in the 1950s and early 1960s one of the few organizational backers for work in racial justice and radical labor education.

One of Vivian Gornick's interviewees for *The Romance of American Communism* was Marian Moran, a Party leader in one of the western states. A woman of integrity, Moran still remained a member of the Party until the 1968 Soviet invasion of Czechoslovakia. Describing her response to the reading of Khrushchev's speech, she writes, Dennis "began to speak at seven o'clock. At eight I began to cry. I sat there, silently weeping, until eleven o'clock. Then I took a plane back to California to tell my people that we had made a great error in learning to depend on anyone but ourselves" (Gornick, 96–97). Gornick, seeking to understand Moran's continued membership in the Party, notes the importance to Moran of the farm labor strikes in California during the 1930s: "What happened to Marian Moran in the Thirties in the United States is what happened to George Orwell in the Thirties in Spain. For a single moment Socialism came to life, for a single moment they each felt themselves at one with all other men and women in the world; the living meaning of a classless society—void of privilege and unequal power, alive with genuine comradeship—sank into them and changed each of them, influencing thought and action for the rest of their lives" (Gornick, 96–97). Living as a Leftist is sometimes to live *within* the Left ideal, to experience during the course of the struggle the society one is struggling to create. After such a powerfully positive experience, it is difficult to break with the organization that called that experience into being.

After the events of 1956 had reduced CPUSA membership and marginalized the Party, the Old Left as a movement was effectively over. The Party continued to organize and to educate, and Party-sponsored organizations provided important training and resources for the New Left of the 1960s.[36] Many leaders of the New Left were "red-diaper babies," that is, the children of Old Left parents, in whose houses they had learned Leftist values and history. So conscious of history was the New Left that it wanted a clean break with the past; in particular, it distanced itself from Russian influence and Russian models and refused to allow theory to dictate strategy.

=== Conclusion ===

Ironically, investigation of un-American activity in the 1950s focused not on people's activities but on their present and more often their past beliefs and allegiances. As in the trial of Sacco and Vanzetti, people were judged not on what they had done but on their politics. Evidence indicates that the CPUSA *did* spy for the Soviet Union during the Cold War, as McCarthy charged. But as Harvey Klehr, John Earl Haynes, and Fridrikh Igorevich Firson note in *The Secret World of American Communism,* "[t]his conspiratorial organization . . . assisted Soviet intelligence and placed loyalty to the Soviet Union ahead of loyalty to the United States. To say this is not to claim that every American Communist was disloyal. Americans became Communists for a wide variety of motives, many of them entirely honorable and decent. . . . The overwhelming majority had nothing to do with espionage."[37] It would be neither accurate nor useful to generalize and portray Communists as either Soviet-directed spies or innocent victims of a witch-hunt; doing so would conflate the Party organization and all of its diverse membership.

The Party's culture of secrecy, its use of front groups, its capacity for duplicity and deception made it easier for Americans to believe that every Communist was a spy or a policy saboteur, and the more cynical manipulators of McCarthyism were happy to foster that impression. Frightened Americans were willing, for a time, to allow flagrant abuse of the civil liberties and protections that are at the heart of American freedom. Once named, people were presumed guilty until they could clear themselves, often an impossibility, as the word of one government witness was sufficiently damning. Those who invoked the Fifth Amendment were presumed guilty and, though safe from criminal prosecution, were labeled Fifth Amendment Communists and almost invariably blacklisted. The HUAC, the SISS, the Government Operations Subcommittee on Investigations (chaired by McCarthy himself), and the various state un-American activities committees all operated as a quasi-judiciary, where the accused had none of the constitutional protections of the real judiciary, and blacklisting was the unspoken sentence for those who could not or would not clear themselves.

The 1940s and 1950s were difficult decades to be a Leftist, as Rose Pesotta's memoir and Tom McGrath's poetry remind us. No clear path ran through the political landscape. Not only was the Left under attack, but the geography of the Left itself seemed to be shifting, with the CPUSA going to CPA and back again, with the Cold War split between Communists and liberals widening, with animosity growing between Communists and the labor movement. As May Sarton illustrates in *Faithful Are the Wounds*, finding ground on which to stand, comfortably, was extremely difficult in that era. In such circumstances, it is easy to feel that, whatever one chooses, one has betrayed someone or something. The image of the spy or the subversive or the agent, such as the rogue CIA operative who figures in the Rome section of *Scoundrel Time*, is recurrent in the popular culture of the 1950s in the writing of Leftists and also in books like Herbert A. Philbrick's *I Led Three Lives: Citizen, "Communist," Counterspy* (1950).[38] Philbrick's memoir, recounting his years as a double agent for the FBI and leading up to his testimony at the trial of the Communist leaders in 1949, was also the basis for a weekly television program in the 1950s.

Waiting to be named, perhaps hoping to avoid the subpoena-server by holding an unlisted phone number, Communists and former Communists and non-Communists who might have supported Left causes lived in fear of being called and accused and blacklisted. Having experienced political reprisals, they must have found the 1956 revelations of Stalin's political crimes all the more galling. A remnant would continue to defend Stalinism and the Soviet model of state Socialism. Others would repent that they had ever been "duped" by Communism and become vociferous defenders of the American way. Still others would continue to be proud of the anti-Fascist, antiracist, prolabor work they had done with the help of the CPUSA and reflect on the point at which "the Party line" became unacceptable either in its policy or in its authoritarianism. Veterans and observers have continued to debate whether the Third Period or the Popular Front best represented the true role of the Party. Debate has continued about the meaning of the movement's demise: does it indicate a failure of leadership? of strategy? of state Socialism? of Socialism generally? In questions such as these the political struggle continues.

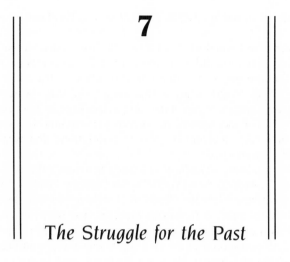

7

The Struggle for the Past

THE POWER TO CHARACTERIZE THE OLD LEFT IS THE POWER TO SAY
what ended when the movement ended, whether that was a foolish dependence on Moscow or an excessive dependence on theory, a premature encounter with history, the enthusiasm for state Socialism, or the Leftist vision
itself. Those on the Right would generally like to read into the passing of the
Old Left and then the New Left the discrediting of all forms of Socialism.
Leftists must necessarily believe that the experience of the Old Left simply
contributes valuable lessons about which forms of government or self-government are desirable and which are not, about appropriate and inappropriate
strategies, and about the relationship between ends and means. A similar
struggle is waged over the characterization of the participants in the Old
Left. If they can be seen as sinister subversives or naive dupes, that characterization discourages sympathy for any Left ideas, program, or movement.
On the contrary, if they can be seen as compassionate, self-sacrificing, and
ultimately victimized, their stature vindicates and elevates the Left. Along
with the struggle to characterize the movement, there continues the struggle

to understand, in human as well as political terms, the experience of the Old Left.

This volume will conclude with a look at three retrospective considerations of the Old Left, from different times and different perspectives. It would be impossible to represent the full range of response to the Old Left without undertaking a book-length study of that alone. The three works chosen do not even represent the extremes of the range. Recent years have seen publication of a number of memoirs of movement participants, but we pass over these in favor of the perspective of later generations and writers neither hostile nor fully supportive.

Lorraine Hansberry's *The Sign in Sidney Brustein's Window*[1] opened at the Longacre Theater in New York City in October 1964 and ran for 101 performances, closing after the death of Hansberry, at age 34, in January 1965. Her previous play, *A Raisin in the Sun,* had won her critical praise and acclaim as the greatest African-American dramatist of her generation. She was an active supporter of the civil rights movement and helped to raise funds to send James Chaney, Mickey Schwerner, and Andrew Goodman to Mississippi, where they were slain for enlisting black voter registration.[2] In such an atmosphere, one might have expected her to write a play about the civil rights movement, but instead she took on a larger political question. Writing about *Sidney Brustein* in an article for the Sunday *New York Times,* she explained:

> I am of the generation which grew up in the swirl and dash of the Sartre-Camus debate of the postwar years. The silhouette of the Western intellectual poised in hesitation before the flames of involvement was an accurate symbolism of some of my closest friends, some of whom crossed each other leaping in and out, for instance, of the Communist Party. Others searched, as agonizingly, for some ultimate justification of their lives in the abstractions flowing out of London or Paris. Still others were contorted into seeking a meaningful repudiation of *all* justification of anything. . . . Mine is, after all, the generation that had come to maturity drinking in the forebodings of the Silones, Koestlers and Richard Wrights. It had left us unprepared for decisions that had to be made in our own time about Algeria, Birmingham or the Bay of Pigs. By the 1960's few enough American intellectuals had it within them to be ashamed that their discovery of the "betrayal" of the Cuban Revolution by Castro just happened to coincide with the change of heart of official American government policy. . . . It is the climate and mood of such intellectuals, if not these particular events, which constitute the core of a play called *The Sign in Sidney Brustein's Window.* (Quoted in Nemiroff, xv–xvi)

The play is set in Greenwich Village in the late spring of 1964. Sidney, in his late 30s, has just folded the Silver Dagger, his folk-music club, because it couldn't compete with all the other folk-music clubs in the Village. His next project is to be a small newspaper that he has recently bought and intends to make a vehicle for discussion of art and ideas, *not* politics. In fact, when Wally O'Hara, a reform candidate for city office, asks for his endorsement, he refuses, saying, "Politics are for people who have those kinds of interests, that's all. I don't happen to have them any more" (Hansberry, 21). Sidney's friend Alton Scales, an African-American ex-Communist, separated from the Party since the Soviet invasion of Hungary in 1956, answers, "There it is, man! We are confronted with the great disease of the modern bourgeois intellectual: *ostrich*-ism. I've been watching it happen to this one; the great sad withdrawal from the affairs of men" (Hansberry, 21–22). Confronted with such mock-accusation, Sidney admits that he has lost the energy that fueled his days as a campus radical: "Since I was eighteen I've belonged to every committee To Save, To Abolish, Prohibit, Preserve, Reserve and Conserve that ever was. . . . I simply can no longer bear the spectacle of the hatchery of power-driven insurgents trying at all costs to gain control—of the refreshment committee!" (Hansberry, 23).

Sidney's wife, Iris, is increasingly discontented with him and with her acting career, which is going nowhere. She hates the sexual impositions and the general indignities foisted on actresses when they read for a part. Sidney confronts her with her refusal even to try to get an acting job, but then tells her that talent isn't always rewarded with success; a lot of people simply get trampled in the rush. She answers that he blames society for everything when in fact people have to take responsibility for themselves. The Brusteins' upstairs neighbor, David, is a gay playwright who believes only in personal integrity. When Gloria, Iris's sister, writes that Alton has asked her to marry him, Sidney and Iris decide to leave it to Gloria to tell Alton that she is a call girl.

Sidney fantasizes about an idealized Appalachian scene of bucolic simplicity and likes Iris to wear her hair long and straight—Appalachian style. But in the real world, he has, predictably, chosen to get involved in O'Hara's campaign. He puts a campaign sign in his window, supports O'Hara in his newspaper, and canvasses for the campaign. David objects that good guy/bad guy politics went out with World War II, but Sidney explains, "The 'why' of why we are here is an intrigue for adolescents; the 'how' is what must command the living. Which is why I have lately become an insurgent again" (Hansberry, 82). He himself is surprised and elated when O'Hara wins.

When Alton finds out that Gloria is a call girl, he writes her a letter of good-bye. Iris gets a commercial selling home permanents and, in preparation, has been sent to an expensive salon to have her hair restyled. Sidney confronts her with the deception involved in this, and she tells him that she just needs to do something in her life and, besides, doesn't he know that O'Hara is really a front for the same old political machine? Can he be so naive? She walks out, and he drinks. He is already drunk when Gloria arrives, gets Alton's letter, and despairingly accepts David's offer that she play a role in his seduction of a young man he very much wants, a man who would like to have her "watching." But instead of going upstairs, she retreats to the bathroom and ends her life as Sidney lies passed out on the sofa.

In the last scene, O'Hara tells Sidney not to work against him or he will lose his newspaper. But Sidney tells him that he will be back out in the streets that very day to begin exposing O'Hara's connections to the machine. Iris comes back to Sidney because he is again whole, and he says that he believes "that people want to be better than they are . . . and that I hurt terribly today, and that hurt is desperation and desperation is—energy and energy can *move* things" (Hansberry, 142).

Thus Hansberry depicts the political malaise of a man disillusioned with organized politics, not only because of Stalinist aggression but also because of power grabs and group infighting over minutiae. She effectively delineates the difficulty of Iris, who does not want to compromise herself in order to work as an actress but is also wary of blaming her stalled career on the commodity culture; having "dropped out," she is purposeless and wonders what she might have done. David finds meaning writing plays about the impossibility of communication, but even his success seems compromised: real people, like Gloria, continue to die, all abstractions aside. Despite being duped by O'Hara, Sidney commits again to a political life, even in the face of the threat to close down his newspaper and in spite of the errors into which political action can lead. His commitment is a local one—for reform in his neighborhood—and not a commitment to world revolution. On the local scene, he can hope for greater clarity and freedom from any party line.

The Sign in Sidney Brustein's Window is Hansberry's analysis of the political passivity that followed the McCarthy era and the revelations of the Twentieth Party Congress as well as the numerous personal disillusionments, like Sidney's, over infighting and ineffectuality. But the characters she portrays are unable to find meaning without political commitment. Sidney's folk club and Iris's acting are both failed attempts to occupy a nonpolitical space, one neither a part of the commodity culture nor in opposition to it. That space, finally, doesn't exist for them. As Hansberry's attempt to redefine useful political activity, *The Sign* met with a strongly positive response from many in the intellectual and theatrical communities. Early reviews were not strong enough, however, to ensure advance ticket sales, and the play survived its 101 performances only with the help of donated funds and services and paid endorsement ads in the *New York Times* (Nemiroff, xxxviii). Produced just before the New Left became a recognized political force, *The Sign in Sidney Brustein's Window* seems to have been a call that Sidney's generation was not sure it wanted to hear.

In a very different tone, John Sayles's "At the Anarchists' Convention" appeared first in the *Atlantic Monthly* in 1979 and was reprinted in the collection *At the Anarchists' Convention* in 1979.[3] The narrator is Leo Gold, who has skipped the last two annual anarchists' conventions because he has been feuding with Brickman, a fellow anarchist, who has now died. Sophie, an old comrade, particularly urges him to attend, and it becomes clear that he will do anything for her. Indeed, his anger at Brickman stems from an affair between Brickman and Sophie years back. The anarchists used to convene at the New Yorker hotel, but it has been taken over by "the Korean and his Jesus children" (Sayles, 21), so they have booked another hotel. This one, however, is owned by the Mormons—mistyped as "Normans" in the protest leaflet got up on the spot. An anarchist cartoonist has festooned the lobby of their meeting room with a poster of Bakunin, throwing a bomb. "Personally, I think it's in bad taste, the bomb-throwing bit. It's the enemy's job to ridicule, not ours," thinks Leo (Sayles, 25). People keep telling Leo they thought he was dead, and he tells them it's a matter of hours. Students from Barnard, armed with tape recorders, are collecting oral history. One conventioneer has scruples about being served by the hotel staff and thinks they all should serve themselves; one has been boycotting grapes so long that she can't stop; factions spring up over whether to elect next year's committee before or after dinner. All the issues are discussed, "At the top of their voices, in the manner of old Lefties." Brickman is remembered in a eulogy, and then his comrades rise to say a few words about him. "Little Papas, who we never thought would survive the beating he took one May Day scuffle . . . stands and tells of Brickman saving the mimeograph machine when they burned our office on 27th Street" (Sayles, 30). Finally, Leo himself rises and gives a tribute to Brickman.

The squabbling over procedure begins to take the heart out of Leo: "Three thousand collective years of frustration in the room, turning inward, a *cancer* of frustration. It's the sound of parents brawling each other because they can't feed their kids, the sound of prisoners preying on each other because the guards are out of reach, the sound of a terribly deep despair" (Sayles, 32). But then the hotel manager arrives and tells them that they will have to move to another room because a mistake has been made and this one had been previously booked by the Rotary Club. As he speaks, Rotarians are gathering edgily around Bakunin in the lobby. The anarchists won't move. One calls the newspaper; one calls for resistance; the Barnard students tape everything. Finally, with no bickering, the conventioneers move into action and barricade the door, singing "We Shall Not Be Moved." Sophie takes Leo's hand, and he feels the old thrill, and even wishes that Brickman were there to add his weight to the good fight.

Two emotions loom large in the story: Leo's despair at fighting within the group, and his profound and lasting affection for his anarchist comrades. Sayles has Leo explain the bickering as an expression of frustration when the group cannot turn outside events their way. It disappears the moment they can mobilize for the fight. The struggle, as always, brings out the best in them. Holding a meeting room against the Rotarians is a pointless exercise, but it is an expression of principle, and giving themselves to that creates once again for the anarchists the community that is, in itself, a realization of the Left ideal.

To Kim Chernin, the Old Left is a generation removed. She wrote *In My Mother's House* (1983) because her mother asked her to write her story.[4] But the book is more than a biography of a Communist organizer, the first person whose citizenship the government tried to revoke during the McCarthy era. It is also the story of a mother-daughter relationship, inextricable from the politics and history of this century. Rose Chernin, born in a Russian shtetl in 1903, became interested in Left politics because of the economic constraints on her own life and those of her mother and sisters. Her husband-to-be gave her a copy of the *Call,* and in New York she joined the circle of radical unionists: "We knew there was something going through the world, the Ladies Garment Workers unionizing, the furriers becoming militant. And of course the Russian Revolution had occurred" (Chernin, 55). Of that she explained, "In Russia, the czar had been the torment of the Jewish people. He had always been there. How could we imagine the people would be able to drive away the czar? Think only. If this could happen to the czar, what now could not happen in a person's life?" (Chernin, 56). In 1928 or 1929, she joined the Communist Party.

For Rose Chernin, the 1930s were an exhilarating time to be doing political work. She recalls the sense of empowerment she felt being one of the huge, chanting crowd at the unemployment demonstration in March 1930 and working for the Unemployed Councils, resisting evictions and organizing rent strikes. She says, "In those years I was happy. In those years I became what I have been all my life since then" (Chernin, 95). Then she and her husband are invited to work in the Soviet Union, and what they see there at that time is the boundless enthusiasm of people for building Socialism: people volunteer for extra hours building the subway; they party in the streets as they complete another length of tunnel; women insist on equal work and get their demands. The murder of Sergei Kirov in 1934, however, worries Rose, because it suggests a conflict within the state, a threat to the society she admires so much.

She returns to live in America again only because she feels that the workers there deserve all the help they can get in the struggle. In 1950, she organizes a group to fight against the threatened deportation of foreign-born Communists. In July 1951, she is arrested under the Smith Act and spends six months in jail because her bail is set at the impossibly high sum of $100,000. Her daughter, Kim, has always admired her mother and wanted to be like her. With her mother's arrest, she finds that she cannot sleep, that her friends at school shun her, that she is at once afraid for her mother and angry at her for being in the situation she is in. When publicity dies down, the "in" crowd at her high school are willing to accept her, and she joins them, glad not to be an outsider but also feeling that she is betraying her mother by associating with a group that tells racist jokes and takes affluence for granted. Reading the Khrushchev report in 1956 and traveling to the Soviet Union in 1957 convince her that the Socialist dream has not been realized there. This change in her political posture creates a gulf between her and her mother. *In My Mother's House* is primarily concerned with the years and the effort it took to bridge that gulf.

To choose the life of a poet over the life of a political activist feels to Kim Chernin like a betrayal of her mother, and it means for her a break with the dreams and the culture in which she was raised. She recognizes, too, that in her rejection of her mother's politics she is punishing her mother for being away from the family so much, for having so much in her life that she could not or would not share with her daughter, even if Rose's motive was to protect her. Political hopes and disillusionments are inseparable from more personal elements of their relationship. Kim writes, "I realize that it is I who have never really forgiven her for remaining a Communist under circumstances that drove me away from the Party and destroyed my faith. But tonight, in a rush of urgent awareness, I realize that the value of her life's work did not depend upon the triumph of Socialism anywhere in the world" (Chernin, 263). Answering a question from her own daughter, she says, "Maybe she's been able to do what she's done because she believes so strongly in something. There are hundreds of people who would have been jailed or deported if it weren't for her. Or some other organizer with the same system of belief. It makes you wonder, should you judge a life by the ideology that inspires it? Or by what that ideology, true or false, inspires the life to do?" (Chernin, 301).

Other children of Old Left parents may still decide to follow their political lead, or they may be bitter that their parents gave so much of themselves outside the family. They may be angry at society for the fear they suffered during the 1950s or angry at their parents for making choices that put them at risk. They may be grateful for growing up with the Left dream or resentful about being raised in an oppositional culture that made them outsiders. *In My Mother's House* is the story of just one lineage of mothers and daughters, but it is an important contribution to the understanding of the Old Left, reminding us that the movement made family history as well as political history. In many ways, *In My Mother's House* is Kim Chernin's story about *not* being a Communist, just as the opening of *The Sign in Sidney Brustein's Window* is structured around the absence of the Old Left political commitment—a palpable absence.

CHRONOLOGY

1912   In January Bread and Roses strike won in the textile mills of Lawrence, Massachusetts. In December Max Eastman takes over editorship of *Masses* and makes it a magazine of revolutionary Socialism.

1917   Russian Revolution overthrows the czar and installs Kerensky government in February (March). (Dates for events in Russia are given first according to the Russian calendar in use in 1917 and then, in parentheses, according to the new calendar. The new calendar matches Western dating.) Bolshevik Party takes control of Russia in October (November).

1918   IWW leaders convicted in a mass trial in Chicago during the summer.

1919   African Americans are targets of violence during the summer as veterans return from World War I and search for scarce jobs. John Reed publishes *Ten Days that Shook the World*. The Communist Party and the Communist Labor Party are founded in the United States during August and September. Emma Goldman and Alexander Berkman are among deportees sent to Soviet Russia on the ship *Buford* in December.

1920   Palmer raids in January result in deportation and jailing of radicals as
        Red Scare continues.

1922   Communist parties in the United States come above ground and unite
        in a single party, then called the Workers (Communist) Party.

1925   A. Philip Randolph begins organizing the Brotherhood of Sleeping Car
        Porters.

1926   *New Masses* begins publication in May. Eugene Debs dies 20 October,
        and Norman Thomas becomes the leader of the Socialist Party.

1927   Sacco and Vanzetti are executed 23 August.

1928   The Communist League of America is founded 27 October, represent-
        ing Trotskyism in America.

1929   Agnes Smedley publishes *Daughter of Earth*. Trade Union Unity
        League (TUUL) is founded in August to replace the Trade Union
        Educational League (TUEL); the change signals the American re-
        sponse to the Third Period, in which reformist organizations were
        targeted as the greatest threat to revolution. Stock market crash in
        October ushers in the era of the Great Depression.

1930   Mike Gold's *Jews without Money* and Mary Heaton Vorse's *Strike!* are
        published. Unemployed stage large demonstrations 6 March, prompted
        by the Communist Party. International Conference of Proletarian-Revo-
        lutionary Writers, held at Kharkov in November, instructs the Ameri-
        can delegates to foster proletarian literature; the John Reed Clubs are
        founded in response.

1931   "Scottsboro boys" are arrested 25 March.

1932   Waldo Frank leads a fact-finding delegation in February to Harlan
        County, Kentucky, scene of conflict over coal miners' organizing. In
        September, 53 artists and intellectuals sign the pamphlet *Culture and
        Crisis,* espousing a radical political approach to American economic
        and social problems.

1933   Jack Conroy publishes *The Disinherited*, an early example of what has
        been called the "proletarian novel." First issue of the *Catholic Worker*
        is published 1 May.

1935   *Waiting for Lefty* is produced. From the spring through the fall, the
        CPUSA joins other Communist parties worldwide in initiating the Pop-
        ular Front era, in which the parties would join anti-Fascist coalitions
        within their countries. The League of American Writers replaces John
        Reed Clubs. A meat boycott during the summer reflects organizing
        among consumers.

1936   James T. Farrell publishes *A Note on Literary Criticism*. The Spanish
        Revolution begins in July.

1937   Sit-down strike at General Motors plant in Flint, Michigan, in January
        establishes that the Congress of Industrial Organizations (CIO) is here
        to stay.

1939   Madrid falls 28 March, ending the Spanish Revolution. Nazi-Soviet non-aggression pact is signed 23 August, ending the Popular Front.

1940   Smith Act is adopted, making it a criminal offense to teach or advocate the overthrow of the U.S. government.

1941   German army invades Soviet territory 22 June, ending the Nazi-Soviet pact and making the CPUSA an enthusiastic supporter of U.S. entry into World War II.

1944   The CPUSA becomes the Communist Political Association (CPA) in May.

1945   Duclos letter prompts return of CPA to CPUSA in April.

1949   Richard Wright and other intellectuals publish their disaffection from Communism in Richard Crossman's *The God that Failed*.

1950   In February Sen. Joseph McCarthy claims to have a list of Communists employed in the State Department.

1953   Julius and Ethel Rosenberg are executed 19 June.

1954   Senate censures Joseph McCarthy 2 December.

1956   At Twentieth Party Congress in February, Nikita Khrushchev accuses Josef Stalin of mass executions, starvations, and deportations.

NOTES AND REFERENCES

Introduction

1. For an overview of the historiography of American Communism, see Maurice Isserman, "Three Generations: Historians View American Communism," *Labor History* 26 (1985): 517–45.

2. On the friction between generations, see Theodore Draper, "American Communism Revisited," *New York Review of Books,* 9 May 1985, 32–37, "The Popular Front Revisited," *New York Review of Books,* 30 May 1985, 44–50, and "The Life of the Party," *New York Review of Books,* 13 January 1994, 45–51; Michael E. Brown, Introduction, in *New Studies in the Politics and Culture of U.S. Communism,* ed. Michael E. Brown, Randy Martin, Frank Rosengarten, and George Snedeker (New York: Monthly Review Press, 1993), 15–44.

3. Walter B. Rideout, *The Radical Novel in the United States, 1900–1954* (Cambridge: Harvard University Press, 1956), vii. Subsequent references to this work will be cited in the text.

4. A. B. Magil, interviewed in 1980 by Paul Buhle for the Oral History of the American Left, series 1, tape 150, Tamiment Library, New York University. Subsequent references to this oral history project will be cited as OHAL.

Chapter 1

1. Richard Flacks, *Making History: The American Left and the American Mind* (New York: Columbia University Press, 1988), 100–101. Subsequent references to this work will be cited in the text.

2. Margaret Anderson, *My Thirty Years' War* (New York: Horizon Press, 1969), 152–53. Subsequent references to this work will be cited in the text.

3. Mari Jo Buhle, *Women and American Socialism, 1870–1920* (Urbana: University of Illinois Press, 1983), 258. Subsequent references to this work will be cited in the text.

4. Daniel Aaron, *Writers on the Left* (1961; reprint, New York: Columbia University Press, 1992), 20. Subsequent references to this work will be cited in the text.

5. Max Eastman, "Knowledge and Revolution," *Masses* 4 (December 1912).

6. Max Eastman, "Editorial Notice," *Masses* 4 (December 1912).

7. Max Eastman, "Confessions of a Suffrage Orator," *Masses* 7 (November 1915).

8. Eugene Wood, "Foolish Female Fashions," *Masses* 8 (December 1912).

9. Mary Heaton Vorse, "The Two-Faced Goddess," *Masses* 4 (December 1912).

10. Floyd Dell, "Feminism for Men," *Masses* 5 (July 1914).

11. Margaret C. Jones, *Heretics and Hellraisers: Women Contributors to the "Masses," 1911–1917* (Austin: University of Texas Press, 1993), 27. Subsequent references to this work will be cited in the text.

12. Anarchist theory has continued to develop in the twentieth century. See Lewis Herber, *Post-Scarcity Anarchism*, (Berkeley: Ramparts, 1971); Lewis Herber, *The Limits of the City*, by Murray Bookchin (1974; reprint, New York: Harper & Row, 1979); and Murray Bookchin, *The Modern Crisis* (Philadelphia: New Society, 1986). See also Susanne Gowan, George Lakey, William Moyer, and Richard Taylor, *Moving toward a New Society* (Philadelphia: New Society, 1976), and Colin Ward, *Anarchy in Action* (London: Freedom Press, 1988).

13. Pierre Joseph Proudhon, *Qu'est-ce que la Propriété?*, 1840, trans. Benjamin Tucker, 1876. See also *Selected Writings of P. J. Proudhon*, ed. Stewart Edwards (New York: Anchor, 1969), and selections in *The Anarchist Reader*, ed. George Woodcock (London: Fontana Press, 1977).

14. Michael Bakunin, *Statism and Anarchy*, trans. and ed. Marshall S. Shatz (Cambridge: Cambridge University Press, 1990); see also selections in *The Anarchist Reader*, ed. George Woodcock (London: Fontana Press, 1977).

15. Karl Marx and Friedrich Engels, *German Ideology*, ed. Roy Pascal (New York: International, 1947), 5:23, 119ff.

16. Karl Marx, *The Poverty of Philosophy* (New York: International, 1963), 196. Whereas capitalists generally argue that an "exchange" of labor for wages or an "exchange" of money for products is fair if both parties agree to it, Marx argues that exchanges under the capitalist system are not fair because labor creates a profit, or "surplus value," for the employer.

17. Peter Kropotkin, *Mutual Aid* (New York: McClure Phillips, 1903), *The Conquest of Bread* (New York: New York University Press, 1972), and *Fields,*

Factories, and Workshops (New York: Putnam's, 1901). See also *The Essential Kropotkin,* edited by Emile Capouya and Keith Tompkins (New York: Liveright, 1975). See also selections in *The Anarchist Reader,* ed. Woodcock.

18. See George Lakey, *A Manifesto for a Nonviolent Society* (Philadelphia: New Society, n.d.).

19. George Woodcock, "Anarchism: A Historical Introduction," in *The Anarchist Reader,* ed. Woodcock, 43.

20. Marian J. Morton, *Emma Goldman and the American Left: Nowhere at Home* (New York: Twayne, 1992), 29. Subsequent references to this work will be cited in the text.

21. Irving Howe, *World of Our Fathers* (New York: Harcourt, Brace, Jovanovich, 1976), 107.

22. Margaret S. Marsh, *Anarchist Women, 1870–1920* (Philadelphia: Temple University Press, 1981), 20–21.

23. Emma Goldman, *Anarchism and Other Essays* (1910; reprint, Port Washington, N.Y.: Kennikat Press, 1963), 230.

24. Alexander Berkman, "Planning Judicial Murder," *Mother Earth,* September 1916, 603.

25. Floyd Dell, *Homecoming* (New York: Farrar and Rinehard, 1933), 69. Subsequent references to this work will be cited in the text.

26. Floyd Dell, *Love in Greenwich Village* (1926; reprint, Freeport, N.Y.: Books for Libraries Press, 1970). Subsequent references to this work will be cited in the text.

27. Floyd Dell, *Women as World Builders* (Chicago: Forbes, 1913).

28. Dan Georgakas, "The IWW Reconsidered," in *Solidarity Forever,* ed. Stewart Bird, Dan Georgakas, and Deborah Shaffer (1985; reprint, London: Lawrence and Wishart, 1987), 6. Subsequent references to this work will be cited in the text.

29. Melvyn Dubofsky, *We Shall Be All: A History of the Industrial Workers of the World,* 2d ed. (Urbana: University of Illinois Press, 1988), 149–51. Subsequent references to this work will be cited in the text.

30. Herb Edwards, interviewed for OHAL, series 1, transcript. Subsequent references to this interview will be cited in the text.

31. Michael Topp, "Lawrence Strike," in *Encyclopedia of the American Left,* ed. Mari Jo Buhle, Paul Buhle, and Dan Georgakas (Urbana: University of Illinois Press, 1990; Illini ed., 1992), 412–13.

32. *I.W.W. Songs: To Fan the Flames of Discontent,* 19th ed. (1923; reprint, Chicago: Charles H. Kerr, 1989).

33. Cynthia Stretch, " 'One Big Union': The *Little Red Songbook* and the Production of Oppositional Community," Twentieth-Century Literature Conference, Louisville, Ky., February 1993.

34. Paul Buhle, *Marxism in the USA: From 1870 to the Present Day* (London: Verso, 1987), 86–88. Subsequent references to this work will be cited in the text.

35. John Graham, "Appeal to Reason," in *Encyclopedia of the American Left,* ed. M. J. Buhle, P. Buhle, and Georgakas, 51.

36. Ernest Untermann, *Marxian Economics: A Popular Introduction to the Three Volumes of Marx's Capital* (Chicago: Kerr, 1907).

37. Walter Rauschenbusch, *Christianizing the Social Order* (New York: Macmillan, 1912).

38. Melvyn Dubofsky, *When Workers Organize: New York City in the Progressive Era* (Amherst: University of Massachusetts Press, 1968), 25–26.

39. Irwin Yellowitz, *Labor and the Progressive Movement in New York State, 1897–1916* (Ithaca: Cornell University Press, 1965), 125–26.

40. Joseph McShane, *Sufficiently Radical: Catholicism, Progressivism, and the Bishops' Program of 1919* ((Washington, D.C.: Catholic University Press, 1986). Subsequent references to this work will be cited in the text.

41. For a discussion of these movements, see Mark Holloway, *Heavens on Earth: Utopian Communities in America, 1680–1880,* 2d ed. (New York: Dover, 1966).

42. For an overview of the debate about the relationship of modernism and radicalism, see Marianne DeKoven, *Rich and Strange: Gender, History, Modernism* (Princeton: Princeton University Press, 1992). DeKoven argues that modernism is not a repudiation of radical politics.

Chapter 2

1. Max Eastman, "Knowledge and Revolution," *Masses* 5 (September 1914).

2. John Reed, "This Unpopular War," *Seven Arts*, August 1917.

3. Max Eastman, "Knowledge and Revolution," *Masses* 6 (October 1914).

4. William English Walling, "Hurray for the German Socialists," *Masses* 6 (October 1914).

5. Arthur Bullard, "To American Socialists," *Masses* 6 (November 1914).

6. Max Eastman, "Revolutionary Progress," *Masses* 9 (April 1917). Subsequent references to this work will be cited in the text.

7. John Reed, "Revolutionary Progress," *Masses* 9 (May 1917).

8. John Reed, "Revolutionary Progress," *Masses* 9 (June 1917).

9. John Reed, "The Russian Peace," *Masses* 9 (July 1917).

10. Max Eastman, "Revolutionary Progress: Syndicalist-Socialist Russia," *Masses* 9 (August 1917).

11. Granville Hicks, *John Reed* (New York: Macmillan, 1936), 244. Subsequent references to this work will be cited in the text.

12. Dorothy Day, *From Union Square to Rome* (Silver Spring, Md.: Preservation of the Faith Press, 1938), 80.

13. Max Eastman, "Revolutionary Progress," *Masses* 9 (September 1917).

14. John Reed, *Ten Days That Shook the World*, intro. A. J. P. Taylor (1919; reprint, London: Penguin, 1977), 9. Subsequent references to this work will be cited in the text.

15. David C. Duke, *John Reed* (Boston: Twayne, 1987), 14. Subsequent references to this work will be cited in the text.

16. Theodore Draper, *The Roots of American Communism* (1957; reprint, Chicago: Ivan R. Dee, 1989), 115. Subsequent references to this work will be cited in the text.

17. Alice Wexler, *Emma Goldman: An Intimate Life* (London: Virago Press, 1984), 235–36. Subsequent references to this work will be cited in the text.

18. Emma Goldman, *My Disillusionment in Russia* (1925; reprint, New York: Crowell, 1970), xliv.

19. For Dell's reflections on this ambivalence, see his *Intellectual Vagabondage: An Apology for the Intelligentsia* (New York: Doran, 1926), and "A Psycho-Analytic Confession," *Liberator* 3 (April 1920): 15–19.

20. Max Eastman, "The Russian Dictators," *Liberator* 1 (March 1918). Subsequent references to this work will be cited in the text.

21. Sidney Lens, *Radicalism in America* (Philadelphia: Crowell, 1966), 258. Subsequent references to this work will be cited in the text.

22. Eugene V. Debs, *The Negro Workers: An Address Delivered October 30, 1923, at Commonwealth Casino, 135th Street and Madison Avenue, NYC* (New York, n.d.), 28–29.

23. Robert H. Brisbane, *The Black Vanguard: Origins of the Negro Social Revolution, 1900–1960* (Valley Forge: Judson, 1970), 73. Subsequent references to this work will be cited in the text.

24. Mark Naison, *Communists in Harlem during the Depression* (1983; reprint, New York: Grove, 1985), 3. Subsequent references to this work will be cited in the text.

25. Thomas C. Holt, "W. E. B. Du Bois," in *The American Radical*, ed. Mari Jo Buhle, Paul Buhle, and Harvey J. Kaye (New York: Routledge, 1994), 116.

26. Tyrone Tillery, *Claude McKay: A Black Poet's Struggle for Identity* (Amherst: University of Massachusetts Press, 1992), 36. Subsequent references to this work will be cited in the text.

27. W. E. B. Du Bois, *Darkwater: Voices from within the Veil* (New York: Harcourt, Brace & Howe, 1920), 159; quoted in Manning Marable, *W. E. B. Du Bois: Black Radical Democrat* (Boston: Twayne, 1986), 108.

28. W. E. B. Du Bois, "Socialism and the Negro," *Crisis* 22 (October 1921): 245–47; quoted in Marable, 108.

29. Philip S. Foner, *American Socialism and Black Americans: From the Age of Jackson to World War II* (Westport, Conn.: Greenwood, 1977), 306–9.

30. Robert A. Hill, Introduction, in *The Crusader* (New York: Garland, 1987), 1:xxiv. Subsequent references to this work will be cited in the text.

31. For a discussion of ambivalence within Marxist theory toward nationalism, see also the entry for "nationalism" in Tom Bottomore, ed., *Dictionary of Marxist Thought* (Cambridge: Harvard University Press, 1983).

32. Cyril V. Briggs, "Bolshevist!!!" *Crusader*, October 1919, 6.

33. Cyril V. Briggs, "Negro First!" *Crusader*, October 1919, 6.

34. Claude McKay, "If We Must Die," *Liberator* 2 (June 1919).

35. Claude McKay, "Africa," *Liberator* 4 (August 1921).

36. Claude McKay, "America," *Liberator* 4 (December 1921).

37. Wayne F. Cooper, *Claude McKay: Rebel Sojourner in the Harlem Renaissance* (1987; reprint, New York: Schocken, 1990), 178.

38. Claude McKay, *A Long Way from Home* (1937; reprint, New York: Arno Press and the New York Times, 1969), 179.

39. James R. Giles, *Claude McKay* (Boston: Twayne, 1976), 33. Subsequent references to this work will be cited in the text.

40. Eugene V. Debs, "The Soul of the Russian Revolution," *Call*, 21 April

1918; reprinted in Philip S. Foner, *The Bolshevik Revolution: Its Impact on American Radicals, Liberals, and Labor* (New York: International, 1967), 90–91.

41. Susan Curtis, *A Consuming Faith: The Social Gospel and Modern American Culture* (Baltimore: Johns Hopkins University Press, 1991), 10.

42. Julia Ruutila, interviewed for OHAL, series 1, tape 217.

43. Ashurst noted that the excerpt he read from the "Songbook" had been taken from an editorial in the *Guardian,* published in Graham County, Ariz. He went on to say that IWW stands for Imperial Wilhelm's Warriors, suggesting that the Wobblies were serving the German war effort.

44. Max Eastman, "Bill Haywood, Communist," *Liberator* 4 (April 1921).

Chapter 3

1. William Weinstone, "Formative Period of CPUSA," *Political Affairs,* September–October 1969; reprinted in *Highlights of a Fighting History: Sixty Years of the Communist Party USA,* edited by Philip Bart, Theodore Bassett, William W. Weinstone, and Arthur Zipser (New York: International, 1979), 15.

2. Howard Zinn, *A People's History of the United States* (1980; reprint, New York: HarperCollins, 1990), 373. Subsequent references to this work will be cited in the text.

3. Michael Gold, *Jews without Money* (New York: Liveright, 1930). Subsequent references to this work will be cited in the text.

4. Michael Brewster Folsom, "The Book of Poverty," *Nation,* 28 February 1966, 242.

5. For an overview of the critical response to *Jews without Money,* see James D. Bloom, *Left Letters: The Culture Wars of Mike Gold and Joseph Freeman* (New York: Columbia University Press, 1992).

6. Morris Dickstein, "Mike Gold: A Centennial Appraisal," Modern Language Association annual meeting, New York, 1992.

7. Michael Brewster Folsom, "The Education of Mike Gold," in *Proletarian Writers in the Thirties,* ed. David Madden (Carbondale: Southern Illinois University Press, 1968), 241–42. Subsequent references to this work will be cited in the text.

8. Agnes Smedley, *Daughter of Earth* (1929; reprint, New York: Feminist Press, 1973). Subsequent references to this work will be cited in the text.

9. Janice MacKinnon and Stephen MacKinnon, *Agnes Smedley: The Life and Times of an American Radical* (Berkeley: University of California Press, 1988), 58.

10. Walt Carmon, "Books," *New Masses* 6 (October 1930): 18.

11. Ruth Norrick, interviewed in 1983 for OHAL, series 1, tape 174. Subsequent references to this interview will be cited in the text.

12. Malcolm Cowley, interviewed in 1981 for OHAL, series 1, tape 56. Subsequent references to this interview will be cited in the text.

13. Herbert Ehrmann, *The Case That Will Not Die* (Boston: Little, Brown, 1969), 43–45.

14. Robert D'Attilio and Jane Manthorn, eds., *Sacco-Vanzetti: Developments and Reconsiderations, 1979* (Boston: Boston Public Library, 1979).

15. Robert K. Murray, *Red Scare: Study in National Hysteria, 1919–1920*

(Minneapolis: University of Minnesota Press, 1955), 267. Subsequent references to this work will be cited in the text.

16. Upton Sinclair, *Boston*, 2 vols. (New York: A. & C. Boni, 1928). Subsequent references to this work will be cited in the text.

17. G. Louis Joughin and Edmund M. Morgan, *The Legacy of Sacco and Vanzetti* (1948; reprint, Princeton: Princeton University Press, 1978), 452–53. Subsequent references to this work will be cited in the text.

18. Malcolm Cowley, "Echoes of a Crime," *New Republic*, 28 August 1935, 79; quoted in Walter B. Rideout, *The Radical Novel in the United States* (Cambridge: Harvard University Press, 1956), 134.

19. Mike Gold, "Let It Be Really New," *New Masses* 1 (June 1926): 20.

20. Camilla Gray, *The Russian Experiment in Art, 1863–1922*, 2d ed., rev. Marian Burleigh-Motley (1962; London: Thames and Hudson, 1986), 224. Subsequent references to this work will be cited in the text.

21. James F. Murphy, *The Proletarian Moment: The Controversy over Leftism in Literature* (Urbana: University of Illinois Press, 1991), 23. Subsequent references to this work will be cited in the text.

22. Mike Gold, "A New Program for Writers," *New Masses* 5 (January 1930): 21.

23. Mike Gold, "Notes from Kharkov," *New Masses* 6 (March 1931): 5.

24. Mike Gold, "Thornton Wilder: Prophet of a Genteel Christ," *New Republic*, 22 October 1930, 266–67.

25. Mike Gold, "America Needs a Critic," *New Masses* 1 (October 1926): 7–9.

26. Harvey Klehr, *The Heyday of American Communism: The Depression Decade* (New York: Basic Books, 1984), 10. Subsequent references to this work will be cited in the text.

27. Christina L. Baker, "Gastonia Strike," in *Encyclopedia of the American Left*, ed. M. J. Buhle, P. Buhle, and Georgakas, 255–56.

28. Dee Garrison, *Mary Heaton Vorse* (Philadelphia: Temple University Press, 1989), 196–203.

29. Mary Heaton Vorse, *Strike!* (1930; reprint, Urbana: University of Illinois Press, 1991), 19. Subsequent references to this work will be cited in the text.

30. Dee Garrison, Introduction, in Mary Heaton Vorse, *Strike!* (Urbana: University of Illinois press, 1991) x. Subsequent references to this work will be cited in the text.

31. Alan Bloch, *Anonymous Toil* (Lanham, Md.: University Press of America, 1992), 75.

Chapter 4

1. Annelise Orleck, " 'We Are That Mythical Thing Called the Public': Militant Housewives during the Great Depression," *Feminist Studies* 19 (Spring 1993): 149. Subsequent references to this work will be cited in the text.

2. *Daily Worker*, 30 December 1930, 4.

3. Elaine Hedges, Introduction, in Meridel Le Sueur, *Ripening*, ed. Hedges (New York: Feminist Press, 1990), 8.

4. Meridel Le Sueur, "Tonight Is Part of the Struggle," in *Salute to Spring*

(1940; reprint, New York: International Publishers, 1989), 138. Subsequent references to this work will be cited in the text.

5. *Culture and Crisis: An Open Letter to the Writers, Artists, Teachers, Physicians, Engineers, and Other Professional Workers of America* (New York: League of Professional Groups for Foster and Ford, 1932).

6. Jack Conroy, *The Disinherited* (1933; reprint, Cambridge: Robert Bentley, 1979), 91. Subsequent references to this work will be cited in the text.

7. John Dos Passos, *The Forty-second Parallel* (1930; reprint, Boston: Houghton Mifflin, 1946).

8. James T. Farrell, *A Note on Literary Criticism* (New York: Vanguard, 1936). Subsequent references to this work will be cited in the text.

9. Mike Gold, "The Keynote to Dos Passos' Works," *Daily Worker*, 26 February 1938, 7; reprinted in Barry Maine, ed., *Dos Passos: The Critical Heritage* (New York: Routledge, Chapman and Hall, 1988), 153.

10. Granville Hicks, "Dos Passos's Gifts," *New Republic*, 24 June 1931, 157–58; reprinted in Barry Maine, ed., *Dos Passos: The Critical Heritage* (New York: Routledge, Chapman and Hall, 1988), 98.

11. Barbara Foley, *Telling the Truth: The Theory and Practice of Documentary Fiction* (Ithaca: Cornell University Press, 1986), 204. Subsequent references to this work will be cited in the text.

12. Michael Clark, *Dos Passos's Early Fiction, 1912–1938* (Selingsgrove: Susquehanna University Press, 1987), 123–24.

13. Bernard Bellush, *The Failure of the NRA* (New York: Norton, 1975), 50. Subsequent references to this work will be cited in the text.

14. Grace Hutchins, "Feminists and the Left Wing," *New Masses* 10 (20 November 1934).

15. Harry Fleischman, "Norman Thomas," in *Encyclopedia of the American Left,* ed. M. J. Buhle, P. Buhle, and Georgakas, 775–76.

16. Kirby Page, "A Socialist Program of Deliverance," *World Tomorrow*, 5 April 1933, 323.

17. Norman Thomas, "New Deal or New Day," *World Tomorrow*, 31 August 1933, 489. Subsequent references to this work will be cited in the text.

18. James P. Cannon, *The History of American Trotskyism* (1944; reprint, New York: Pathfinder, 1972), 41. Subsequent references to this work will be cited in the text.

19. James P. Cannon, "Our Policy and Present Tasks," *The Militant*, 23 December 1930.

20. Constance Myers, *The Prophet's Army: Trotskyists in America, 1928–1941* (Westport, Conn.: Greenwood, 1977), 49. Subsequent references to this work will be cited in the text.

21. Kirby Page, "What Is Behind the United Front," *World Tomorrow*, 26 October 1933.

22. Kirby Page, "A Socialist Program of Deliverance," *World Tomorrow*, 5 April 1933, 325.

23. Reinhold Niebuhr, "A Reorientation of Radicalism," *World Tomorrow*, July 1933, 444. Subsequent references to this work will be cited in the text.

24. Reinhold Niebuhr, "A New Strategy for Socialists," *World Tomorrow*, 31 August 1933, 491.

25. Dorothy Day, *The Long Loneliness* (1952; reprint, New York: Harper & Row, 1981), 38. Subsequent references to this work will be cited in the text.

26. Conference on the Catholic Worker Movement, Holy Cross College, 2 May 1983, OHAL, series 1, tape 41. Subsequent references to this conference will be cited in the text.

27. James Allen, Introduction, in *Race Hatred On Trial* (New York: Communist Party, 1931); reprinted in *Highlights of a Fighting History*, ed. Bart, Bassett, Weinstone, and Zipser, 80–81.

28. Arnold Rampersad, *The Life of Langston Hughes, Volume I, 1902–1941* (New York: Oxford University Press, 1986), 5.

29. Saunders Redding, Foreword, in *Good Morning Revolution: Uncollected Social Protest Writings by Langston Hughes*, ed. Faith Berry (New York: Lawrence Hill & Co., 1973), ix.

30. A recent publication of *Billy Sunday and Other Poems* (San Diego: Harcourt Brace, 1993) reveals a more politically radical Sandburg than does previously published work.

31. Langston Hughes, "My Adventures as a Social Poet," *Phylon* 8 (3d Qtr., 1947): 205–12.

32. Langston Hughes, "Christ in Alabama," *Contempo*, September 1931; reprinted in *Good Morning Revolution*, ed. Berry, 138.

33. Langston Hughes, "Brown America in Jail: Kilby," *Opportunity* (1932); reprinted in *Good Morning Revolution*, ed. Berry, 51.

34. Langston Hughes, "Southern Gentlemen, White Prostitutes, Mill-Owners, and Negroes," *Contempo* (1931); reprinted in *Good Morning Revolution*, ed. Berry, 49.

35. Langston Hughes, "Good Morning, Revolution," *New Masses* 8 (September 1932); reprinted in *Good Morning Revolution*, ed. Berry, 5.

Chapter 5

1. Vivian Gornick, *The Romance of American Communism* (New York: Basic Books, 1977), 110. Subsequent references to this work will be cited in the text.

2. David Madden, Introduction, in *Proletarian Writers of the Thirties* (Carbondale: Southern Illinois University Press, 1968), xv.

3. Mike Gold, "A Letter to the Author of a First Book," *Daily Worker*, 29 January 1934): 215–16.

4. Stuart Cosgrove, "Prolet-Buhne: Agit-Prop in Amerika," in *Performance and Politics in Popular Drama: Aspects of Popular Entertainment in Theatre, Film, and Television, 1800–1976*, ed. David Bradby, Louis James, Bernard Sharrett (Cambridge: Cambridge University Press, 1980), 207.

5. Clifford Odets, *Waiting for Lefty*, in *Six Plays by Clifford Odets* (New York: Modern Library, 1939), 12. Subsequent references to this work will be cited in the text.

6. Gerald Weales, "Already the Talk of the Town below the Macy-Gimbel Line," in *Odets: The Playwright* (London and New York: Methuen, 1985); reprinted as "Waiting for Lefty," in *Critical Essays on Clifford Odets*, ed. Gabriel

Miller (Boston: G. K. Hall, 1991), 151. Subsequent references to this work will be cited in the text.

7. Joseph Wood Krutch, ["*Waiting for Lefty* and *Till the Day I Die*,"] *Nation*, 10 April 1935; reprinted in *Critical Essays on Clifford Odets*, ed. Miller, 15.

8. Gabriel Jackson, Introduction, in *The Spanish Civil War* (Chicago: Quadrangle Books, 1972), 10. Subsequent references to this work will be cited in the text.

9. Esther Dolgoff, interviewed for OHAL, series 1, tape 67. Subsequent references to this interview will be cited in the text.

10. *The Good Fight: The Abraham Lincoln Brigade in the Spanish Civil War*, prod. Noel Buckner, Mary Dore, and Sam Sills, 1984; dist. First Run Films and Kino International, New York. Subsequent references to this work will be cited in the text.

11. Frederick R. Benson, *Writers in Arms: The Literary Impact of the Spanish Civil War* (New York: New York University Press, 1967), 17; see also Burnett Bolloten, *The Spanish Civil War* (Chapel Hill: University of North Carolina Press, 1991), 563. Subsequent references to these works will be cited in the text.

12. Ernest Hemingway, *For Whom the Bell Tolls* (1940; reprint, New York: Scribners, 1968). Subsequent references to this work will be cited in the text.

13. John Dos Passos, *The Adventures of a Young Man* (Boston: Houghton Mifflin, 1939). Subsequent references to this work will be cited in the text.

14. Josephine Herbst, "The Starched Blue Sky of Spain," *The Noble Savage*, n.d., 2; reprinted as *The Starched Blue Sky of Spain*, intro. Diane Johnson (New York: HarperCollins, 1991). Subsequent references to this work will be cited in the text.

15. Meridel Le Sueur, "Women Know a Lot of Things . . . That They Don't Read in the Papers, and They're Acting on What They Know," *Worker*, March 1937; reprinted in her *Ripening*, ed. Hedges (New York: Feminist Press, 1990), 171.

16. Douglas P. Seaton, *Catholics and Radicals* (Lewisburg: Bucknell University Press, 1981), 22. Subsequent references to this work will be cited in the text.

17. "How the Meat Strike Started in Hamtramck," *Party Organizer*, September 1935.

18. Michael Honey, "Fighting on Two Fronts," *Labor's Heritage* 4 (Spring 1992): 50–66. Subsequent references to this work will be cited in the text.

19. Earl Browder, "Building the Democratic Front: Report to the Tenth Convention, CPUSA" (New York: Workers Library Publishers, 1938); reprinted in *Highlights of a Fighting History*, ed. Bart, Bassett, Weinstone, and Zipser, 176.

20. Abner Berry, interviewed by Mark Naison in September 1977 for OHAL, series 1, tape 16. Subsequent references to this interview will be cited in the text.

21. Adam Hochschild, "The Secret of a Siberian River Bank," *New York Times*, 28 March 1993, 40, 78.

22. Maurice Isserman, *Which Side Were You On? The American Communist Party during the Second World War* (Middletown: Wesleyan University Press,

1982; reprint, Urbana: University of Illinois Press, 1993), 36. Subsequent references to this work will be cited in the text.

23. Lillian Hellman, *Watch on the Rhine*, in *Six Plays by Lillian Hellman* (New York: Modern Library, 1960; reprint, 1979).

24. Katherine Lederer, *Lillian Hellman* (Boston: Twayne, 1979), 54. Subsequent references to this work will be cited in the text.

25. Thomas McGrath, interviewed in 1971 for OHAL, series 1, tape 168. Subsequent references to this interview will be cited in the text.

26. Discussion of Popular Front culture, led by Paul Buhle, October and December 1977, OHAL, series 1, tape 193, Tamiment Library, New York University. Subsequent references to this discussion will be cited in the text.

Chapter 6

1. Joseph Norrick, interviewed in March 1983 for OHAL, series 1, tape 174.

2. Rose Pesotta, *Bread upon the Waters* (1944; reprint, Ithaca: ILR Press, 1987). Subsequent references to this work will be cited in the text.

3. Sydney Stahl Weinberg, *The World of Our Mothers* (Chapel Hill: University of North Carolina Press, 1988), 74. Subsequent references to this work will be cited in the text.

4. Elaine Leeder, *The Gentle General: Rose Pesotta, Anarchist and Labor Organizer* (Albany: State University of New York Press, 1993), xiii. Subsequent references to this work will be cited in the text.

5. Ann Schofield, Introduction, in *Bread upon the Waters*, vii. Subsequent references to this work will be cited in the text.

6. Paul Buhle, "ILGWU—International Ladies Garment Workers Union," *Encyclopedia of the American Left*, ed. M. J. Buhle, P. Buhle, and Georgakas, 368–71.

7. On the summer school for working women at Bryn Mawr, see *The Women of Summer*, prod. Suzanne Bauman and Rita Heller, 1986; dist. Filmmaker's Library, New York.

8. Richard Wright, ["Richard Wright,"] in *The God That Failed*, ed. Richard Crossman (New York: Harper & Bros., 1949), 115–62. Subsequent references to this work will be cited in the text.

9. Constance Webb, *Richard Wright: A Biography* (New York: Putnam's, 1968), 141. Subsequent references to this work will be cited in the text.

10. Thomas McGrath, *To Walk a Crooked Mile* (New York: Swallow Press, 1947). Subsequent references to this work will be cited in the text.

11. E. P. Thompson notes that McGrath left the Communist Party after a disagreement with the West Coast leadership between 1955 and 1957. He was then an independent Leftist and took a brief interest in the Progressive Labor Party. See Thompson's "Homage to Thomas McGrath," in *The Revolutionary Poet in the United States: The Poetry of Thomas McGrath*, ed. Frederick C. Stern (Columbia: University of Missouri Press, 1988) 104–49.

12. Joseph Starobin, *American Communism in Crisis, 1943–1957* (Cambridge: Harvard University Press, 1972), 59. Subsequent references to this work will be cited in the text.

13. Robin D. G. Kelley, *Hammer and Hoe: Alabama Communists during the Great Depression* (Chapel Hill: University of North Caroline Press, 1990), 225.

14. Richard M. Fried, *Nightmare in Red: The McCarthy Era in Perspective* (New York: Oxford University Press, 1990), 7. Subsequent references to this work will be cited in the text.

15. Curtis D. MacDougall, *Gideon's Army* (New York: Marzani and Munsell), 2:434.

16. Robert Griffith, *The Politics of Fear: Joseph R. McCarthy and the Senate* (Lexington: University of Kentucky Press, 1970), ix.

17. Mary Sperling McAuliffe, *Crisis on the Left: Cold War Politics and American Liberals, 1947–1954* (Amherst: University of Massachusetts Press, 1978).

18. Seymour Martin Lipset and Earl Raab, *The Politics of Unreason: Right-Wing Extremism in America, 1790–1970* (New York: Harper & Row, 1970), 237–38.

19. M. J. Heale, *American Anti-Communism: Combating the Enemy Within, 1830–1970* (Baltimore: Johns Hopkins University Press, 1990), 155. Subsequent references to this work will be cited in the text.

20. Tony Hiss, "My Father's Honor," *New Yorker,* 16 November 1992, 100–106.

21. Walter Schneir and Miriam Schneir, *Invitation to an Inquest* (New York: Pantheon, 1983).

22. For the cultural "uses" of the Rosenberg case, see Virginia Carmichael, *Framing History: The Rosenberg Story and the Cold War* (Minneapolis: University of Minneapolis Press, 1993).

23. Dan Georgakas, "Hollywood Blacklist," *Encyclopedia of the American Left,* ed. M. J. Buhle, P. Buhle, and Georgakas, 326–29.

24. "Revised Credits," *Chicago Tribune;* reprinted in *Indianapolis Star,* 6 December 1992.

25. "Blacklisted Writers Finally Receiving Credit," *Indianapolis Star,* 6 December 1992.

26. Victor S. Navasky, *Naming Names* (New York: Viking, 1980; reprint, New York: Penguin, 1981), 200–206. Subsequent references to this work will be cited in the text.

27. David K. Dunaway, "Songs of Subversion: How the FBI Destroyed the Weavers," *Village Voice,* 21 January 1980, 40. Subsequent references to this work will be cited in the text.

28. Doris Willens, *Lonesome Traveler: The Life of Lee Hays* (New York: Norton, 1988) 151–64.

29. Fred Hellerman, in *Wasn't That a Time,* dir. Jim Brown, 1981; dist. MGM/UA Home Video, New York, 1983.

30. Ellen W. Schrecker, *No Ivory Tower: McCarthyism and the Universities* (New York: Oxford University Press, 1986), 93. Subsequent references to this work will be cited in the text.

31. May Sarton, *Faithful Are the Wounds* (1955; reprint, New York: Norton, 1985). Subsequent references to this work will be cited in the text.

32. Lillian Hellman, *Scoundrel Time* (Boston: Little, Brown, 1976; reprint,

Boston: Bantam, 1977). Subsequent references to this work will be cited in the text.

33. Murray Kempton, "Witnesses," *New York Review of Books*, 10 June 1976, 22–25.

34. Sidney Hook, "Lillian Hellman's *Scoundrel Time*," *Encounter* 48 (February 1977): 82–91.

35. Alan M. Wald, *The New York Intellectuals: The Rise and Decline of the Anti-Stalinist Left from the 1930s to the 1980s* (Chapel Hill: University of North Carolina Press, 1987), 3–5. Subsequent references to this work will be cited in the text.

36. See James Miller, *Democracy Is in the Streets* (New York: Simon and Schuster, 1987), and Todd Gitlin, *The Sixties: Years of Hope, Days of Rage* (New York: Bantam, 1987).

37. Harvey Klehr, John Earl Haynes, and Fridrikh Igorevich Firson, *The Secret World of American Communism* (New Haven: Yale University Press, 1995), 323.

38. Herbert A. Philbrick, *I Led Three Lives: Citizen, "Communist," Counterspy* (New York: Grosset and Dunlap, 1952).

Chapter 7

1. Lorraine Hansberry, *The Sign in Sidney Brustein's Window,* intro. Robert Nemiroff (New York: Random House, 1965). Subsequent references to this work will be cited in the text.

2. Robert Nemiroff, Introduction, in *The Sign in Sidney Brustein's Window.* Subsequent references to this work will be cited in the text.

3. John Sayles, "At the Anarchists' Convention," *Atlantic Monthly*, 28 February 1979, 48–52; reprinted in *The Anarchists' Convention* (Boston: Little, Brown, 1979). Subsequent references to this work will be cited in the text.

4. Kim Chernin, *In My Mother's House* (1983; reprint, New York: Harper Colophon, 1984). Subsequent references to this work will be cited in the text.

SELECTED BIBLIOGRAPHY

PRIMARY SOURCES

Chernin, Kim. *In My Mother's House*. 1983. Reprint, New York: Harper Colophon, 1984.

Conroy, Jack. *The Disinherited*. 1933. Reprint, Cambridge: Robert Bentley, 1979.

Day, Dorothy. *The Long Loneliness*. 1952. Reprint, New York: Harper & Row, 1981.

Dell, Floyd. *Love in Greenwich Village*. 1926. Reprint, Freeport, N.Y.: Books for Libraries Press, 1970.

Dos Passos, John. *Adventures of a Young Man*. Boston: Houghton Mifflin, 1939.

———. *The Forty-second Parallel*. 1930. Reprint, Boston: Houghton Mifflin, 1946.

Farrell, James T. *A Note on Literary Criticism*. New York: Vanguard, 1936.

Gold, Michael. *Jews without Money*. New York: Liveright, 1930.

Hansberry, Lorraine. *The Sign in Sidney Brustein's Window*. (Produced 1964.) New York: Random House, 1965.

Hellman, Lillian. *Scoundrel Time*. 1976. Reprint, Boston: Bantam, 1977.

———. *Watch on the Rhine*. (Produced 1941.) Reprinted in *Six Plays by Lillian Hellman*. New York: Modern Library, 1979.

Hemingway, Ernest. *For Whom the Bell Tolls*. 1940. Reprint, New York: Scribners, 1968.

Herbst, Josephine. "The Starched Blue Sky of Spain." N.d. Reprinted as *The Starched Blue Sky of Spain*. New York: HarperCollins, 1991.

Hughes, Langston. "Christ in Alabama." *Contempo*. September 1931. Reprinted in *Good Morning Revolution: Uncollected Social Protest Writings by Langston Hughes*, edited by Faith Berry. New York: Lawrence Hill & Co., 1973.

———. "Good Morning, Revolution." *New Masses* 8 (September 1932).

I.W.W. Songs: To Fan the Flames of Discontent. 19th ed. 1923. Reprint, Chicago: Charles H. Kerr, 1989.

Le Sueur, Meridel. "I Was Marching." *New Masses*. September 1930.

———. "Tonight Is Part of the Struggle." In *Salute to Spring*. 1940. Reprint, New York: International Publishers, 1989.

McGrath, Thomas. "The Heroes of Childhood." *To Walk a Crooked Mile*. New York: Swallow Press, 1947.

McKay, Claude. "If We Must Die." *Liberator*. June 1919.

Odets, Clifford. *Waiting for Lefty*. (Produced 1935.) Reprinted in *Six Plays by Clifford Odets*. New York: Modern Library, 1939.

Pesotta, Rose. *Bread upon the Waters*. 1944. Reprint, Ithaca: ILR Press, 1987.

Reed, John. *Ten Days That Shook the World*. 1919. Reprint, London: Penguin, 1977.

Sarton, May. *Faithful Are the Wounds*. 1955. Reprint, New York: Norton, 1985.

Sayles, John. "At the Anarchists' Convention." *Atlantic Monthly,* 28 February 1979. Reprinted in *The Anarchists' Convention*. Boston: Little, Brown, 1979.

Sinclair, Upton. *Boston*. New York: Boni, 1928.

Smedley, Agnes. *Daughter of Earth*. 1929. Reprint, New York: Feminist Press, 1973.

Vorse, Mary Heaton. *Strike!* 1930. Reprint, Urbana: University of Illinois Press, 1991.

Wright, Richard. ["Richard Wright."] In *The God That Failed*, edited by Richard Crossman. New York: Harper & Bros., 1949.

SECONDARY SOURCES

Archival Resources

Documents of the Communist Party, West Coast. Finn Hall. Berkeley, Calif.

Oral History of the American Left (OHAL). Tamiment Library. New York University.

Reference Works

Buhle, Mari Jo, Paul Buhle, and Dan Georgakas, eds. *Encyclopedia of the American Left*. Urbana: University of Illinois Press, 1990; Illini ed., 1992.

Buhle, Mari Jo, Paul Buhle, and Harvey J. Kaye, eds. *The American Radical*. New York: Routledge, 1994.

Histories of American Radical Movements

Buhle, Paul. *Marxism in the USA*. London: Verso, 1987.

Draper, Theodore. *The Roots of American Communism*. 1957. Reprint. Chicago: Ivan R. Dee, 1985.

Dubofsky, Melvyn. *We Shall Be All: A History of the Industrial Workers of the World*. 2d ed. Urbana: University of Illinois Press, 1988.

Flacks, Richard. *Making History: The American Left and the American Mind*. New York: Columbia University Press, 1988.

Isserman, Maurice. *Which Side Were You On? The American Communist Party during the Second World War*. Middletown: Wesleyan University Press, 1982. Reprint, Urbana: University of Illinois Press, 1993.

Klehr, Harvey. *The Heyday of American Communism: The Depression Decade*. New York: Basic Books, 1984.

Lens, Sidney. *Radicalism in America*. Philadelphia: Crowell, 1966.

Starobin, Joseph. *American Communism in Crisis, 1943–1957*. Cambridge: Harvard University Press, 1972.

Surveys of Radical Literature, Writers, or Literary Theory

Aaron, Daniel. *Writers on the Left*. New York: Harcourt, Brace and World, 1961. Reprint, New York: Columbia University Press, 1992.

Bloch, Alan. *Anonymous Toil*. Lanham, Md.: University Press of America, 1992.

Foley, Barbara. *Telling the Truth: The Theory and Practice of Documentary Fiction*. Ithaca: Cornell University Press, 1986.

Gilbert, James Burkhardt. *Writers and Partisans: A History of Literary Radicalism in the United States*. New York: Wiley & Sons, 1968.

Murphy, James F. *The Proletarian Moment: The Controversy over Leftism in Literature*. Urbana: University of Illinois Press, 1991.

Nelson, Cary. *Repression and Recovery: Modern American Poetry and the Politics of Cultural Memory, 1910–1945*. Madison: University of Wisconsin Press, 1989.

Pells, Richard. *Radical Visions and American Dreams: Culture and Social Thought in the Depression Years*. New York: Harper, 1973.

Rideout, Walter B. *The Radical Novel in the United States, 1900–1954*. Cambridge: Harvard University Press, 1956.

Specialized Historical Studies

Bart, Philip, Theodore Bassett, William W. Weinstone, Arthur Zipser, eds. *Highlights of a Fighting History: Sixty Years of the Communist Party USA*. New York: International, 1979.

Bird, Stewart, Dan Georgakas, Deborah Shaffer, eds. *Solidarity Forever: The IWW, An Oral History of the Wobblies*. Chicago: Lake View Press, 1985. Reprint, London: Lawrence and Wishart, 1987.

Bolloten, Burnett. *The Spanish Civil War*. Chapel Hill: University of North Carolina Press, 1991.

Brown, Michael E., Randy Martin, Frank Rosengarten, George Snedeker, eds.

New Studies in the Politics and Culture of American Communism. New York: Monthly Review Press, 1993.

Gornick, Vivian. *The Romance of American Communism*. New York: Basic Books, 1977.

Klehr, Harvey, John Earl Haynes, and Fridrikh Igorevich Firsov. *The Secret World of American Communism*. New Haven: Yale University Press, 1995.

Myers, Constance. *The Prophet's Army: Trotskyists in America, 1928–1941*. Westport, Conn.: Greenwood, 1977.

Naison, Mark. *Communists in Harlem during the Depression*. 1983. Reprint, New York: Grove Press, 1985.

Orleck, Annelise. " 'We Are That Mythical Thing Called the Public': Militant Housewives during the Great Depression." *Feminist Studies* 19 (Spring 1993): 147–72.

Shaffer, Robert. "Women and the Communist Party, USA, 1930–1949." *Socialist Review* 9 (May–June 1979): 90–100.

Wald, Alan M. *The New York Intellectuals: The Rise and Decline of the Anti-Stalinist Left from the 1930s to the 1980s*. Chapel Hill: University of North Carolina Press, 1987.

Zeigler, Robert H. *American Workers, American Unions, 1920–1985*. Baltimore: Johns Hopkins University Press, 1986.

Specialized Literary Studies

Benson, Frederick R. *Writers in Arms: The Literary Impact of the Spanish Civil War*. New York: New York University Press, 1967.

Bloom, James D. *Left Letters: The Culture Wars of Mike Gold and Joseph Freeman*. New York: Columbia University Press, 1992.

Jones, Margaret C. *Heretics and Hellraisers: Women Contributors to the "Masses," 1911–1917*. Austin: University of Texas Press, 1993.

Joughin, G. Louis, and Edmund M. Morgan. *The Legacy of Sacco and Vanzetti*. 1948. Reprint, Princeton: Princeton University Press, 1978.

Madden, David. *Proletarian Writers on the Thirties*. Carbondale: Southern Illinois University Press, 1968.

Nekola, Charlotte, and Paula Rabinowitz, eds. *Writing Red: An Anthology of American Women Writers, 1930–1940*. New York: Feminist Press, 1987.

INDEX

Abbott, Leonard, 11

Abern, Martin, 100

Abraham Lincoln Battalion. *See* Abraham Lincoln Brigade

Abraham Lincoln Brigade, 125

Actists. *See* Association of Catholic Trade Unionists

AFL. *See* American Federation of Labor

African Blood Brotherhood, 46

agitprop, 74–75, 120, 121, 122, 141

Agricultural Adjustment Act (AAA), 97, 125, 134

Alexander, Charles, 107

Alger, Horatio, 92

Allen, James: *Race Hatred on Trial,* 108

amalgamation, 77

American Communist Party. *See* Communist Party USA

American exceptionalism, 42, 78

American Federation of Labor (AFL), 16, 17, 18, 19, 25, 41, 42, 53, 54, 77, 78, 101, 114, 124, 131, 132, 135, 139, 145, 147, 150, 160

American Labor Party, 135

American Legion, 165

American literary naturalism, 93–94

American Protective League, 42

American Railway Union, 20

American Workers Party, 100, 101, 102, 107, 173

American Writers Congress, 117

anarchism, 7, 8, 10, 11, 12, 35, 39, 69, 105, 124, 126, 145

anarchist movement, 83, 145

anarcho-syndicalism, 10
Anderson, Margaret, 4, 11; *My Thirty Years War*, 4
Anderson, Sherwood, 91; *Winesburg, Ohio*, 4
Anvil, 91
Appeal to Reason, 21
Arvin, Newton, 91
Ashley, Jessie, 4
Ashurst, Sen. Henry Fountain, 50
Association of Catholic Trade Unionists (ACTU), 107, 132–33, 159
Atlantic Monthly, 180
Attentat, 10

Baginski, Max, 11
Bakunin, Michael, 8, 9, 181
Balabanoff, Angelica, 37
Barnes, Cornelia, 5
Beal, Fred, 79
Becker, Maurice, 5, 91
Bell, Josephine, 31
Bellamy, Edward: *Looking Backward*, 25, 26
Bellows, George, 5
Benson, Frederick R.: *Writers in Arms: The Literary Impact of the Spanish Civil War*, 127
Bentley, Elizabeth, 162, 164
Berger, Victor, 21
Berkman, Alexander, 10, 11, 13, 31, 35, 49, 124, 185
Bernstein, Karl, 40
Berry, Abner, 136, 151
Bishop's Program of Social Reconstruction, 48–49, 106, 113
black belt self-determination, 110
blacklist, 164, 166, 170, 171, 172, 175, 176
Bloch, Alan, *Anonymous Toil*, 81
Bogdanov, Alexander, 73
Bolshevik Party, 32, 35, 185
Bolshevik revolution, vii, 3, 12, 26, 27, 35, 37, 41, 44, 45, 51, 69, 101
Bolsheviks, 32, 33, 34, 35, 37, 39, 42, 43, 50, 51, 53, 90
boring from within, 77, 104, 114, 147

Bradley, Mary: "A Stranger in the City," 7
Bread and Roses strike. *See* Lawrence, Massachusetts, textile strike
Briggs, Cyril, 45, 46, 107
Brooks, Cleanth, 153
Brookwood Labor College, 100, 148
Brotherhood of Sleeping Car Porters, 45, 135, 186
Browder, Earl, 77, 83, 104, 115, 133, 135, 140, 144, 155, 156, 157, 173
Brown, Michael, viii
Bryan, William Jennings, 95
Bryant, Louise, 4, 37
Bryn Mawr Summer School for Women Workers, 148
Budenz, Louis, 161
Buhle, Paul, 141
Bukharin, Nicolai, 78, 137
Bullard, Arthur, 29, 30
Bulletin de la Presse, 34

Caballero, Largo, 126
Cahiers de Communisme, 156
Caldwell, Erskine, 91
Call, 48, 62, 63, 104, 105
Camus, Albert, 178
Cannon, James P., 50, 54, 78, 100, 101, 102
Carlists, 125
Carmon, Walt, 63
Carnegie, Andrew, 95
Carnegie Endowment for International Peace, 162
Catholic Worker, 106, 186
Catholic Worker movement, 104–7, 132–33
Chambers, Whittaker, 162, 163
Chaney, James, 178
Chaplin, Ralph, 19
chauvinism, 108, 110
Cheney, Ralph, 91
Chernin, Kim: *In My Mother's House*, 182–83
Chernin, Rose, 182
Christian Socialism, 25, 48, 67, 99, 103, 168

Christian Socialist, 25
Christian Socialist Fellowship, 25
Churchill, Winston, 47, 154
Cincinnati Reds, 160
CIO. *See* Congress of Industrial
    Organizations
Civilian Conservation Corps, 131
Clark, Michael, 96
Cold War, vii, 156–58, 160, 161, 167,
    173, 175, 176
collective novel, 95, 119, 141
Comintern (Third International), viii,
    43, 46, 47, 50, 53, 54, 55, 63, 77,
    78, 83, 84, 90, 98, 100, 101, 102,
    107, 108, 133, 140, 154, 161;
    Sixth World Congress of, 100
Committee for Industrial
    Organization, 132
Commonweal, 105
Communism, vii, viii, 2, 27, 37, 41,
    46, 52, 54, 59, 72, 73, 74, 78, 79,
    83, 90, 104, 105, 112, 145, 151,
    167, 168, 169, 173, 174
Communist Information Bureau
    (Cominform), 159
Communist Labor Party, 42, 54, 185
Communist League of America, 100,
    101, 186
Communist Manifesto, 30, 121
Communist Party. *See* Communist
    Party USA
Communist Party of America, 54
Communist Party USA (CPUSA), vii,
    viii, ix, 1, 3, 51, 52, 53–54, 55,
    60, 62, 63, 64, 65, 67, 72, 74, 76,
    77, 79, 82, 83, 84, 87, 88, 89, 90,
    91, 96, 97, 99, 101, 102, 103,
    108, 109, 113, 115, 117, 118,
    120, 122, 125, 128, 129, 130,
    132, 133, 134, 136, 139, 140,
    142, 143, 144, 145, 147, 152,
    153, 154, 155, 159, 161, 165,
    170, 172, 173, 175, 176, 186,
    187; founding of, 40–43;
    membership, 83, 98, 115, 116,
    138, 145, 155, 174
Communist Political Association

(CPA), 155–56, 161, 173, 176,
    187
Comstock Act, 13
Confederacion Nacional del Trabajo
    (CNT), 123, 125
Conference for Progressive Labor
    Action, 100
Congress of Industrial Organizations
    (CIO), 131–34, 135, 138, 140,
    141, 143, 144, 145, 147, 149,
    150, 159, 160, 186
Conroy, Jack, 88; *The Disinherited,*
    91–95, 113, 118, 186
constructivists, 73, 120
Contempo, 111
Cook, George Cram, 4
Cooper, Gary, 128
Corey, Lewis. *See* Louis Fraina
Councils (Soviets) of Workingmen's
    and Soldiers' Delegates, 31
Cowley, Malcolm, 65, 71–72, 84, 90,
    91, 96, 97, 116, 117, 136, 142
CPUSA. *See* Communist Party USA
Cripple Creek miners' strike, 16
Crisis, 44, 135
Cronaca Sovversiva, 66
Crosley, George. *See* Whittaker
    Chambers
Crossman, Richard: *The God That
    Failed,* 151, 187
Crusader, 45, 46
Cullen, Countee, 91
Cultural and Scientific Conference for
    World Peace, 170
Culture and Crisis, 90–91, 110, 112,
    186
Czolgosz, Leon, 10, 11

Daily Worker, 60, 75, 96, 116, 118,
    119, 132, 136, 150, 156, 161, 166
Darwin, Charles, 9
Davies, Joseph E.: *Mission to
    Moscow,* 144, 164
Day, Dorothy, 4, 30, 104–7, 113, 133;
    The Long Loneliness, 104–7
de Cleyre, Voltairine, 11
Debs, Eugene Victor, 17, 20, 21, 41,
    43, 48, 95, 98, 104, 186

Debs Column, 125
DeLeon, Daniel, 17
Dell, Floyd, 4, 6, 13, 30, 31, 83;
    Homecoming, 13; *Love in
    Greenwich Village,* 14–16,
    37–39, 49, 51, 70; *Women as
    World Builders,* 15
Democratic centralism, 63
Democratic Front, 133, 135
Democratic Party, 133, 135, 157, 160
Democratic Socialism, 78
Dennis, Eugene, 133, 140, 156, 173,
    174
Detroit, Michigan, race riot, 157
Dewey, John, 5, 96
Dewey, Thomas, 158
dialectical materialism, 74
Dickstein, Morris, 59
dictatorship of the proletariat, 2, 127
Die Freiheit, 10
Dies, Martin, 140
Dodge, Mabel, 4
Dolgoff, Esther, 124
Dollfuss government, 115
Donne, John: "Meditation XVII," 128
Dos Passos, John, 90, 91, 128, 131;
    The Adventures of a Young Man,
    127, 128–30; *The Forty-second
    Parallel,* 95–96, 119, 128;
    Manhattan Transfer, 96
Douglas, Kirk, 165
*Draft Program of the Communist
    International: A Criticism of
    Fundamentals,* 100
Draper, Theodore, vii, 54; *The Roots
    of American Communism,* 34, 42,
    43, 55
Dreiser, Theodore, 11, 90
Du Bois, Dr. W. E. B., 44
dual union, 42, 77, 79, 147, 148
Dubinsky, David, 147
Dubofsky, Melvyn: *We Shall Be All: A
    History of the Industrial
    Workers of the World,* 18
Duclos, Jacques, 156
Duclos letter, 156, 158, 187
Duke, David C., 34
Dulles, John Foster, 162

Eastman, Crystal, 4, 39
Eastman, Max, 4, 5, 6, 28, 29, 31, 37,
    39, 40, 48, 83, 185
Eaton, Jeannette: "Rebellion," 7
Edison, Thomas, 95
Edwards, Herb, 18, 49
Ehrmann, Herbert: *The Case That
    Will Not Die,* 66
Emerson, Ralph Waldo, 3, 11, 26
Encounter, 172
End Poverty in California, 68
Engels, Friedrich, 30
Espionage Act (1917), 30, 41
Ettor, Joseph, 6, 16, 18

Falange (Falangists), 123, 125
Farm-Labor Party, 43, 54–55, 115,
    133
Farrell, James T., 95, 96, 119, 141; *A
    Note on Literary Criticism,* 119,
    186; Studs Lonigan trilogy, 119
Fascism, 90, 102, 103–4, 113, 117,
    124, 125, 126, 128, 131, 133,
    141, 143, 144, 170
Federal Council of Churches, 24
Federal Negro Theater, 152, 153
Federal Writers' Project, 152
fellow travelers, 2, 96, 115
Fellowship of Reconciliation, 98, 100,
    103
feminism, 15
Fifth Amendment, 167, 171, 175
Firson, Fridrikh Igorevich (and
    Harvey Klehr and John Earl
    Haynes): *The Secret World of
    American Communism,* 175
First Amendment, 166
First International, 8
Fischer, Louis, 151
Flacks, Richard, 2, 65; *Making
    History: The American Left and
    the American Mind,* 64
Flint, Michigan, General Motors
    strike, 132, 186
Flynn, Elizabeth Gurley, 3, 16, 19,
    60, 76
Foley, Barbara, 96
Folsom, Michael, 59

Foner, Philip S.: *American Socialism and Black Americans,* 45
Ford, James, 91, 115
Foreman, Carl: *The Bridge on the River Kwai,* 165
Fortas, Abe, 170
Foster, William Z., 50, 77, 83, 87, 91, 96, 133, 137, 155, 156, 173
Fourth International, 102
Fraina, Louis, 37, 42, 83, 91
Franco, Gen. Francisco, 123, 124
Frank, Waldo, 90, 91, 186
Free Speech League, 11
French Communist Party, 156
French Social Democratic Party, 101
French turn, 101, 102
Frick, Henry Clay, 10
Fried, Richard M., 160; *Nightmare in Red,* 158
Friends of the Soviet Union, 109
Fuchs, Klaus, 163, 164
Fuller, Gov. Alvan T., 66

Gandhi, Mohandas Karamchand, 103
Garland, Charles, 72
Garland Fund, 72
Garrison, Dee, 81, 82
Garvey, Marcus, 45, 46
Gastonia, North Carolina textile strike, 79, 81
General Motors. *See* Flint, Michigan, General Motors strike
General Strike, 13, 17, 41, 50, 145, 149
George, Harrison: *Red Dawn,* 50
German Social Democratic Party (SDP), 30, 40, 104
Gibson, Lydia, 7
Gide, André, 151
Gilbert, James Burkhart, viii
Gilbert, Joseph, 122
Gilbert, Ronnie, 166
Gilman, Charlotte Perkins: *Herland,* 26
Giovannitti, Arturo, 6, 11, 16, 18
Gitlow, Ben, 37, 42
Glaspell, Susan, 4
Glintenkamp, H. J., 31

Godwin, William: *An Inquiry Concerning Political Justice,* 7
Gold, Harry, 163, 164
Gold, Mike, 40, 56, 61, 64, 70, 72, 74, 75, 76, 83, 94, 96, 118, 119; *Jews without Money,* 55–60, 76, 83, 95, 186
Goldman, Emma, 4, 7, 10, 11, 12, 13, 31, 34, 35, 37, 49, 124, 145, 148, 185; *Anarchism and Other Essays,* 12; *My Disillusionment in Russia,* 35; *My Two Years in Russia,* 35
Gompers, Samuel, 77, 101, 132
Goodman, Andrew, 178
Gordon, Sarah, 116
Gornick, Vivian: *The Romance of American Communism,* 174
Government Operations Subcommittee on Investigations, 175–76
Granich, Itshok Isaac. *See* Mike Gold
Great Depression, 55–56, 74, 76, 84, 87, 89, 90, 93, 98, 104, 107, 112, 116, 125, 126, 142, 170, 186
Great Migration, 43
Greenglass, David, 163, 164
Greenglass, Ruth, 163
Greenwich Village, 4, 11, 12, 13, 14, 20, 22, 34, 37, 39, 63, 79, 104, 178
Griffith, Robert: *The Politics of Fear,* 160
Group Theatre, 120, 165
Guardian, 141
Guernica, 125
Guild Socialism, 49
Guthrie, Woody, 166

Haggerty, Thomas J., 16
Hammett, Dashiell, 170
Hamtramck meat boycott, 134, 186
Hansberry, Lorraine: *A Raisin in the Sun,* 178; *The Sign in Sidney Brustein's Window,* 178–80, 183
Hapgood, Hutchins, 4, 11
Harlan County, Kentucky, miners' strike, 89–91

Harlem Renaissance, 45, 110
Hathaway, Clarence, 108
Havel, Hippolyte, 11
Haymarket Riot, 10, 16, 149
Haynes, John Earl (and Harvey Klehr
    and Fridrikh Igorevich Firson):
    *The Secret World of American
    Communism*, 175
Hays, Lee, 166–67
Haywood, William ("Big Bill"), 4, 16,
    19, 50, 51, 95, 153
Heap, Jane, 4
Hellerman, Fred, 166
Hellman, Lillian, 138, 173;
    Pentimento, 138; *Scoundrel
    Time*, 139, 170–72, 176; *Watch
    on the Rhine*, 138–39, 170
Hemingway, Ernest, 61, 117, 127,
    131; *The Fifth Column*, 127; *For
    Whom the Bell Tolls*, 127–28,
    130; *The Spanish Earth*, 131;
    The Sun Also Rises, 81; *To Have
    and Have Not*, 127
Herbst, Josephine, 74, 118; "The
    Starched Blue Sky of Spain,"
    127, 130–31
Herndon, Angelo, 110
Herrmann, John, 91, 130, 131
Hervé, Edouard, 17
heterodoxy, 4
Hicks, Granville, 30, 91, 96
*Highlights of a Fighting History:
    Sixty Years of the Communist
    Party USA*, 98
Hill, Joe, 19
Hill, Robert A., 46
Hillquit, Morris, 21
Hindenburg, Paul von, 104
Hiss, Alger, 162, 163
Hitler, Adolf, 101, 114, 115, 116, 124,
    126, 137
Hollywood Ten, 162, 164
Homestead steel strike, 10
Hook, Sidney, 91, 172, 173
Hoover, Herbert, 87, 97
Hoovervilles, 87
Hopper, Edward, 93
House Un-American Activities

Committee (HUAC), 2, 161, 162,
    163, 164, 165, 166, 170, 171,
    172, 173, 174, 175
housewives' movement, 134
HUAC. *See* House Un-American
    Activities Committee
Hughes, Langston, 91, 110–13;
    "Brown America in Jail: Kilby,"
    111; "Christ in Alabama," 111,
    113; "Good Morning,
    Revolution," 112, 113; "My
    Adventures as a Social Poet,"
    111; "Southern Gentleman,
    White Prostitutes, Mill-Owners,
    and Negroes," 111–12
Hutchins, Grace, 97

Ibarruri, Dolores (La Pasionaria), 126
Iberian Anarchist Federation, 123
ILGWU. *See* International Ladies
    Garment Workers Union
individualistic novel, 119, 141
Industrial Workers of the World
    (IWW), 3, 4, 5, 6, 10, 11, 12, 13,
    16, 17, 18, 19, 20, 31, 38, 39, 41,
    42, 49, 50, 54, 62, 63, 66, 77, 78,
    79, 83, 84, 87, 95, 105, 124, 125,
    145, 149, 153, 172, 185
Insurgents, 124, 125, 126
Internal Security Act. *See* McCarran
    Act
International Brigades, 124, 126, 127
International Bureau of Revolutionary
    Literature, Second World Plenum
    (Kharkov conference), 74, 84,
    103, 119, 120, 130, 186
International Labor Defense, 107,
    108, 109
International Ladies Garment
    Workers Union (ILGWU), 145,
    147, 148, 149, 150
International Literature, 151
International Union of Revolutionary
    Writers, 75
International Workers' Dramatic
    Union, 120
International Workingmen's

Association. *See* First International

internationalism, 28, 30

Isserman, Maurice, viii, 155; *Which Side Were You On? The American Communist Party during the Second World War,* 144

IWW. *See* Industrial Workers of the World

Jefferson, Thomas, 11, 20

Jewish Daily Forward, 21, 145

Jewish Socialist movement, 83

John Reed Clubs, 74, 75, 88, 116, 117, 118, 151, 152, 186

Johnson, Diane: introduction, "The Starched Blue Sky of Spain," 131

Jones, Margaret C.: *Heretics and Hellraisers: Women Contributors to the "Masses," 1911–1917,* 6

Jones, Mother (Mary Harris), 16

Joughin, G. Louis (and Edmund M. Morgan): *The Legacy of Sacco and Vanzetti,* 70, 71

Kamenev, Lev Borisovich, 33, 137

Kandinsky, Vassily, 73

Kazan, Elia, 165, 171

Kelley, Harry, 11

Kempton, Murray, 172

Kendrick, John R., 50

Kerensky, Alexander, 31, 32, 33, 35, 97, 185

Kharkov conference. *See* International Bureau of Revolutionary Literature, Second World Plenum

Khrushchev, Nikita, 137, 173, 174, 183, 187

Kirov, Sergei Mironovich, 137, 182

Klehr, Harvey (and Fridrikh Igorevich Firson and John Earl Haynes): vii; *The Secret World of American Communism,* 175

Koestler, Arthur, 151, 178

Kornilov, General, 31–32

Kristallnacht, 138

Kronstadt massacre, 35, 37

Kropotkin, Peter, 9, 104, 105; *Mutual Aid,* 10

Krutch, Joseph Wood, 122

Ku Klux Klan, 44

Kushnarev, Theodore, 145

Labor Party. *See* Farm-Labor Party

LaFollette, Philip, 133

Lausche, Gov. Frank, 166

Lawrence, Massachusetts, textile strike, 6, 16, 18–19, 79, 100, 185

Le Sueur, Meridel, 132; *Salute to Spring,* 88–89, 102–3, 112

Leadbelly, 136

League of American Writers, 117, 118, 138, 142, 143, 186

League of Struggle for Negro Rights, 111, 135

Leeder, Elaine, 147

Left Front, 152

Left Front of Art (LEF), 74, 75

Lenin (Vladimir Ilyich Ulyanov), 32, 33, 40, 41, 53, 54, 73, 74, 78, 118

Levy, Louis, 147

Liberal Club, 14

liberals, 158, 162, 168, 172, 176

Liberator, 39, 40, 46, 50, 72

Liebkneckt, Karl, 30

"Little Red Song Book," 19–20, 50, 87

London, Jack, 14; *The Iron Heel,* 47

Loray Mill. *See* Gastonia, North Carolina, textile strike

Lovestone, Jay, 78, 147

Lovestoneite heresy, 78

Lowell, A. Lawrence, 67

Loyalists (Republicans), 124, 126, 136, 138, 150, 165

loyalty oaths, 167

Lumpkin, Grace, 91

Lunacharsky, Anatoly, 73, 74

Madden, David, 118; *Proletarian Writers of the Thirties,* 118

Madeiros, Celestino, 66

Madrileños, 124

Magil, A. B., 74

Malevich, Kasimir, 73
Maltz, Albert, 170; *Broken Arrow*, 165
Marsh, Margaret S.: *Anarchist Women, 1870–1920*, 11
Marshall Plan, 158
Marx, Karl, 8, 21, 25, 29, 30, 40, 46, 53, 92, 153; *The German Ideology*, 9; *The Poverty of Philosophy*, 9
Marxism, 7, 35, 78
Masses, ix, 3, 5, 6, 7, 11, 13, 28, 29, 30, 31, 39, 72, 104, 105, 151, 185
Matusow, Harvey, 166
Maurin, Peter, 104–7
McAuliffe, Mary Sperling: *Crisis on the Left: Cold War Politics and American Liberals, 1947–1954*, 160
McCarran Act, 161, 162
McCarthy, Sen. Joseph, 159, 162, 168, 171, 175, 187
McCarthyism, 159–68, 170, 172, 173, 175
McGrath, Tom, 140–42, 153–54, 176; *Longshot O'Leary's Garland of Practical Poesy*, 153; *To Walk a Crooked Mile*, 153–54
McKay, Claude, 40, 46, 47, 51, 111; *A Long Way from Home*, 47
McKinley, William, 10
McShane, Joseph: *Sufficiently Radical*, 26
Mencken, H. L., 91
Mesabi Iron Range, 13, 21, 79
Messenger, 45, 110
Michigan Group, 42
Militant, 101
Minneapolis, Minnesota, truck drivers' strike, 101, 102
Minor, Robert, 144
modern schools movement, 124
Monthly Review, 141
Mooney, Tom, 13
Moore, Fred, 66
Moore, Richard, 108
Moran, Marian, 174

Morelli gang, 66
Morgan, Edmund M. (and G. Louis Joughin): *The Legacy of Sacco and Vanzetti*, 70, 71
Morton, Marian, 10
Moscow Art Theatre, 120
Most, Johann, 10; *Die Freiheit*, 10
Mother Earth, 11, 12, 13
Mother Earth Bulletin, 35
Munich Pact, 126
Murphy, James F.: *The Proletarian Moment*, 75, 119
Mussolini, Benito, 124
Muste, A. J., 100, 101, 102, 107, 127, 161

NAACP. *See* National Association for the Advancement of Colored People
Naison, Mark, viii
Nation, 122
National Association for the Advancement of Colored People (NAACP), 44, 45, 78, 109, 110, 113, 135
National Association of Manufacturers, 5, 48, 49
National Civic Federation, 49
National Committee for the Defense of Political Prisoners, 90
National Industrial Recovery Act (NIRA), 97, 144, 149, 150
National Labor Board, 101, 158
National Lawyers Guild, 138
National Maritime Union, 144
National Miners Union (NMU), 89, 90
National Negro Congress (NNC), 135, 138
national question, 46
National Recovery Act (NRA), 97, 99, 131
National Textile Workers Union (NTWU), 79
Nationalist Clubs, 26
Navasky, Victor, *Naming Names*, 166–67

Needle Trades Workers Industrial Union, 147, 148–49
Negrin, Juan, 126
Nemirovich-Danchenko, Vladimir, 120
New Criticism, viii
New Deal, 87, 96–98, 99, 101, 102, 103, 105, 112, 113, 123, 131, 132, 133, 134, 136, 138, 144, 148, 155, 157, 158, 159, 160, 162, 163, 165
New Economic Policy, 53, 73
New Leader, 99
New Left, 175, 177
New Masses, 60, 63, 74, 75, 76, 83, 88, 97, 102, 112, 118, 119, 153, 186
New Negro Movement, 44
New Republic, 75, 96
New South, 135
New Theatre League, 120
New York Review of Books, 172
New York taxi strike, 119, 122
New York Times, 34, 50, 178, 180
Niebuhr, Reinhold, 24, 104
Nin, Andres, 126, 130
Nineteenth Amendment, 22, 60
NMU. *See* National Miners Union
non-aggression pact of 1939 (Hitler-Stalin pact), 137–41, 187
Norrick, Ruth, 25, 65, 98, 167
Norris, Frank, *The Octopus*, 13
North Atlantic Treaty Organization (NATO), 158

Odets, Clifford, 171; *Six Plays of Clifford Odets*, 121; *Waiting for Lefty*, 119–22, 141, 165, 186
On the Dissolution of the American Communist Party. See Duclos letter
One Big Union Monthly, 50
Open Shop Association, 76
Opportunity, 111
Oral History of the American Left, 65, 90, 91, 96, 97, 98, 107, 116, 117, 125, 136, 141, 142, 151, 153, 154, 167

Organizer, 148
Orwell, George, 71, 174

Page, Kirby, 99, 104
Pageant of the Paterson Strike, 34
Paine, Thomas, 11
Palmer, Atty. Gen. A. Mitchell, 51
Palmer Raids, 51, 65, 186
Pankhurst, Sylvia, 46
Parker, Dorothy, 117
Partisan Review, 75, 118, 119, 172
Party Organizer, 134
Pasaic, New Jersey, textile strike, 79
La Pasionaria. *See* Dolores Ibarruri
Paterson, New Jersey, silk workers strike, 19, 34
Penney, Owen, 37
people's economy, 87
Pesotta, Rose, 176; *Bread upon the Waters*, 145–50
Philbrick, Herbert A.: *I Led Three Lives: Citizen, "Communist," Counterspy*, 176
Phillips, William, 119
Picasso, Pablo, 125
Plekhanov, Georgy, 74
polycentrism, 154
Pope Leo XIII, 26
Popular Front (against Fascism), ix, 99, 115, 117, 119, 123, 129, 132, 133, 135, 136, 140, 141, 142, 143, 176, 186, 187
Popular Front government of France, 124
production for use, 97
Program of the Russian Social Democratic Labor Party, 31
Progressive Era, 22, 25
Progressive Party, 133, 158–59
proletarian literature, 74, 84
proletarian novel, 55, 113, 117–20, 186
Proletcult (Organization for Proletarian Culture), 73, 74, 75
Proudhon, Pierre Joseph, 8, 10; *The Philosophy of Poverty*, 9
Provincetown Players, 79, 105
Pullman strike, 20

pumpkin papers, 163
Pure Food and Drug Act, 67

Radek, Karl Bernardovich, 37
Rahv, Philip, 119
Rand School, 99
Randolph, A. Philip, 45, 135, 186
Rauh, Ida, 4
Rauh, Joseph, 170, 172
Rauschenbusch, Walter:
    Christianizing the Social Order,
    24
Rebel Poet, 91
Red-baiting, 67, 159, 162, 168
*Red Channels: Communist Influence
    on Radio and Television,* 166
red-diaper babies, 175
Red International. *See* Comintern
Red Scare, 41, 48, 51, 52, 53, 54, 66,
    67, 71, 76, 82, 145, 186
Reed, John, ix, 4, 6, 11, 29, 30, 31,
    37, 42, 50, 60; *Ten Days That
    Shook the World,* 32–35, 51, 185
Reitman, Ben, 13
reportage, 103, 113
Republican Party, 157
Republicans. *See* Loyalists
Rerum Novarum, 26, 48, 49, 105,
    106, 113, 148
Reuther, Victor, 132, 133
Reuther, Walter, 132, 133
revisionism, 40
Rideout, Alan, viii; *The Radical Novel
    in the United States, 1900–1954,*
    117, 118
Rodchenko, Alexander, 73
Rodman, Henrietta, 4, 14
Rogers, Merrill, 31
Roman Catholic Church, 26, 48, 49,
    105, 123, 126, 150
Roman Catholic Left, 104, 113
Roman Catholicism, 105
Roosevelt, Franklin Delano, 90, 97,
    98, 115, 123, 133, 136, 139, 143,
    144, 154, 156, 163
Rosanova, Olga, 73
Rosenberg, Ethel, 162, 163, 187
Rosenberg, Julius, 162, 163, 164, 187

Russian Association of Proletarian
    Writers (RAPP), 74
Russian Left Opposition, 100
Russian Revolution, 29, 30, 33, 34,
    39, 48, 53, 62, 98, 182, 185
Ruthenberg, Charles, 42
Ruuttila, Julia, 49
Ryan, Fr. John Augustine, 48

Sacco, Nicola, 65–70, 72, 83, 84, 128,
    145, 164, 175, 186
Salsedo, Andrea, 65, 66
Sandburg, Carl, 111
Sanger, Margaret, 4
Sanger, William, 4
Sarton, May: *Faithful Are the
    Wounds,* 168–70, 176
Sartre, Jean Paul, 178
Sayles, John: *At the Anarchist's
    Convention,* 180–82
Schmidt, Johann Kasper. *See* Max
    Stirner
Schofield, Ann, 147
Schrecker, Ellen W., viii; *No Ivory
    Tower: McCarthyism and the
    Universities,* 167
Schwerner, Mickey, 178
Scottsboro boys, 107–13, 165, 186
Scottsboro Unity Defense Committee,
    109
SDP. *See* German Social Democratic
    Party
Seattle cooperatives, 87, 134
Second International, 28, 40, 51, 92
Second Period, 114
sectarianism, 76, 98
Sedition Act (1918), 41
Seeger, Peter, 166–67
Senate Internal Security
    Subcommittee (SISS), 161, 167,
    175
Seven Arts, 29
sewer Socialism, 21
Shachtman, Max, 100
show trials, 136
Silone, Ignazio, 151, 178
Sinclair, Upton, 104; *Boston,* 67–71,
    81, 84; *The Jungle,* 67, 104

Slim, T-Bone, 19
Sloan, John, 5
Smedley, Agnes, 65, 70, 83; *Daughter of Earth*, 60–64, 186
Smith Act, 139, 182, 187
Sobell, Morton, 163, 164
Social Creed of Churches, 24
Social Democrat, 69, 84
Social Gospel, 3, 24, 25, 26, 98, 100, 107
Social Security, 133
social-fascism, 78
Socialism, ix, 6, 7, 22, 25, 29, 51, 67, 95, 98, 100, 104, 105, 133, 141, 147, 174, 176, 177, 185
Socialism in one country, 100, 113
Socialist Labor Party, 42
Socialist Party, 3, 5, 11, 13, 17, 19, 20, 21, 22, 24, 25, 30, 31, 39, 40, 41, 42, 43, 44, 45, 46, 62, 63, 67, 77, 78, 83, 90, 96–97, 98, 99, 100, 102, 103, 104, 113, 114, 115, 125, 145, 186; Militants, 99; Old Guard, 99
Socialist Realism, 73
Socialist Workers Party, 102, 139
Solidarity, 50
Sorel, Georges, 17
Southern Tenant Farmers' Union, 98
Southern Worker, 110
Spanish Civil War. *See* Spanish Revolution
Spanish Communist Party, 124, 125, 126
Spanish Republic, 123, 127
Spanish Revolution, 123–31, 142, 166, 186, 187
Spender, Stephen, 151
Spragovsky, Anatoly, 137
St. John, Vincent, 16
Stachel, Jack, 90, 140
Stalin, Josef, 73, 78, 100, 101, 113, 136, 137, 154, 158, 159, 173, 174, 176, 187
Stanislavsky, Konstantin, 120
Starobin, Joseph, vii; *American Communism in Crisis, 1943–1957*, 155

steel strike of 1919, 79
Steffens, Lincoln, 30, 37, 91
Steinbeck, John, 117
Stirner, Max, 9; *The Ego and His Own*, 7
strategic poetry, 153
Subversive Activities Control Board, 161
Suprematists, 73
syndicalism, 90

tactical poetry, 153
Taft-Hartley Bill, 158, 159
Tatlin, Viktor, 73
Taxi Drivers Union of Greater New York (TDU), 122
Teheran Conference, 154
Teheran Declaration, 155, 156
Telluride, Colorado, strike, 16
Tenth Convention of the CPUSA, 135
Thayer, Judge Webster, 66
Theatre Union, 120
Third International. *See* Comintern
Third Period, 77–78, 78, 84, 88, 97, 101, 107, 109, 176, 186
Thomas, Norman, 98, 99, 100, 103, 186
Thompson, Louise, 109
Thompson, William, 66
Thoreau, Henry David, 3, 11, 20, 26
Tillery, Tyrone, 47
Time Out, 166
Toledo Auto-Light strike, 100
Trade Union Educational League (TUEL), 77, 114, 147, 148, 186
Trade Union Unity League (TUUL), 77, 78, 89, 90, 186
Transport Workers Union, 145
Tresca, Carlo, 19
Trotsky, Leon, 32, 78, 100, 101, 126, 137; *Literature and Revolution*, 119
Trotskyism, 100–103
Trotskyists, 96, 103, 113, 125, 126, 129, 132, 140, 153
Truman, Harry, 156, 158, 159, 160

Trumbo, Dalton, 170; *The Brave One,* 165; *Gun Crazy,* 165; *Roman Holiday,* 165; *Spartacus,* 165
Tsar Nicholas II, 31
Tucker, Benjamin, 11; *Liberty,* 11
Twelfth Comintern Plenum, 114
Twentieth Party Congress, 173–75, 180, 187

UMW. *See* United Mine Workers
unemployment demonstrations, 87, 105, 108, 186
UNIA. *See* Universal Negro Improvement Association
Union General de Trabajadors (UGT), 123, 125
United Communist Party, 54
United Electrical, Radio, and Machine Workers, 144
United Front, 104
united front from below, 114
United Front of Struggle, 115
United Libertarian Organizations (ULO), 124
United Mine Workers (UMW), 89
Universal Negro Improvement Association (UNIA), 45, 46
Untermann, Ernest: *Marxian Economics: A Popular Introduction to the Three Volumes of Marx's Capital,* 22, 24
Untermeyer, Louis, 6
Urban League, 44, 109, 110, 113, 135

Vanguard, 124
vanguard party, 51
Vanzetti, Bartolomeo, 65–70, 72, 83, 84, 128, 145, 164, 175, 186
Vermont resolution, 159
Vlag, Piet, 5
Volkogonov, Gen. Dmitri, 163
Voorhis Act, 140
Vorse, Mary Heaton, 6, 83, 90, 105; *Strike!,* 79–83, 186

Wagenknecht, Alfred, 108

Wagner Act, 131, 133
Wald, Alan, 173
Wall Street Journal, 162
Wallace, Henry, 156, 158, 159, 170
Walling, William English, 6, 30
War Labor Board (WLB), 144, 157
Ward, Harry F., 24
Washington, Booker T., 44, 47
Weales, Gerald, 121, 122
Weavers, 166
Webb, Constance, 152
Weinstone, William, 54
WEVD, 99
White, Josh, 136
Whitman, Walt, 3, 14
Wiggins, Ella Mae, 79, 82
Wilder, Thornton, 76, 94; *The Women of Andros,* 75
Willard, Frances, 25
Williamson, John, 156
Wilson, Edmund, 90, 91
Wilson, Michael: *The Bridge on the River Kwai,* 165
Wilson, Woodrow, 44, 172
Winter, Alice Beach, 5
Winter, Ella, 91
Wobbly. *See* Industrial Workers of the World
woman suffrage, 5, 12, 79, 88, 104
Women's Christian Temperance Union, 25
Women's National Committee of the Socialist Party, 21
Wood, Eugene, 6
Woodcock, George, 10
Workers' Dreadnought, 46
Workers Party, 99, 101, 102, 161
Workers' Party (of 1920s; later CPUSA), 40, 55, 72
workers' theatres, 120
Works Progress Administration (WPA), 97, 98, 131, 135, 152
World Tomorrow, 99, 103, 104
World War I, 12, 13, 22, 26, 27, 28–29, 35, 40, 41, 44, 45, 48, 49, 50, 67, 68, 76, 95, 103, 127, 137, 144, 157

World War II, viii, 118, 143, 147, 153, 154, 157, 160, 187
WPA. *See* Works Progress Administration
Wright, Richard, 88, 150–54, 178, 187; *Black Boy,* 151, 153; *Native Son,* 151; *The Outsider,* 151; in *The God That Failed,* 151
Writers Guild of America, 165

Yakovlev, Anatoli, 164
Yalta Conference, 162
Yokinen, August, 108
Young, Art, 31
Young, Nedrick: *The Defiant Ones,* 165

Zinn, Howard: *A People's History of the United States,* 87
Zinoviev, Grigory, 33, 37, 137

THE AUTHOR

Julia Dietrich received her Ph.D. from University of Cincinnati in 1976 and is now Professor of English at the University of Louisville, where she teaches in the undergraduate program and in the doctoral program in Rhetoric and Composition. Her scholarly interest is in the historical uses of literature as social persuasion.